8/11

Schmitt

Seduced by *Twilight*

Seduced by *Twilight*

The Allure and Contradictory Messages of the Popular Saga

NATALIE WILSON

McFarland & Company, Inc., Publishers
Jefferson, North Carolina, and London

LIBRARY OF CONGRESS CATALOGUING-IN-PUBLICATION DATA

Wilson, Natalie, 1971–
    Seduced by Twilight : the allure and contradictory messages
of the popular saga / Natalie Wilson.
        p.   cm.
    Includes bibliographical references and index.

    ISBN 978-0-7864-6042-7
    softcover : 50# alkaline paper ∞

    1. Meyer, Stephenie, 1973– Twilight saga series.   2. Young
adult fiction, American — History and criticism.   3. Youth —
United States — Attitudes — History — 21st century.   I. Title.
PS3613.E979Z98   2011
813'.6 — dc22   2011005068

BRITISH LIBRARY CATALOGUING DATA ARE AVAILABLE

Front cover image © 2011 Shutterstock

Manufactured in the United States of America

McFarland & Company, Inc., Publishers
  Box 611, Jefferson, North Carolina 28640
    www.mcfarlandpub.com

To Naomi and Shane.
You dazzle me.

Table of Contents

Preface and Acknowledgments

My immersion in the *Twilight* saga began when I read the series along with my then-nine-year-old daughter. Were it not for her, I might never have been introduced to Bella, Edward, and Jacob — indeed, I may have become a "Twi-hater" who, never having read the series, was convinced its popularity signaled the looming demise of humanity (and certainly of "good literature").

Thanks to my daughter's insistence that she simply *must* read the books, I bought her the first novel as a Valentine's Day present, not realizing at the time just how fitting this gift was, given that the saga functions as an overwhelming devotion to love. While I myself did not fall for the saga in the head-over-heels way Bella falls for Edward, I will admit that I read it at breakneck speed.

In the beginning I readied myself for a slog through the *long* books while holding myself back from hurling them towards the trash. Later, only emerging for necessities like food and water, my reading finally slowed due to the irksome maternal martyrdom meme of *Breaking Dawn* (not to mention Bella's love for a black and blue body, "decorated" by Edward). Sure, the repetitive adjective use bothered the wordsmith in me. The lack of symbolism and complexity left my more literary mind hungry. Yet, I couldn't stop turning the pages. What would Bella do? I, like large segments of the planet, had become transfixed by the saga.

After being selected to deliver three talks at *Summer School in Forks*, I decided to pen a book-length analysis of the series— in no minor part due to the fans and scholars I met at that conference who inspired me to take a deeper look at the texts and their appeal. From there I attended and presented at *Twi-Con* and began to study the *Twi*-net world — that vast and lively array of blogs, podcasts, and websites devoted to Stephenie Meyer's saga. I interviewed fans at Comic-Con, at movie premieres, at bookstores, and at *Twilight* conventions. I surveyed my college students, my children's teachers and classmates, my friends and family. *Twilight* even highjacked my daughter's fifth grade field trip when the teacher discovered I was writing a book on the series and couldn't stop talking

1

to me about it. It took over discussions with my mother, who dutifully began reading the series once she learned of my study. It nearly made me miss a flight when a woman spied one of the books under my arm and *had* to talk to me about "all that sex" in *Breaking Dawn*. It infiltrated talks with friends, dinner table discussions, and workplace gatherings—it even made its way into my advanced feminist theory seminar.

Arguing that readers are drawn to the series because it offers a virtual smorgasbord of messages that speak to the contemporary moment, the following book will analyze the saga and the surrounding fandom, suggesting that fans are not the dribbling, insipid, Edward addicts they are often made out to be. Rather, as a discussion of the surrounding cultural contexts will reveal, fans are drawn to the series because it offers a vast textual landscape that echoes the world in which they live—a landscape replete with conflicting messages about abstinence and sexuality, about femininity and masculinity, about race, class, morality, and religion. Maintaining that the saga's grounding in specific contemporary contexts is what produces its mass appeal, *Seduced by* Twilight will explain why these particular books have taken the world by storm.

Indeed, the *Twilight* franchise looks to be immortal, just like the undead vampires at its narrative core. In fact, the *Twilight* franchise is so popular that many bookstores, Barnes and Noble and Borders among them, have special *Twilight* sections. Allowing readers to immerse themselves in a world of supernatural, super-hot characters, *Twilight* is a modern fairy tale replete with heroes, villains, and happily ever afters. Yet, it also explores much deeper themes— trust, betrayal, the meaning of family, the institution of marriage, the source of evil—kind of like the Bible, but with vampires.

Arguing that the series' messages about gender, race, class, sexuality, and belief are as unstable as Bella's moods, the following book will explore the contradictory messages of *Twilight*, a series that presents neither a subversive nor a conservative view of larger social contexts but an ambiguous mixture of both. This vacillation, I contend, is precisely why the saga allures everyone from the prepubescent eight-year-old to the knitting grandma.

As a professor, scholar, blogger, mother, and critical fan, I have set out to offer an assessment of the seductive sway the saga holds over the contemporary moment. With a deep scholarly interest in how popular trends allow people to negotiate larger societal issues and ideologies, I am eager to discuss how and why *Twilight* seduces us.

While there are a number of existing analyses of the series, many of them are religious in focus (such as *Touched by a Vampire* by Beth Felker Jones and *Spotlight: A Close-Up Look at the Artistry and Meaning in Stephenie Meyer's Twilight Novels* by John Granger), others take a particular disciplinary approach (such as *Twilight and Philosophy* and *Twilight and History*), some serve as "guides" to love (such as *Everything I Need to Know About Women I Learned by Reading Twilight: A Vampire's Guide to Eternal Love* by Jim Lee), and a few are multi-authored compilations of essays (such as *Bitten by Twilight*, as well as my anthology, co-edited with Maggie Parke, *Critical Essays on Stephenie Meyer's Twilight Saga and its Impact on Popular Culture*).

Though *Seduced by Twilight* is the first single-authored work to examine the saga from a feminist cultural studies lens, this work would not have been possible without the encouragement and support of many other scholars and authors. My work is heavily influenced by scholars such as Susan Bordo, Janice Radway, Tania Modleski, Susan Douglas, Jane Caputi, Angela McRobbie, and Barbara Creed, as well as by the many excellent vampire scholars that think so deeply about our enduring fasincation with the undead.

Neither would the current work be possible without all the support and encouragement I have received from mentors and colleagues. I owe a large part of my PhD to Bonnie Zimmerman, my master's thesis advisor, who encouraged me years ago to pursue an academic career. As I hammered away at my dissertation and slogged back and forth from the University of London Library while trying to juggle daycare and preschool drop-offs and pick-ups, her encouraging words often spurred me on. More recently, as I tried to cram writing and research into the hours my two children were away at school, I received daily encouragement from family and friends— Rachel, Patty, Graham, Lezlie, Tracy, Sarah, and Elyse each deserve medals for all the vampire talk they had to endure!

I want to offer my appreciation to the *Twi*-scholars who I have thankfully formed lasting friendships with — Ananya Mukerhjea, Angela Tenga, Natalia Cherjovsky, Melissa Miller, Simon Bacon, Karen Smythe, Maggie Parke, Tanya Erzen — many of whom read earlier drafts of part or all of this book. My work is better thanks to their careful and insightful commentary.

My work also benefitted from the many fans, bloggers, and vampire afficionados who were willing to share their reasons for loving (or hating) the saga. Thanks to them, I was inspired to launch the blog *Seduced by Twilight*, where I continue to offer *Twilight*-related analysis and commentary. I owe particular gratitude to Renee Martin, of *Womanist Musings*, for offering me a guest column at her blog, to the editors of *Ms. Magazine* and the *Ms. Magazine Blog*, Michele Kort and Jessica Stites, for their dedication to helping scholars such as myself breach the academic/publishing divide, and to Brian Frost and Yvette Nolasco, middle school teachers extraordinaire, who helped me distribute endless *Twilight* surveys.

The academic leave I was granted from Cal State San Marcos made writing this possible, as did the support of colleagues such as Pamela Redela, Linda Pershing, Dawn Formo, Sheryl Lutjens, and Martha Stoddard-Holmes. I also owe a great deal of gratitude to my students, who encourage me daily to be a better scholar, teacher, blogger, and author. Their enthusiasm and willingness to examine the world from a gender studies lens in my women's studies classes inspires me to continue on in this sometimes sparkly vampire-like sometimes zombie-like world of academia.

And finally, I dedicate this book to my daughter Naomi, one of my very favorite feminists, whose witty *Twilight* comics carried me through many a hard day of editing the manuscript, and to my son Shane, who, unlike Edward or Jacob, wields sarcasm and humor to great effect and would *never* suggest being female is tantamount to being "silly." To both of them I do not offer Edward's advice to "be safe"—rather, I say, be bold, be adventuresome, be yourselves and—above all—please don't ever choose life with an undead sparkly vampire over college!

Introduction:
A Post-*Twilight* World

I fully expected to hate Stephenie Meyer's *Twilight Saga* when I was dragged, kicking and screaming, to read it by my then-nine-year-old daughter. She claimed that she was the only child on the planet not reading Meyer's books and regaled me with stories of how *all* the kids at her school clutched one of the four books to their person at recess, and I began to wonder why *Twilight* had come to such cultural prominence. I was aware large segments of the planet (and particularly large portions of the female population) had been bitten by the *Twilight* bug. However, until I delved a little deeper, I didn't realize just how large a phenomenon Meyer's series had launched.

I had heard the usual claims: the books are badly written, once you start reading them you can't put them down, Edward was *to die for*. Aware of discussions about the age appropriateness of the series given the "sex stuff" (as my daughter put it), I assumed the legions of 9- to 11-year-old girls wearing *Twilight* T-shirts at my daughter's elementary school were drawn to the "mature content" that our abstinence-only culture insist they *not* be aware of. While I anticipated sexual content was what had parents in a dither, this was not ultimately what worried me — rather, I was concerned about what I had heard were the very regressive messages regarding gender roles. Would Bella be just another weak wallflower? Would Edward's apparent irresistibility lead my daughter to forget her love of feisty female protagonists and head down the path of future Harlequin romance addiction? I need not have worried, as her relationship with the series was much like a crush.

She fell headlong into the first book, feverishly turning the pages. With the second book, the honeymoon period started to fade. She began to complain about Bella — her lack of character, her clumsiness, her stereotypical femininity. By the third book, she had just as many dislikes as likes. Then, as her *Twi*-break-up loomed, she slogged through book 4. Now that a few years have passed, she is able to look at her *Twi*-crush more clearly. She has seen the existing film adaptations several times, and laughs heartily at Bella's earnestness, at the clumsy dialogue, at Edward's overdone emotion (and lip gloss). While I feared

I would have a "*Twi*-hard" on my hands, I need not have — she, like me, has a love/hate relationship with the saga.

Such a relationship to popular texts is common for feminist cultural theorists, as evidenced by Susan Bordo's fittingly titled *Twilight Zones*. Bordo documents her "personal love/hate struggle" with popular culture, noting her "rebellious but often dazzled, beguiled but skeptical, always intimate relationship with cultural images" (1). Her work emphasizes that all of us are enmeshed in culture — even though many academics like to act as if they can use "high-powered theory to cut like a scythe" through the maze of cultural images (1). Drawing on Plato's "Allegory of the Cave," Bordo examines the seductiveness of illusions, noting that in the present cultural moment "bedazzlement by created images is no metaphor; it is the actual condition of our lives" and insisting that "if we do not wish to remain prisoners of these images, we must recognize that they are not reality" (2).

While many *Twilight* fans admittedly fail to recognize their devotion to the saga, the majority are not prisoners to its allure. Rather, they are able to have critical distance, mocking the texts' and films' more ridiculous moments and analyzing the series' often less-than-stellar messages. Indeed, as I educated myself more about the series itself and various responses to it, I was surprised by all the different ways *Twilight* seduces its readers. Tapping into our cultural love affair with romance, the books *seduce* readers not only because they rely so heavily on archetypal character types and alluring supernatural figures, but also because they reflect various cultural shifts and trends.

Fans live at a time where, as Mark Collins Jenkins explains, "vampires have never appeared more sensitive or romantic" (7). Surrounded by not only the likes of Edward Cullen, but also Bill, Eric, and Pam of *True Blood*, Stefan, Damon, and Pearl of *The Vampire Diaries*, and the sympathetic vampires of *Underworld*, *Daybreakers*, *Being Human*, and *The Gates*, is it any wonder that so many seem so smitten with the undead? While Collins argues that "American culture is in the midst of a vampire epidemic," I would counter that American culture is *in love* with vampires rather than *afflicted* by them (as the word *epidemic* suggests) (8). Vampires have become, rather than the dangerous warnings they once were, contemporary culture's sexy drug of choice.

While medicating ourselves with immersions into the world of the undead comes with some negative side effects (such as convincing us to value youth, beauty, and power and romanticize violence), it also has its benefits — especially when we analyze our dependence and "manage" our addictions. Even in the more conservative, regressive vampire narratives there is space to enact subversive readings.

And *Twilight* is no exception.

As cultural theorist John Fiske asserts, culture can both promote societal norms *and* be a site of resistance. Noting de Certeau's metaphor of the text as a supermarket "from which readers select the items that they want, combine them with those already in their cultural 'pantry' at home, and cook up new meals or new readings according to their own needs," Fiske's work (and the work of other cultural studies scholars) reveals that culture is never only a site of consumption or manipulation but also allows for productive, tactical, and even subversive engagements with even the most conservative of texts/ideologies.[1] Texts, according to Fiske, are "'completed only by the productivity of popular readers and by their relevant insertion into readers' everyday lives" (108). *Twilight* is being "inserted" into readers' everyday lives in myriad ways— some of which accord with regressive cultural ideologies, such as the pro-family and traditional marriage movements, others of which challenge normative social constructions in regards to gender, sexuality, and race.[2]

Females in particular are the targets of the conservative and fundamentalist bent permeating contemporary culture, as has been the case historically.[3] With that in mind, it is imperative we analyze texts such as *Twilight*, which undoubtedly has caught the female cultural imagination. As Rosalind Wiseman admits, "Even the most emancipated women can't escape the impact of all those messages our culture sends us about what we have to be," and we, living in this *Twilight* moment, need to put on our critical lenses in order to examine this impact (105). Like the episode from the *Twilight Zone* television series in which everyone had to choose between a few available face and body models, we are being exhorted to choose from a limited selection of ways to be in the world.[4] Instead of going into a futuristic apparatus and emerging moments later as exact replicas of one of the model choices (as in the *Twilight Zone* episode), we are surrounded by constant cultural messages that exhort us to become the *right* kind of body and person — white, heterosexual, God-fearing, middle class, and so on. We must resist these seductive messages. While we may not be able to leave our cultural cave of illusions, we can certainly, as Bordo suggests, "turn a light on *in* it" (14).

The present book is an attempt to turn a light on Meyer's series and its widespread popularity. I hope that it will prompt readers to question Bella's desire to wed herself to the Cullen vampire lifestyle as well as to question their own attraction to the seductive messages *Twilight* offers.

We need not deny our attraction to the saga (or to its many sparkly vampires and hunky werewolves), but we would be well served to turn a critical eye on our enmeshment in vampire culture. Rather than moving into a Snow White–like cottage in the Forks woods for a happily ever after as a forever young, forever beautiful wife and mother, we should endeavor to become not sidekick Lois Lanes, but Super(wo)men, able to see through the illusions of our culture with a laser-like gaze. We may indeed be seduced by *Twilight*, but our awareness of the many ways in which the saga, its characters, and its messages seduce us will allow us to be more of an empowered Eve than a soporific Sleeping Beauty. Our world may be far from the post-racial, post-feminist utopia some claim, but it can at least be post–*Twilight* if we, as critical readers of our culture, refuse the seductive message that falling in love with a sparkly vampire will solve all our problems.

While *Twilight*'s popularity is usually traced to the mysterious romance at the series' core, the way the saga is centered around Bella's choice to become a vampire certainly also appeals to contemporary readers schooled in the rhetoric of *empowerment*. The cultural championing of *choosing* abstinence, the continuing sexualization of women and girls, the backlash against feminism, the bolstering of certain types of masculinity, the political and religious turn to the right, the exhortation to be consumer citizens—all of these are important social contexts that further foster *Twilight*'s appeal and make it, to use a popular *Twi*-ism, as addictive as heroin.

As attitudes about marriage, family, parenting, gender roles, and race relations are being jolted by cultural shockwaves, it is not surprising that a series exploring these issues appeals to so many. Further, the open, rather blank writing allows readers to project their own ideas onto the narrative: those who seek a "typical romance" are able to live vicariously as the damsel in distress saved by the uber-hot Edward; those who frame their lives in terms of religious belief are able to view the series as a Christian allegory; those with more political sensibilities are able to read the human/vampire/werewolf triad as negotiating difference, hierarchies, and societal inequalities. *Twilight* provides such narrative pleasure because it is able to offer different things to different readers. It is like a Vegas buffet—there is something for everyone. Most readers return to *Twilight*, either through repeated book reads, blog discussions, attending conferences, or buying every "so the lion fell in love with the lamb" trinket possible. They stuff themselves silly, gorging down enough vampire and werewolf to repulse those who somehow remain immune to the series allure—the *Twi*-haters.

These haters dislike the book for a multitude of reasons, but one recurring complaint is their simplicity. In the books, the contentious debates over "family values" dominating the cultural landscape become the idealized Cullen family. The mixed messages given to girls to be "good" yet hypersexual is embodied in Bella—the ultimate good girl who teeters constantly on the edge of "badness." The collective guilt of our war-ridden society morphs into an epic vampire battle where good wins out against evil. Consumer capitalism on over-drive is given a flattering *Twi*st via the opulent world of vampires who have no monetary impediments, such as outsourcing or inflation.

Arguing that the series' messages about gender, race, class, sexuality, and belief are as unstable as Bella's moods, the present study will explore the contradictory messages of *Twilight*, a series that presents neither a subversive nor a conservative view of larger social contexts but is an ambiguous mixture of both. This vacillation, I contend, is precisely why the saga appeals to such a varied readership. Most of the messages in the saga are rather old-fashioned, encouraging the largely female fan base to head back to the kitchen. The series speaks for the likes of Glenn Beck, who recently told Sarah Palin to "make him some stew." Yet, some of the textual strands are transgressive, suggesting that religious and cultural mores of sexuality and gender are too strict. Others imply that some of the more delimiting aspects of the current culture — namely, the abstinence-only imperative, the cult of beauty, and the sexualizaton of women and the violence done to them — are acceptable. This textual vacillation not only can be traced to the author's status as a female Mormon, but also is indicative of contemporary American culture. We are a society that cannot quite make up its mind about our principles and beliefs. We are Puritanical devotees dedicated to hard work and morality and simultaneous crazed consumer gluttons driven by desires for the perfect body, the perfect product, the newest gagdet. Neither can we make up our minds about gender, sexuality, race, and class. We are a "post-racial" society obsessed with race and ethnicity, a "post-feminist" society trying to roll back women's rights, a "secular" society fanatical about religion. *Seduced by Twilight* will investigate these conflicting ideologies shaping American culture, using *Twilight* as a lens through which to view our culturally inconsistent ways of thinking.

Bella, in particular, embodies cultural inconsistencies with regard to gender; she speaks to our culture's rampant sexualization of females on the one hand and obsession with abstinence and purity on the other. Our cultural fascination with "MILFs," "cougars," and "hot moms" also takes fictional form in *Twilight*. In the fandom, this translates into a bevy of "*Twilight* Moms" who are just as much (or more) smitten with the series than their daughters. The claims that our society is "post-racial" and "post-feminist" are tidily fictionalized in a world in which vampires, werewolves, and humans get along and battles for gender equality need not be fought. Emerging at a cultural moment colored by conservative politics and religion, by consumer capitalism, and the explosion of internet culture, *Twilight* is both a product of and a reaction to these trends. As many technological shifts impede human contact and physical interaction, as we spend more time at keyboards, on Facebook, and on eBay, as we are encouraged to avoid physical contact via purity balls and pandemic fear-mongering, as we are encouraged to shop our way out of both "terrorist attacks" and economic downturns, as we chatter into cell phones, text, and Twitter, we are profoundly distanced from face-to-face contact. Thus, the series speaks to our innate desire for connection. This is how sociologist Ananya Mukherjea explains the draw of the series, arguing that *Twilight* offers a collective experience for readers and fans.[5]

While some might argue that the young fan base of *Twilight* does not care for the more weighty issues the saga circulates around, this assumption denies the very complex interaction between readers and texts. Moreover, the predominately young fan base is not the vapid, only-caring-about-iPods bunch they are made out to be. It may seem youth culture is not concerned nor engaged with the bigger issues shaping the world, but their devotion to books that speak to these bigger issues—such as *The Harry Potter Series*, the *Lord of the Rings Trilogy*, and, yes, *Twilight*—belies this claim. Each of these series, while very different, speaks to enduring sociocultural issues. *Twilight*, coming out during an era of extreme cultural anxiety, salves readers' fears and ignites their desires.

On the plus side, the series has a female protagonist at the helm and many female characters—a factor that in itself is still a rarity in both printed and visual narratives. It covers topics that are too often put under erasure-violence against women, rape culture, female sexuality, changing codes of masculinity. It has male characters who talk and feel, female characters that refuse to live by the purity-ball paradigm, storylines that metaphorically grapple with inter-racial relationships. Its focus on the obsessive and even dangerous components of romance, as well as on sexuality, has encouraged readers to discuss what con-stitutes a healthy relationship.

On the more problematic side, the series champions rather conventional notions of gender, sexuality, race, class, and belief. It focuses obsessively on true love, a focus that also romanticizes violence, polices female sexuality, and promotes abstinence. It is imbued with racialized representations that do not take white privilege or racism to task. The saga offers an uncritical (even glow-ing or — more aptly — sparkling) depiction of patriarchal capitalism. It upholds norms in relation not only to gender and class, but also body and beauty, giving the message that youth and physical attractiveness should be pursued at all costs. It is underpinned by an unspoken but pervasive religious subtext, one shaped by the Mormonism of the author specifically and our cultural turn to the religious right more generally.

As a reader, while part of me enjoyed escaping into Bella's world, another part of me never stopped analyzing the deeper messages and implications of the series. I am wary of some of the more stereotypical, conservative, and disempowering messages the series circulates around. Though I have been warned that fans don't want to hear anything critical about their beloved *Twi*-texts, I hope I am correct in giving fans more credit than this. I agree with Buffy scholar Lorna Jowett that "it might even be true that fans are more likely to be critical, not less, since they regularly engage in discussion and analysis" (1). I have found this to be true at the many *Twilight* events I have attended. It is also certainly true in the lively *Twi*-net world — that collection of blogs, websites, discussion groups, and fan-fiction sites that regularly and enthusias-tically discuss and analyze *Twilight*. These "*Twilight*ers" have taken the message of cultural studies theorists and feminist scholars to heart (though they most likely don't realize it) that critical analysis of popular texts is important — that it reveals a great deal about our human condition and our place in social real-ity.

The *Twilight* saga is popular by any standard, breaking best-seller lists and sales ranks the world over. Like the *Book of Mormon*, which "was ignored by literary critics" yet "brought several hundred thousand immigrants to America in the 19th century," *Twilight* will likely ultimately be recognized as an important cultural text worthy of academic study — indeed, this realization is already in evidence not only in the present study but in other recently published titles (Brodie 67). In particular, cultural studies and feminist scholars have already recognized the saga's social importance. As the former is a field that insists popular cultural forms are worthy of academic study, it is a discipline particularly conducive to the study of the *Twilight* texts and fandom.

In *Anatomy of Criticism*, Northrop Frye claimed all texts are equally worth academic attention, paving the way for an expansion of what types of texts counted as "worthy" of scholarly study (186). Frederic Jameson later argued we can use texts to find "clues which lead us back to the concrete historical situation of the individual text itself," and that "allow us to read its structure as ideology, as a socially symbolic act, as a protopolitical response to a historical dilemma" (157). If we read the *Twilight* saga in this vein, we can see it as a "symbolic act" engaging in complex ways with its "concrete historical situation." Both the author and readers enact "protopolitical" responses to historical dilemmas relating to gender norms, the structure of the family, and acceptable sexuality, among other things. If we take Janice Radway's model, and look at "what a literary text can be taken as evidence for," we might argue that *Twilight* proves we have yet to become post-feminist or post-racial, let alone post–Puritanical (2). As Jackson Katz asserts, "One of the central insights of the relatively young discipline of cultural studies is that questions of identity ('Who am I?') and ideology ('How does the world work and how do I fit into it?') are intimately connected to the stories that circulate in a culture and give answers to these deeply human concerns" (151). Yet, as Radway reminds us, drawing on Stanley Fish, texts do not have any one meaning or intrinsic value — rather, readers *construct* meaning. However, "whatever the theoretical possibility of an infinite number of readings," Radway writes, "there are patterns or regularities to what viewers and readers bring to texts in large part because they acquire specific cultural competencies as a consequence of their particular social location. Similar readings are produced ... because similarly located readers learn a similar set of reading strategies and interpretive codes that they bring to bear upon the texts they encounter" (8).

Thus, *Twilight* readers, located in the early 21st century, will undoubtedly answer "how does the world work" types of questions through their particular sociohistorical lens. As Radway explains, "Just as one might want to ask what sorts of social grammars prepare adolescent boys to understand and take interest in slasher films like those in the *Halloween* series, so one might also want to ask what competencies prepare certain women to recognize romances as relevant to their experience and as potential routes to pleasure" (10). In regards to explaining the allure of *Twilight*, we might ask what draws readers to its particular "routes to pleasure"— or, to put it in the terms of *Twilighter* fans, what makes someone a "*Twi*-hard" or a "*Twi*-addict." There is of course a deep connection "between social location and the complex process of interpretation," and thus those actively located within religious belief systems will interpret differently to those who are not, and so on (8).

Feminist scholars and critics draw on these insights of cultural studies to enact a more thorough and conscious analysis of patriarchy and gender norms, as indeed they are beginning to do with *Twilight*. Popular fiction (and reader's responses to it) often represents, as Radway argues, a "very real dissatisfaction and embodies a valid, if limited, protest" (220). Given that even those of us who define ourselves as feminist, including myself, often find fiction such as *Twilight* appealing, we need to examine what this attraction suggests. Tania Modleski, noting that "feminist critics seem to be strenuously disassociating themselves from the seductiveness of feminine texts," makes a similar claim, emphasizing that romances increase in popularity during socially tumultuous times (14). In current times, why and how are our real-world contexts fueling *Twilight*'s massive appeal? Such questions demand attention. As Elana Levine declares, "It is only by understanding the gendered appeals of the present that we might shape the social, political, and cultural dimensions of the future" (285). It is these "gendered appeals," among others, that the present study sets out to explore. Among the specific question this book will address are:

- Why are vampires so compelling at this particular historical juncture?
- What does the particular representation of romance say about our cultural notions of love, romance, sexuality, and desire, particularly in relation to our abstinence-only culture?
- What messages do the textual representation of gender, race, class, sexuality, and belief send to readers? How are these messages a reflection of cultural trends and ideologies?
- What characterizes the *Twilight* fandom? How can we account for the popularity of the series across generations, genders, and belief systems?
- How does the popularity of the saga further the norms and practices of consumer culture, and, further, what does the massive franchising of *Twilight* portend?
- How does *Twilight* criticize the social order from which it springs? Or does it?
- Alluring as they are, how might some of the messages of the series be problematic?

These and other questions will frame the present study, with each of the chapters reading the texts and their cultural impact in relation to surrounding sociohistorical contexts.

Chapter 1 delves into how Meyer's saga both accords with and departs from traditional representations of the vampire. The chapter asserts that the series introduces us to a new breed of sympathetic vampire and lusty wolf, one that promotes rather conservative notions of race, class, gender, and sexuality yet has some traces of subversive messages.

Chapter 2 explores how the romantic packaging of the series is very seductive — though many of its messages seek to repress and render passive — its female audience. Arguing romance narratives such as *Twilight* carry on a long tradition of conditioning females to actively pursue the very types of relationships that have resulted in their social and cultural subordination, this chapter examines both the more positive and the more delimiting messages at the series' romantic core.

Chapter 3 asserts that the series and reactions to it serve as a fascinating testament to our cultural ambivalence about females. Exploring the representations of femininity and motherhood the saga enacts, the chapter questions in what ways the saga supports regressive gender norms and in what ways it critiques the social systems that keep women socially subordinated.

Chapter 4 examines how the saga engages with changing conceptions of masculinity, arguing the series presents neither a subversive nor a conservative view of masculinity, but, rather, a contradictory mixture of both. As readers, the chapter contends, we are encouraged to root for a white, wealthy hetero vampire, yet we are also introduced to likeable wolves-of-color and tenderhearted father figures.

Chapter 5 argues that the narrative offers rather incongruous representations and ideas about sexuality. Exploring how the series depicts female sexuality as a dangerous threat that needs be tamed via vampirism (which, in the saga, is also representative of religion and its emphasis on heterosexual reproductive married monogamy), this chapter focuses on cultural contexts such as violence against women, abstinence-only education, and arguments over "traditional" marriage.

Chapter 6 investigates the ways in which Mormon theology undergirds the text. Paying particular attention to Mormonism's beliefs regarding race and gender, the chapter contends that white, male Mormon vampires are held up as heroic, angelic, and godly, while non-white, non-male, and non-religious characters are presented as needing to be "converted" to vampirism (which is the symbolic equivalent, the chapter posits, of Mormonism).

Chapter 7 explores the ways in which the series champions and bolsters hegemonic white masculinity, especially via its presentation of the sparkly white vampires and the "russet-colored" Quileute wolves. Examining the systems of power and privilege that permeate society, the chapter argues that via Bella's desire to become vampire, readers are encouraged to also desire the wealth, beauty, and privilege of the Cullen vampire lifestyle.

Chapter 8 documents the ways in which the *Twilight* phenomenon speaks to the consuming desires of the contemporary moment and explores the franchising and corporatization of the books, films, and actors. The chapter also observes the productive engagement of the fandom, contending that *Twilighters* are not merely passive consumers but also active, sometimes subversive, fans who resist cultural norms via their engagement with the *Twilight* phenomenon.

Overall, *Seduced by Twilight* insists that we need to examine what the popularity of the series means and to forge ways to respond to the zeitgeist that promotes critical discussion. The saga, much like any text, is neither wholly regressive nor progressive, neither all positive nor all problematic. More to the point, to ignore its cultural impact or write it off dismissively as "just a girl thing" not only would participate in the sexism that still shapes wider culture, but also would deny us the opportunity to discover how, why, and to what end we are seduced by *Twilight*.

Indeed, the title of the saga, though not the one Meyer intended, is ultimately a quite fitting metaphor for the seductive appeal of the saga. "Twilight" literally refers to the time between night and day, when the sun is still below the horizon. It is an in-between time, serving as the bookmark to both parts of the day, marking the time between dawn and sunrise as well as that between sunset and dusk. The light provided by the upper atmosphere, rather than by direct sunlight, offers a muted quality, a sort of natural "romantic lighting." Just as *twilight* is an in-between time that refuses to accord to the either/or dualistic thinking that so shapes our world, so is the saga "in between" many key cultural dichotomies— it is neither feminist nor anti-feminist, neither fundamentalist nor anti-religion, neither progressive nor conservative. At the level of content, it also circulates around various binaries such as human/vampire, good/evil, moral/immoral, civilized/uncivilized. It explores the in-between space of these constructions, suggesting that "*Twilight*" is a better place to be, is indeed the place we inhabit as humans who are neither wholly good nor wholly evil. The fact that "*Twilight*" has become the name used to refer to the saga as whole reflects how apt this title is. For the purposes of the present study, "*Twilight*" will similarly be used to refer to the entire series. Further, for purposes of brevity, when referencing page numbers of specific quotes, the abbreviations *T* (for *Twilight*), *NM* (for *New Moon*), *E* (for *Eclipse*), and *BD* (for *Breaking Dawn*) will be used.

I hope that you find this exploration of *Twilight* seductive, that you are willing, like Little Red Riding Hood, to stray from the straight and narrow path into the darker wooded areas that allow for explorations of the less sparkly aspects not only of the *Twilight* series, but also of its cultural milieu.

Chapter 1

The Allure of the Vampire,
the Danger of the Wolf
Or, Why to Avoid Big,
Bad Shape-shifters in Favor of
Knights in Sparkling Armor

So much of what lures us about the vampire also, when viewed from a different light, repels us. Immortality, in our imaginations, is often latched onto as an impossible but very desirable dream. We do not tend to think of the bored, listless immortals of Swift's *Gulliver's Travels* but rather about avoiding death and all it entails, about having super strength or speed, about amassing wealth or power. When it comes to the vampire, the immortality of this creature's existence is the shiny bauble that blinds us from the harsher realities of a revenant existence — killing, blood-drinking, sleeping in coffins, avoiding sunlight, watching those we love wither and die around us. Instead of these factors, we focus on defying aging and the promise of eternal, undying love.

Though vampires emerged in much lore as rather gruesome creatures, they have become increasingly sympathetic figures over the years. Montague Summers (whom Meyer quotes in *Twilight*), in his paradigmatic *Vampire: His Kith and Kin*, refers to the vampire as "a pariah even among demons," noting that "there is no figure so terrible, no figure so dreaded and abhorred, yet dight with such fearful fasincation, as the vampire" (xxi, 1). Yet, as vampire lore spans the globe, reaching far back into dateless antiquity, vampire myths and legends, and the resulting fiction, films, and television shows they have spawned, vary a great deal. While their most enduring characteristic is that of undead bloodsucker, their other common attributes (fangs, speed, strength, and susceptibility to sunlight, garlic, crosses, and stakes) vary across cultures, time periods, and medium. As Paul Barber explores in *Vampires, Burial, and Death*, the vampire of folklore bears "precious little resemblance" to that of fiction (2). Maintaining that the folkloric vampire emerged as a way to explain disease, death, and bodily dissolution in preindustrial societies, Barber's work details the vast differences between vampires of lore and those that later came to grace our pages and screens.

In contemporary times, the vampire is rarely an evil walking corpse with a cruel and insatiable lust for blood, which s/he sucks from the victim's heart (like the vampires of folklore), nor is s/he an undead plump peasant who brings death to her/his neighbors and drinks cattle blood — rather, s/he is usually a tortured outcast, a lonely immortal longing for love, family, and approval.[1] Meyer's 21st-century vampires, in particular, are more angelic than monstrous. The Cullen vampires are far from the blood-thirsty killers or hairy-palmed coffin sleepers that populated early lore and literature. They are not defined by the more ick-inducing factors of vampire existence. They don't kill humans. They don't sleep in coffins (they don't even need to sleep). They are not harmed by sunlight (as so many celluloid vampires have been from *Nosferatu* on), but are illuminated by it. They are not afflicted with beaked noses or unsightly fangs as were Count Dracula and Count Orlack.[2] To the contrary, they are preternaturally gorgeous creatures, their ice-cold ultra–white bodies not off-puttingly corpse-like, but incarnations of the body beautiful; they are more Greek god than revivified corpse. Indeed, the Cullen vampires function as extreme versions of the sympathetic vampire.[3]

Vampires that Matter: The Sympathetic Vampire and Cultural Outsiderdom

The 20th century (and now the 21st) has seen an increasing number of such sympathetic vampires. The late 20th century, for example, saw a number of sympathetic vampires. Black, queer, working class, and/or fat, vampires often came to embody an intersectional otherness that worked to interrogate societal norms and hierarchies.[4] Patrick Day notes this sympathetic vampire became particularly pervasive in the last third of 20th century with well over a thousand narratives featuring such revenants (33). Arguing this time period transformed the vampire from monster into an outsider figure with utopian aspirations not in keeping with "conventional middle-class American society," Day names this shift the "liberation of the vampire" (33). Milly Williamson similarly reads the modern vampire as "a misfit with a good image" (186). In narratives such as *The Gilda Stories* and *The Vampire Tapestry*, the vampire figure is utilized in order to variously explore racism and capitalism, while popular vampire shows and films such as *Buffy the Vampire Slayer*, *The Lost Boys*, and *Near Dark* depict alternative gender, sexual, and family formations. More recently, *True Blood* and *The Vampire Diaries* portray humanized vampires who are concerned with love and romance just as much as (if not more than) with killing or power. Films and television have greatly influenced modern conceptions of the vampire, as

Stacy Abbot documents in her work *Celluloid Vampires*, bringing her/him out of the coffin (so to speak) and into the (post)postmodern world of rapidly changing global, national, and local formations.

As many texts and films attest, the vampire offers a "way of inhabiting difference," for embracing otherness and the "painful awareness of outsiderdom" (Williamson 1–2). This interrogation of outsiderdom that vampire narratives frequently enact is fitting for a global world undergoing reconfigurations of race, class, gender, and sexual norms. This aspect of vampire tales has led various scholars to read the vampire as a boundary-breaking, transgressive, even queer, figure.[5] As Kathryn Kane argues, "The vampire is a queer figure because it is disruptive; the vampire breaks down categories, transgresses boundaries, and upsets the very premises upon which systems of normality are structured" (103). Noting this is true of *most* vampires, Kane's work explores how Meyer's vampires "clearly and firmly refuse the queerness typically associated with the figure" (103). While many vampires are transgressive figures, I would counter that just as many vampire tales work to demonize the transgressions of the vampire in order to bolster rather than subvert societal norms. Where *Twilight* is different is in its use of vampires who are themselves very traditional and conservative. Though horror often serves a conservative function (as will be discussed below), the figure of the vampire has most often been used to represent a transgressive threat. This is why, as Williamson points out, at the core of the vampire is the "desire to signify," "to *matter* in the light of day and not just in the shadows"—to not be, in short, an outsider (2). We see this desire to signify in relation to matters of sexuality (as in *Carmilla, The Vampire Chronicles, Nadja, The Addiction, The Hunger*), race (*The Gilda Stories, Blade, Blacula, Vampire in Brooklyn, Blood: The Last Vampire*), and class/community (*Dracula, Near Dark, The Lost Boys, Daybreakers*). We also see the desire to *matter* to other people, to family, to society as a whole.

The sympathetic vampire, in short, signifies our desires to become what Judith Butler terms "bodies that matter"—or beings that are not abject outsiders or abhorred others but rather accepted, desired, and respected individuals with the agency to act as viable subjects (16). Though Summers argues that the vampire "is a thing which belongs to no world at all," the sympathetic vampire often rejects her/his Othered status, trying to fit into societal norms—to, for example, be allowed to marry (as in *True Blood*) or to have children (as in *Twilight*) (1). Such storylines often validate various social formations—marriage, family, monogamy, and/or heterosexual reproduction (though *Twilight* admittedly does far more validating of social norms than does *True Blood*). This validating function of the vampire mythos is, according to James Twitchell, what makes it so enduring. As he contends, in order to endure, a myth "must do more than inform or validate some social order; it must suggest specific behavior that maintains both the social order and bolsters the individual's sense of worth" (85).

Along their travels from antiquity to contemporary times, vampires have variously supported and resisted the social order, sometimes behaving in ways that bolster societal norms and sometimes revealing those norms to be unjust, outdated, or in need of change. Likewise, their permutations have dealt with relations between self and other as well as between self, society, family, religion, nation, and so on. Abbott's work contends that vampires have come to represent the experience of modernity, which she defines as the "eternal present" (5). This formulation seems particularly fitting for a figure that changes to reflect her/his social milieu and, as such, lives constantly in the "eternal present." Or, as Nina Auerbach puts it, "Every age embraces the vampire it needs" (145). This also explains why vampires have a tendency to proliferate during periods of social change and unrest — they, as our undying, eternally changing metaphors, reflect back to us truths about the contemporary moment — whether that moment be the Victorian era, the 1970s, or the early 21st century — and, in particular, they "go where the power is" so as to interrogate shifting societal formations (Auerbach 6). Indeed this is why, according to Auerbach, vampires flourished in the United States in the 20th and 21st centuries. But if Meyer's vampires are the type of undead that our contemporary moment "needs," what does this say about our era? If they indeed "go where the power is," does this mean that power is located in a clumsy, low-self–esteem teenager living on the Olympic Peninsula? Well, yes and no. Bella is hardly power incarnate, yet her character serves as a means through which to interrogate various nodes of power of the contemporary moment — religion, sexuality, gender, race, and class. Edward, as the white vampire knight, *does* represent power — a power that can be linked to conservative religious and political movements that very much want to maintain (and extend) their power. In this regard, *Twilight* vampires speak to our cultural need to come to terms with not only teenage sexuality but also shifting political and religious power structures.

Patriarchal Vampires, Submissive Females, and Chaste Heterosexuality: The Conservative Function of Vampire Narratives

On a mythic level, *Twilight* validates patriarchal capitalism and suggests that married monogamy creates a stable society while at the same time bolstering readers' worth by feeding longstanding beliefs such as "true love conquers all." This indeed is a powerful myth. According to Tricia Clasen, the series circulates around four key romantic myths: love at first sight, love is forever, love is the most important relationship, and love requires mind reading (120). Though Clasen notes that "myths establish and reveal the values and preferred actions of a society," her article does not examine how the vampire mythos is combined with romantic myths in order to foster very particular values and preferred actions (120). If, as Twitchell similarly claims, "myths embody and convey the most sacred truths a society can first produce and then protect," *Twilight* vampire mythos conveys that patriarchy — and the white, male, heterosexual privilege it fosters — is "sacred" and must be protected at all cost — even at the cost of one's mortality and soul (85).

Yet, as myth, the vampire has often been utilized to explore how non–traditional sexuality and/or family arrangements threaten so-called civil life and normal families. Indeed, the vampire has been put into play in order to allow for expression of those desires that civil society represses — the "aberrant" sexuality and gender performances where female/male, heterosexual/homosexual, penetrating/receiving all become blurred and open to contestation–even the boundaries of the body become open (through the vampire's bite) — with the mixing and drinking of blood representing racial, sexual, and gender transgressions. Horror generally and vampires specifically thus contribute to our understanding of social norms and ideologies.

Twitchell explores the mythic function of horror, arguing that horrific motifs are "more than just fear-jerkers to the culture that animates them; they are invariably the most subtle projections of buried and repressed fear" (25). Claiming that such motifs are "drawn from a combination of individual and group repressions," Twitchell draws on Freud's theory of compulsive repetition to explain how that which we fear/repress we also desire (77–78). Horror, in effect, functions as a release valve, allowing us to work through these fears and desires in a way that does not threaten the comforting grand narratives of our social reality. The vampire myth, as discussed above, explores norms (and the transgression of them) in relation to sexuality, death and aging, gender, and family. Sometimes the vampire is the sexual predator, sometimes the undead beauty, sometimes the phallic woman, sometimes the evil father figure who refuses to relinquish control (or women) to his sons/younger men.

Though in our technologically saturated age we often overlook the enduring presence of myths in our lives, they are nevertheless there, teaching us how to be, who to be, who to love. Taking off where fairy tales end, horror myths have a similarly conservative function; they "conserve culture *and* protect the individual" (Twitchell 92). Or, as Stephen King puts it, "the horror story ... is really as conservative as an Illinois Republican in a three-piece pinstriped suit.... Its main purpose is to reaffirm the virtues of the norm by showing us what awful things happen to people who venture into taboo lands" (368). In *Twilight*, we are indeed taught that awful things will happen when we venture outside the norm — things such as rape, incarceration, murder, damnation, the breakdown of the family. Though more romance than horror, *Twilight*'s dalliance with terror — the terror of the unknown, of death, of powerlessness—conveys that if we avoid "taboo lands" we can live "happily ever after" — as indeed Bella and Edward do (and even the epic vampire battle with the Volturi has a happy ending). Thus, though monster scholar David Skal claims the horror genre deals with the impossibility of the American Dream, *Twilight* does not acknowledge this impossibility. Instead, the saga presents us with the Cullen vampires, who embody undead versions of the dream.[6] In contrast to horror's focus on "disenfranchisement, exclusion, downward mobility," where "the family is a sick-joke, its house more likely to offer siege instead of shelter," *Twilight* offers inclusion into the Cullen family lifestyle and the upward mobility that it brings (Skal 354). As King further writes, "The melodies of the horror tale are simple and repetitive, and they are melodies of disestablishment and disintegration ... but another paradox is that the ritual outletting of these emotions seems to bring things back to a more stable and constructive state again" (26). In Meyer's saga, disestablishment and disintegration are indeed the consequences of not playing by the rules— of being too sexual, too rebellious, or simply not properly feminine, as the "aberrant" lifestyles of the James/Laurent/Victoria/newborn army as well as the Volturi portray. The horrors these bad vampires represent are laid to rest with the comforting promise that the good vampires will win out in the end, and that all any woman needs to be happy is a good man. This message relies on normative constructions of gender, power, race, and class— all is "right" by the end (as is the case with most horror and romance), meaning that existing power structures continue unchallenged — that white male privilege remains in its lofty tower — or, more aptly, its gleaming vampire mansion.

As such, *Twilight* accords with what Williamson argues is the raison d'être of vampires: "The vampires of the West exist to frighten us into acquiescence, to reassert patriarchy, racial superiority, family values and chaste heterosexuality" (1). But *Twilight* vampires don't so much frighten us into acquiescence as lure us into it — if we love the likes of Edward, the saga promises, we, too, can have all the privileges Bella accrues by the saga's end — love, wealth, beauty, eternal youth. Here, the series also accords with King's definition of horror as an "out–letting and a lancing" that functions as "a nationwide analyst's couch" (26). In effect, Meyer beckons reader's to lay back and share their fantasies and fears, then to be lulled into sedation with promises of love and happiness. If many vampires shock us into acquiescence, Meyer's vampires *drug* us into it; they become our brand of heroine, the fix that promises to dampen our fears and soothe our anxieties. While *Dracula* valued progress and rationalism, ending with "the reinstatement of Victorian middle-class social and moral structure," *Twilight* values regression and romanticism — a retreat not into Van Helsing–style rationalism, but into Bella's emotions (Hollinger 206). Like *Dracula*, the saga ends with the restoration of middle-class values; like much popular fiction, *Twilight* educates us to accept norms and does so, significantly, via the condemnation of femininity and the valorization of masculinity.

Literature often performs this function, encouraging readers to accept prevailing social formations, as Ken Gelder so cogently explores in relation to the vampire figure in his *Reading the Vampire*. And if "monsters are metaphors," as Franco Moretti similarly argues, the Cullens seem to be held up as representative of the ideal — the ideal lovers, the ideal family, the ideal appearance. However, this suggestion has the ancillary outcome of suggesting that other ways of existence pale in comparison to the ideal — including other family formations, sexualities, socioeconomic configurations, and racial/ethnic identities. As readers don't tend to recognize the monster as a metaphor but read the monster literally (as Moretti further points out), their zealous identification with the Cullen vampires results, for many, in a widespread desire to become — or to become loved by — a Cullen.

This desire to become a vampire of course has a long history, with some people claiming they are true to life vampires, others living a "vampire lifestyle," and still others immersing themselves in vampire fandoms and vampire–related events.[7] However, these vampiric quests have usually been associated with outsiderdom and difference, with an embrace of subverting societal norms in terms of dress, demeanor, and desire. With an emphasis on black clothing, overt sexuality, and/or dalliances with violence/blood, vampire aficionados often aim to be transgressive rather than mainstream. As Catherine Spooner points out in her study, *Fashioning Gothic Bodies*, dressing up as (or merely admiring) vampires is not always subversive but "is often dependent on formula, convention, and mass-market images" rather than "a radical gesture against the norm" (167). The conventional dependence on mass-market images certainly allies to *Twilight* culture, where fans' actions accord with and support social norms in relation to consumerism. Readers' desires for romantic monogamy, for true love, for family, for belief — all of these also concur with accepted social formations. Further, fans' adherence to the love-struck fan-model and their willingness to spend, spend, spend on the franchise supports the consumer capitalist society of which *Twilight* is a part. Finally, their admiration for the abstinence-only message at the core of the series is in keeping with our culture's sexually regressive turn. Granted, readers and fans do not have a monolithic response, and many do question rather than support societal norms via their love of *Twilight* (e.g., through insisting on eroticizing its content and/or refusing to buy into its messages about gender and sexuality); nonetheless, overall, the fandom is not resistant to major trends and beliefs of the contemporary moment — it is not so much a counter–culture fandom as a pro-culture fandom, supporting as it does traditional notions of romance, family, and belief. As such, it makes Auerbach's claim that vampires have been co–opted by "a conservative social enterprise" ring true (186).

Other scholars claim that the vampire has not so much been co–opted but rather s/he has always been a figure related to restoring the social order, a figure exploring "the relationship between violence, social cohesion, and justice" (McClelland 30). For example, McClelland, in *Slayers and Their Vampires*, posits that stories of good and evil "tend to represent the status quo and help to maintain the current distribution of power," that when the vampire is killed, social categories are healed (169). However, in *Twilight*, the vampire is not killed—rather, the human is. Killing Bella, turning her vampire, restores her "proper" sexuality and ensconces her within the good Cullen family. Those vampires that are killed, though—James, Victoria, Laurent, and the newborns—posed a threat to normative social formations. In effect, the Cullens (and the humans and wolves that help them) become vampire *slayers*—killing other vampires in order to preserve things as they are (which is exactly what McClelland names as a primary function of the slayer figure).[8] Thus, if, as Twitchell and others argue, "the vampire myth, like all horror stories, is conservative," we might read the slaying of vampires as the laying to rest that which threatens to change the social order (139). Or, to put it another way, the vampire can function as a *progressive* figure that can provide a catalyst to break out of social normativity, threatening to change/infect the status quo with her/his venomous, infecting bite. Indeed, Summers names this "craving to pass on the horrible pollution" as "the most dreaded quality of the vampire" (168). Most often, this bite is associated with changing the vampire's victim into a lustful, insatiable creature who will no longer abide by societal rules, especially in regards to female sexuality. Yet in *Twilight* this trend is reversed: Bella's change to vampire, instead of turning her into a more lustful creature, ultimately turns her into a chaste and devoted wife and mother, as well as into a valued member of the Cullen family. The saga thus displays a distinct yearning for romantic love, but also for familial love.

Vampire Family Values

Though the vampire, due to her/his need for blood and thus either violence or murder, has often been presented as necessarily solitary and nomadic, the Cullen vampires long for family and stability. In contrast to Count Dracula, who traveled to London from the east, or Gilda from Jewelle Gomez' novel, who travels across the United States, never permanently settling anywhere, or even the vampire family from *Near Dark* who race from sundown to sundown in their sun–shielded vehicles, the Cullen vampires have made Forks home. Yet, like many of their vampire predecessors, they, too, traveled from east to west, finally settling on the western-most outpost of the Olympic Peninsula. In a new amalgam of Western and road movie, the saga circulates around travel, movement, and liberation from social constraints. Abbott notes how many vampires include such an admixture of the Western and road movie genres, focusing particularly on *Near Dark* and *The Lost Boys*. Bella, unlike Caleb from *Near Dark*, must not choose between "the nocturnal, urban lifestyle of the vampires" and her family—instead, she is able to become part of the extended Cullen family *by becoming a vampire* (Abbott 28). Granted, she could have chosen to remain human (and to possibly have a future life in La Push with Jacob, as she pictures in *Eclipse*). Indeed, she can be read as choosing between a figure that was a staple in Western films—the noble savage—and the gothic hero/rake Edward. Instead of choosing the "freedom of the expansive landscape" celebrated in both Western films and road movies, Bella chooses "the social constraints of civilization" that the Cullens conform to (i.e., traditional conceptions of the family, sexuality, gender, belief, and so on) (Abbott 164, 170). Her choice is interesting also in terms of the Gothic conventions that it both harkens and subverts. While the Western and the road movie focus on open, sprawling space and frontier landscapes, Gothic conventions focus on creepy old edifices, claustrophobic spaces, dark passageways, and secret chambers.

While *Twilight* is in keeping with the Gothic emphasis on an endangered heroine, a dubious hero, and atmospheric weather, it departs from such conventions in its representation of nature (and particularly the forest) as more dangerous than the Cullen mansion (which is a far cry from the crumbling, musty castles of Gothic novels). Forks is associated with nature and bad weather, with Bella referring to its dark sky as "like a cage" (*T* 11). She calls Forks "my personal hell on Earth" and is particularly damning of its forests, describing them as "murky and ominous" and filled with dangerous roots and branches (*T* 26, 116). In the saga, the forests are aligned to the Quileute wolves and also to the non–Cullen vampires who wish to kill Bella (James, Laurent, Victoria, and later the Volturi), who "ghost" across the forest like Gothic visions incarnate. Significantly, whenever Bella is depicted as enjoying the forest she is either being carried on Edward's back and is "above" nature, surveying it from his angelic heights (as the *Twilight* film adaptation makes particularly clear) or else bounding through it as a newborn vampire, controlling nature rather than succumbing to its "emerald confines" (*T* 117). In this regard, the saga toys with conventions of the Gothic, the Road Movie, and the Western and does so, significantly, in ways that repeatedly bolster rather than subvert social norms. For example, as opposed to most vampires, who are unable to (or do not wish to) "settle down," the Cullens play at being human as best they can so as to participate in that most human (and Mormon) of goals—love and family. Though vampire narratives often entail an acute longing for communal or familial belonging, *Twilight* makes such longing *the* focus of the saga and, in so doing, loses the vampire genre's regular emphasis on horror, transgression, and social dissolution. Admittedly, many vampires, as Patrick Day documents, "aspire to love, family and community far more than revolution" (34). Yet, Day insists that vampires also dream of liberation, especially in their attempts to "assert that the true fulfillment of humanity results when all aspects of our identity become liberated from the various forms of repression dominating middle class society" (34).

Yet, in *Twilight*, Meyer's Cullens certainly aspire to love, family, and community more than to revolution. Moreover, they are not keen to escape the norms of middle-class society—though they do in fact do one better by according to upper-class or aristocratic norms and, in so doing, bolster the notion that a society stratified by wealth and class standing is not a problematic night-mare but instead an uber–American (vampire) dream. In addition to being good upper-class citizens and consumer capitalists, the Cullens can also be read as incarnations of nomadic Mormons, exiled further and further west in a long history of religious persecution (a topic to be explored in detail in chapter 6). As contemporary incarnations of the sympathetic undead, the Cullen vampires consist of a good-hearted doctor and benevolent patriarch (Carlisle), a formerly abused single mother (Esme), a tortured genius (Edward), a beautiful rape vic-tim (Rosalie), a strong, gorgeous, and funny hunk (Emmett), a psychic female labeled insane (Alice), a shell-shocked war vet (Jasper), and, ultimately, a self–effacing, jaded young woman convinced she is both unimportant and unlovable (Bella). These vampires have come to haunt the popular imagination as they, like most vampires, are embedded within their cultural contexts—contexts such as abstinence-only education, a so-called post–racial and post–feminist society, and a political turn to the conservative, religious right.[9]

This component of vampires—wherein they seem imminently able to adapt to changing times, makes them, as Auerbach argues, "perfect survivors" (1). She, like many other vampire scholars, argues that our "mutating vampires" reflect their respective sociohistorical epochs (1). Similarly, Brian Frost empha-sizes that "perhaps the most remarkable characteristic of the vampire is its ability to adapt to changing social and environmental conditions" while the anthology *The Vampire as Metaphor in Contemporary Culture* argues for the vampire as "a creature who can take on the allegorical weight of changing times and collective psyches" (1, 4). As Auerbach contends, "The alacrity with which vampires shape themselves to personal and national moods is an adaptive trait their apparent uniformity masks" (5). Though they often share a number of key traits—such as fangs, a desire for human blood, an aversion to garlic, sun-light, and crosses—they also are so adaptable as to accommodate the changing sociocultural and religious mores of different time periods. While, as Auerbach puts it, "ghosts, werewolves, and manufactured monsters are relatively change-less, more aligned with eternity than with time," vampires "blend in the chang-ing cultures they inhabit" (6). By extension, vampire mythology, as Twitchell argues, is able to "continually re–magnetize ... around the audience's changing lodestones" (110). In regards to *Twilight*, one of the key lodestones it magnetizes around is societal attitudes towards sex and sexuality.

Twilight *as Fable: Or, the Moral of the Story Is: No Sex Before Marriage*

Twitchell, arguing that horror maintains "the social stability of culture" and "plays out the 'do's' and 'don't's' of adolescent sexuality explaining to the

soon-to-be-reproductive audience exactly how to avoid making horrible mis-
takes," could feasibly be writing about *Twilight* specifically (though he is not)
(65–66). Meyer's saga indeed aims to maintain social stability and offers a list
of do's and don'ts—do fall in love, don't have sex before marriage, do marry
and procreate. These messages, which Twitchell suggests are at the heart of all
horror, account for what he names "the ultra–conservative nature of horror
myths" (65). Horror stories, in effect, are fairy tales for grown ups, teaching
people "what is sexually permissible and what is sexually damaging" (Twitchell
139). Just as some versions of *Little Red Riding Hood* teach one not to lose that
little red cap to the first man one meets, so does *Twilight* teach that sex can
equal death, especially sex with a wolf![10]

If we consider that the aim of fairy tales and horror is "biological efficiency"
or "repression in the service of protecting established reproductive patterns,"
we can see why these tales are so appealing and enduring—they speak to the
very heart of our being—to our desires for love, affection, sex, belonging
(Twitchell 139). Meanwhile, they converse in a way that is often parental,
instructing us to "be safe" much in the same way Edward instructs Bella (*T*
249). Further, such tales do so in a way that speaks to our collective psyche, to
our social selves, to that part of our being that has been so thoroughly instructed
(and constructed) to live life in accordance with cultural dictates. This collective
aspect of our response to fairy and horror tales has a "contagious resonance"
due to its non–solitary nature and the ways in which it responds to repressed
desires and fears (Auerbach 3). This aspect of narratives is alluring, as it revolves
around our psychosexual cultural beliefs, functioning as an ongoing and
expanding "fable of sexual initiation" (Twitchell 126). Such fables are introduced
to us as children, through *Little Red Riding Hood* and the like, and then continue
on via romance novels, horror films, young adult fiction, and so on. *Twilight*—
as a series that appeals to those from 8 to 80—appears to be a cross-generational
fable, one that circulates around issues of sexual initiation as well as sexual
activity, relationships, and love.

From a patriarchal perspective, many such myths warn about the dangers
of "polymorphously perverse sexual activities," about the threat females (supposedly) pose to reason, civility, and male dominance, and about the (supposed)
need to maintain the nuclear family and the heterosexual monogamy society
is built upon (Aldiss x). However, such warnings are often not overt but hidden.
Further, in such tales, women often bear the weight of being the true monsters
and/or the pure maidens who must be protected. *Twilight*, with Victoria, Jane,
Bella, and so on, carries on the war against femininity and gender equality in
a narrative package that is incredibly seductive to the very people its messages
wish to repress. Though Meyer and many of her fans deny any such agenda,
the antifeminine, pro-patriarchy messages of *Twilight* are in line with many a
vampire tale. As Bram Dijkstra argues, "The writers of contemporary Gothic novels, the makers of vampire movies, as well as the many men and women who are

virtually addicted to these narratives, pronouncing them harmless fun or simply campy entertainment, are still unconsciously responding very directly to an antifeminine sensibility established in its modern form and symbolic structure by the sexist ideologues among the nineteenth-century intelligentsia" (340–41). Here, in the 21st century, readers are similarly responding to the "antifeminine sensibility" that continues to be established by ideologues—especially in relation to abstinence, heteronormativity, and the *need* to maintain traditional marital and family formations.

As Twitchell and others contend, the vampire myth is very much about "proper reproductive sex" and is thus a conservative myth in many regards, holding up the "good father" and the nuclear family (159). In *Twilight*, Carlisle is the good father, modeling for Edward how to create a stable patriarchal family of his own (which, by the saga's end, Edward is well on his way to creating with Bella as wife, and Renesmee and Jacob as heterosexually paired daughter/son). Jacob, in contrast, is the younger, racialized suitor who endangers Bella's purity and harkens from a nontraditional family "pack." Various other males in the text (Mike, James, Laurent, Aro) also threaten the perfect unit Bella and Edward represent, some due to their youth (Mike) and others due to their nontraditional family formations (Jacob, James, Laurent, and Aro). The vampire story, at its core, often "explains whom not to get into bed with," and Bella (and her readers) are duly instructed NOT to get into bed with immature humans, lusty wolves, or dangerous (as opposed to "pure") vampires (Twitchell 160).

However, in addition to circulating around the horror of inappropriate sexual pairings, vampire tales circulate around the horror of unnatural creation. The newborns in *Twilight*, much-like Frankenstein's monster, are abominations that threaten "normal" reproduction — we cannot, *Twilight* assures us, allow women such as Victoria to create on their own, nor allow nontraditional groups (such as the Volturi, the wolves) to create familial structures that threaten the patriarchal good life.[11] While some vampire tales have suggested that patriarchy may not be so fine and dandy, especially for women, *Twilight* is not one of these. In contradistinction to the representation of the vampire figure as a threat to whiteness, maleness, and heterosexuality — as well as to the stability of the societal as well as the individual body — *Twilight* constructs a new breed of vampire that *promotes* and *perpetuates*, rather than undercuts, these norms.[12] Not only does it accord with messages to keep women in their place (a message that has become more insistent in our "post–feminist" age), but it also is in harmony with our era's focus on keeping marriage "traditional" and bolstering heteronormativity.

The vampire, as noted above, has historically been related to such messages. In the 19th century, for example, the "the stable notion of nature as natural and of the natural has good made it possible to configure same-sex desire as unnatural — thus monster — thus vampire," as Sue-Ellen Case notes in "Tracking the Vampire" (395). As David Skal similarly points out, homosexuals have been represented as "evil predators with the Draculean powers to corrupt and transform the sexually straight and virtuous" (346). Skal quotes Anita Bryant's claim that "the male homosexual eats another man's sperm. Sperm is the most concentrated form of blood. The homosexual is eating life," and notes the erroneous historical belief that "they have to recruit, because they can't reproduce their own kind," which he notes has been "a common refrain on the right" (346). This refrain echoes in subdued form in *Twilight*—though there are no overt representations of homosexuality, its absence and the accompanying championing of heterosexual monogamy serve to subtly suggest that the only way to live the good (vampire) life is via heterosexual marriage and reproduction. Given the author's devout Mormonism, such a refrain is to be expected.

Further, given that vampires and religion have long shared an association — though usually not a friendly one — Meyer's depiction of the vampire as a tortured soul is hardly unique. As an initially anti–Christian figure considered to be a demon with no soul (and thus no reflection), the vampire was said to be susceptible to Christian talismans such as holy water and the cross.[13] The vampire mutated over the years, ultimately ending up in Meyer's universe as a Mormon figure seeking out eternal progression and life within an eternal family (see chapter 6 for more on this argument). While David Skal claims that "the symbolic flesh-eating and blood-drinking of the Catholic mass has the same ancient roots as vampire legends," we might argue that *Twilight* draws on Mormon theology to similarly explore the symbolic links (as well as differences) between the human and the divine. If, as Judith Weissman argues, "vampirism is only an extreme version of the evils of the body against which Christians have been told to fight for almost two thousand years," *Twilight* vampirism offers us a means to resist the "evil" of promiscuity and lust, depicting Mormon conceptions of the eternal family as able to tame the evils of the flesh (74, 348). Meyer's vampires function as ideal Mormons/Christians who rightly disavow sinful bodily pleasures—so much so, in fact, that a plethora of evangelical books on using *Twilight* as a sort of guide to being a better Christian abound.[14]

Post-post–Imperial Vampires: The Cullen Clan's Obeisance to Cultural Norms

While the vampire has often been used in the service of social maintenance (and certainly is put to this usage in *Twilight*), s/he has also been a transgressive, subversive figure. What Gelder names a "post–imperialist" reading of vampires problematizes binaries such as self/other and good/evil. While an imperial or conservative reading sees vampires as evil, as outsiders who should be feared, a post–imperial reading instead draws on "the vampire's positive effects," where "the vampire is to be redeemed" and "the problem lies, instead, with the upstanding heroes" (66). Gordon and Hollinger, along similar lines, find it apt that the vampire "thrives in this postmodern milieu of dissolving borders, between the virtual and the real, between private and public personae, in the breaking down of cultural and national boundaries" (4). In her writing on what she names "the postmodern vampire," Hollinger argues that vampires texts "'mirror' aspects of that peculiar human condition which has come to be termed 'postmodern,'" a decentering condition that, as she notes, "puts into question the grounds on which so many human behaviors and beliefs have previously been secured" ("Fantasies of Absence" 199). Defining postmodernism as "about approaching categories like Good and Evil with a certain ironic skepticism," Hollinger suggests the figure of the vampire is able to "emphasize the more liberating implications of this absence of the transcendent" (202). While I agree with her reading of the vampire, and while there has certainly been a number of "postmodern vampires" gracing page and screen in the late 20th and early 21st century, *Twilight* vampires are not of this type. Rather, they reify phallocentric, Western norms and grand narratives, and, far from approaching dichotomies such as good/evil with "ironic skepticism," they revel in the maintenance of a clearly delineated "you are either with us or against us" view of the world. The saga upholds this dualistic view of the world by grounding itself around various key binary oppositions— male/female, human/vampire, good vampire/bad vampire, and vampire/wolf.[15]

Possibly what has allowed for the widespread popularity of *Twilight* vampires even more, though, is the way in which they speak, in somewhat muted form, to their 21st-century moment. In the same way that Moretti reads *Dracula* as "a refined attempt by the nineteenth-century mind not to recognize itself," so too does Meyer's saga seem to function as a fiction in which not only does the author not recognize herself, but also neither do many readers recognize the way the series reflects the 21st-century mindset (102). Meyer has rather consistently denied she was penning any sort of Mormon creed, let alone texts with any sort of purposeful authorial intent. Indeed, she insists regularly that *Twilight* was born of a dream — projecting the story onto her sleeping, subconscious mind in way so many authors have in order to uphold an "I couldn't help it, it came to me in a dream" justification.[16] This claim also circumvents allegations regarding the saga's derivative nature — at least to an extent. By maintaining the story came to her in a dream, Meyer deflects responsibility regarding how her saga echoes earlier vampire texts.[17]

However, though Meyer denies ever having read *Dracula*, her saga and Stoker's novel share a number of similarities. *Dracula*, published in 1897, has often been read as revealing a great deal not only about Stoker's unconscious, but also about the sociocultural contexts from which the Count et al. emerged — much in the same way *Twilight* is currently being read in relation to Meyer's unconscious and her social milieu.[18] Like *Twilight*, *Dracula* has been similarly accused of not being good literature. James Twitchell argues as much, noting the "cardboard characters, dull asides, and desultory plotting" (127). He, like many other literary theorists, accounts for *Dracula*'s popularity due to its focus on "social and sexual taboos" (127). *Twilight* has been similarly maligned, with critics noting its purple prose, flat characters, and repetitive adjective use. Despite claims by many regarding the inferior writing of Stoker and Meyer, their texts have widespread popularity.[19] While Dracula has endured for over 100 years, *Twilight*'s popularity thus far, in an age of constant media saturation and rapidly changing trends, is nevertheless impressive. I contend that each of these respective fictions are so alluring because they speak specifically to continuing notions about femininity, to the "need" for patriarchy, and to the dangers of unregulated (female) sexuality.

Vampire Eves: Monstrous Femininity from *Dracula to* Twilight

Bram Dijkstra explores *Dracula* as an antifeminine text in his 1986 book *Idols of Perversity*, asserting that Stoker's novel responds to the "period's suspicions about the degenerative tendencies in woman" and arguing that Stoker penned, perhaps without even realizing it "a narrative destined to become the looming twentieth-century basic commonplace book of the antifeminine obsession" (342). Noting that Count Dracula operates in a world of women, Dijkstra maintains that "the two women on whom the count sets his bloodshot eyes, Lucy Westenra and Mina Harker, represent the success and failure of modern man's arduous attempts to acculturate woman to the civilized world" (344). While *Twilight* is not as overtly antifeminine as *Dracula*, its focus on civilizing women via incorporating them into the patriarchal fold (represented both by the patriarchal vampire world of which Bella becomes a part and via her attachment and eventual marriage to Edward) echoes that of the earlier Stoker text.

Both Stoker's novel and Meyer's series also link their female characters to Eve. While Lucy and Mina represent "the two faces of Eve," Bella and other female *Twilight* characters similarly straddle the good/evil divide (Dijkstra 344). Bella, Esme, and Alice function as good Eves while Victoria, Jane, and Tania function as evil Eves. And, much like Mina, who blames her inability to resist temptation on the fact that for women "some of the taste of the original apple ... remains still in our mouths," Bella likens herself to Eve, noting, when she meets Edward for the first time, "He didn't know me from Eve" (Stoker 220; *T* 24). Both these fictional Eves have a bit of a rebellious streak about them. Mina, as evidenced in the above scene where she deliberately supplies Van Helsing with the short-hand version of her diary, which she knows he cannot read, can't resist the "temptation of mystifying" the men around her (Stoker 220). Bella, whose inner monologue becomes the entire *Twilight* saga (apart from the section Jacob narrates in *Breaking Dawn*) does not so much deliberately mystify men as refuse to obey them. Though she is compliant for the most part, she disobeys Charlie's orders not to see Edward, she allows Edward into her bedroom every night, and she subsequently disobeys Edward's directive not to see Jacob.

Both of these female characters are also significantly aligned to the vampire, a word that is defined in the Oxford English Dictionary as "an alluring woman who exploits men." However, both are also saved from the sexually licentious, predatory monstrosity associated with female sexuality (and the female vampire)—Mina by the male "crew of Light" and Bella by being first married to a "virginity warrior" and then turned into pure, angelic vampire.[20] In an echo of *Dracula*'s Crew of Light, which consists of five males, Bella also has five male protectors—Charlie, Edward, Jacob, Billie, and Carlisle.[21] While Twitchell reads *Dracula* as about a band of boys against a domineering father (*Dracula*) who are joined by wise, good father (*Van Helsing*), *Twilight* might more aptly be read as a band of good vampires (or a benevolent vampire patriarchy) working against evil vampires. The Volturi, like evil vampires through the ages, are greedy, violent, and power-hungry predators. They delight in controlling others and inflicting pain. They are not a traditional family (like the Cullens) but are more of a hierarchical dictatorship. While the Volturi are thus associated with organized greed and power, Victoria and her newborn army are contrastingly associated with rebellious, uncivilized behavior and lust.

As such, we might read Victoria and the newborns as contemporary incarnations of the female vampire—a figure that has historically been associated with wantonness, monstrosity, lust, aberrant sexuality, and a refusal to abide by patriarchal norms. An overarching theme in many vampire (and other) texts is, as Dijkstra points out, that "women become beasts in the absence of men" (340). For example, the Lamia figure from classical mythology, which is described variously as a serpent with a head and breasts of a female and/or as a female vampire, ate children and sucked the blood from men. Further, as Dijkstra documents, the Lamia figure was linked to that most monstrous of creatures—the feminist. She was represented as "a bisexual, masculinized, cradle-robbing creature" who "was seeking to arrogate to herself male privileges, refused the duties of motherhood, and was intent upon destroying the heavenly harmony of feminine subordination in the family" (Dijkstra 309). In *Dracula*, Lucy becomes such a figure. Not only does she "cradle-rob" as the so-called Bloofer lady, but, as various critics have argued, she also represents the threat of the "New Woman" (Roth 58). Her murder is often read as the most overtly misogynist moment in novel, a moment that reveals the more latent hatred toward sexually independent women that permeates the rest of *Dracula*. Or, as Gelder pronounces, "women, rather than Dracula, are the central horror in the novel: the vampire is simply the means by which that horror can be realized" (77).

In both *Dracula* and *Twilight*, sexuality is what makes females particularly horrific. While in *Dracula* this sexuality must be staked through the heart (Lucy), in *Twilight*, it is safely contained in the marital bed (Bella). The arch female villain in Meyer's saga, Victoria, is in keeping with the sexually wanton Lucy — her red hair redolent of a vixen, she avenges her lover's murder by stalking Bella — or, in other words, the wanton whore threatens to kill the angelic virgin, making the way for Edward, the heroic vampire knight, to save the virginal Bella. Victoria defies the patriarchal structure that the novel upholds as beneficial, taking power into her own hands and creating an army of newborns (a nod to the fact that when females create outside of patriarchal rule, the results are monstrous). While this strand of Meyer's saga seems to echo Stoker's representation of nonreproductive sexual activity as horrific (and thus participates in the long tradition of making sexuality that does not ally to the production of the family taboo), it also circulates around the enduring representation of women as inherently evil (and especially so when not aligned with a male). Meyer's *The Short Second Life of Bree Tanner* continues this representation with Bree safely paired with Diego— once he is killed, leaving her single, she is destroyed by Felix upon Jane's orders. It seems female vampires without male mates or caretakers (such as Victoria and Bree) need be annihilated.

From Eve to Lilith to Medusa: The Fate of Females Who Defy Male Rule

While Eve, a prime symbol of females' capacity for evil, is used by both Stoker and Meyer, with Mina and Bella functioning as descendants of this female apple biter, we might also read Lucy and Victoria as fictional incarnations of Lilith, who, "in her unwillingness to play second fiddle to Adam, was ... widely regarded as the world's first virago" (Dijkstra 309). Lucy and Victoria are both unwilling to play second fiddle to a man, and the alliance of each with not one man but with multiple men signifies their lustful, vixen-like ways. Both, it seems, might also be read as Medusa figures. Lucy is specifically likened to Medusa in *Dracula*, while Victoria's serpentine red locks and ultimate decapitation are redolent of Medusa's beheading. Such linkages are particularly interesting in terms of Medusa's long association with dangerous female sexuality and the vagina dentata. Dijkstra, writing of an "ultimate siren" whose "snake hair" coils "into a bright bouquet of pointy-toothed pink labia ... a veritable nightmare visualization of woman as predatory sexual being," suggests that we might think of Medusa as vampiric (310). Frost similarly reads Lilith as an early vampire, noting that according to the Talmud, Adam mated with Lilith and "begot flesh-eating devils"— much like Victoria's creation of her newborn army (6).

According to rabbinical doctrine, Lilith came to Adam in his dreams as succubus, a figure that "haunted the dreams of young men, magically undermining their vitality and draining their potency" (Frost 6). Significantly, Dijkstra reads the female vampire Carmilla as a descendent of these evil figures, noting that the horror in LeFanu's text emanates from "the never-ending evil of all women — their blood link with the animal past" (342). If we read Carmilla as representing the eternal animal in woman, we might also read many later female vampires similarly. While male vampires are often aristocratic and even sympathetic (the Count, Weyland, Edward Cullen), female vampires are often more evil, bestial, and predatory (the three red-lipped ladies that attempt to seduce Jonathon Harker, the seductress Miriam Blaylock from *The Hunger*, Victoria and Jane from *Twilight*.) Though female vampires are sometimes sympathetic and noble, they are generally so only when they are safely ensconced within patriarchy and either ruled by or sexually paired with a male (as with the many good female revenants in *Twilight*).

Female figures can avoid their fate as evil temptresses, it seems, if they are virginal and angelic — like Mina and Bella. They are not to exude the sexual power of Lilith or Medusa, but rather they exist more as sleeping beauties or lovely corpses. Dijkstra writes at length about this "sleep-death equation" prominent in art and literature, arguing it allows for nonthreatening sexual fantasies, or for male readers/viewers to immerse themselves in "thoughts of sensual arousal by a woman who appeared to be safely dead" (62). This "ideal of woman as sexless sacrificial virgin" that Dijkstra explores in relation to fin-de-siècle art emerges regularly throughout literature (63). For our purposes here, the ways in which the ideal sexless/dead woman allies to vampire texts is most pertinent. In *Dracula*, the Count seems to need to feed on these "sexless sacrificial virgins" — or as Dijkstra puts it, Dracula "feeds on the blood of young girls to grow young again" (343). Such an act has historical precedent in the exploits of Elisabeth Bathory, the Hungarian countess who, in the early 1600s, killed some 650 young girls, as she was convinced of the restorative powers of virginal blood. Bathory supposedly believed bathing in their blood would stave off aging — much like drinking virginal blood staves off death for many a vampire. The virginal woman as prime prey lives on in many texts that came after *Dracula* and also has historical precedent in the long-standing belief that female sexuality poses a danger to males. For example, in 1922, William Robinson penned *Married Life and Happiness*, claiming normal women should be satisfied with sex once every ten days (or relieved they don't have to endure sex more often given that they are not supposed to enjoy it). Robinson claims,

> There is the opposite type of woman, who is a great danger to the health and even the very life of her husband. I refer to the hypersensual woman, to the wife with an excessive sexuality. It is to her that the name vampire can be applied in its literal sense. Just as the vampire sucks the blood of its victims in their sleep while they are alive, so does the woman vampire suck the life and exhaust the vitality of her male partner — or victim. And some of them — the pronounced type — are utterly without pity or consideration [qtd. in Dijkstra 334].

Significantly, these "hypersensual women" are "literal" vampires, sucking the vitality from males. Noting the "scientific commonplace" that there was indeed "a direct equation between woman's supposed hunger for seminal substance and her bestial blood lust," Dijkstra contends that the vampire figure arises as an incarnation of the fear of the monstrous feminine (334). However, we might also surmise that the male vampire arises to control or contain the female — as when he attacks virgins, "saving" them from becoming dangerously sexual women.[22] Though Mina and Lucy become *more* sexual post–vampire bite, the attraction/repulsion to the sexualized female Stoker's novel enacts suggests that while sexual women may be desirable, they are dangerous — so dangerous that they need to be either subdued by a band of men (the crew of Light) or staked through the heart (Lucy). Reading staking through the heart as symbolizing the killing of Lucy's awakened sexual desire, Dijkstra's work reveals the ways that fears of female sexuality, the female body, and female blood coalesce in the figure of the vampire (342). Or as Dijkstra puts it,

> The womb of woman was the insatiable soil into whose bottomless crevasses man must pour the essence of his intellect in payment for her lewd enticements. The hunger of the beast was in her loins, and the hunger of the beast was the hunger for blood.... The conjoining of bestial woman with the remnant of the beast in man could only spawn human animals ... blood lusting vampires all [335].

Perhaps this coalescence is nowhere better exemplified than in Baudelaire's 1857 poem "Metamorphoses of the Vampire," wherein a serpentine woman lures a man with words "potent as heavy sent," telling him, "My lips are moist and yielding" before she drains him of his "very marrow" (79). Post-coitus, the man realizes she seems "to have replenished her arteries from my own" and turns to her to find "a hideous /Putrescent thing, all faceless and exuding pus" (79). Here, the seemingly beautiful naked woman is displayed as an evil seductress, one whose fluid mouth will suck the life from men, revealing her true self — a faceless monster woman or vagina dentata. As is so often the case, the female vampire is presented here as an evil seductress — a woman able to lure men from reason into the dark abyss of sexuality. For sexual acts to be safe, women (especially during the Victorian era but true also of many 1980s teen vampire films) need to be properly submissive — avoiding any sort of phallic act/penetration — any, if you will, bite. Indeed, women are often construed as naturally desiring such metaphorical bites — as in the 1886 work of Richard von Krafft-Ebing, who wrote at length about the natural inclination for women to be sexually passive. Krafft-Ebing claims nature has given woman

> an instinctive inclination to voluntary subordination to man; [who] will notice that exaggeration of customary gallantry is very distasteful to woman, and that any deviation from it in the direction of masterful behavior, though loudly reprehended, is often accepted with secret satisfaction. Under the veneer of polite society the instinct of feminine servitude is everywhere discernible [qtd. in Dijkstra 101].

This inclination certainly seems evident in *Twilight*, wherein Bella seems to like Edward's gallantry for the first three books and does not balk at his more "masterful behavior." Then, in the final text, we see her taking great pleasure in this "masterful behavior," luxuriating in her post–coital black and blue body. Her "instinct" for "feminine servitude" becomes even more apparent when she agrees to Edward's marital demands and enthusiastically adopts the mantle of motherhood. She, in effect, lives up to what is referred to as the "holy trinity of womanhood — mother, wife, and daughter" (Dijkstra 64). As such, *Twilight* adds a new twist to the vampire tale — rather than Bella's affiliation with vampires turning her to lustful beast (as Lucy's links to the Count did), her relationship with Edward turns her into a chaste wife and mother — she is, in fact, more lustful *before* she is a vampire. This change, however, does not ultimately change the surrounding narratives about patriarchy/family that many horror stories enact. As with *Dracula*, where women are shown to be civilized and saved by men and their capitulation to role of wife and mother, in *Twilight*, Bella is similarly saved by Edward and her entry into his patriarchal vampire clan via marriage. This conservative bolstering function of such tales of course extends well beyond vampire narratives, but vampire mythos certainly revolves explicitly and intriguingly around issues linked to such fortification. While in many tales the vampire is the dangerous Other who must be repudiated to "save" culture, in *Twilight* the vampires function to bolster race, class, and gender norms.

Edward Cullen, Vampire God of the Icy Cold Yet Über-Hot Body

Edward functions as the apex of vampire flawlessness in the saga, seducing both our self–effacing narrator Bella and readers alike. He is a vampire of honor, a sparkling knight who abhors the thought of harming humans as much as his own monstrous nature. His golden eyes, tireless loyalty, and gentlemanly demeanor exude masculine perfection of the type Jane Eyre and Elizabeth Bennett dreamed of. He is wealthy but not snobby, highly educated but not self–important, dashingly handsome but not vain. More Dr. Jekyll than Mr. Hyde, he makes immortality look like a dream come true — an endless existence of education, music, art, travel, and love. His need for blood is rendered adventurous and noble — he hunts like a lion rather than a hyena. He also makes insomnia particularly appealing: pre–Bella we are led to assume his nights consisted of listening to his vast music library and reading books; post–Bella he watches his beloved sleep in the witching hours, protecting and comforting her — something parents and lovers wish they could do for those whom they so desperately wish to shield from harm.

Edward is also a monster perfectly fitting for our post–9/11, anxiety-ridden age. He holds out the nostalgic promise that love can conquer all — even terrorist-like Volturi vampires. With his impervious body like a living shield, he suggests we need not worry about terror alerts. His intellect and wealth speak to our desires to know all the secrets of existence while living a life of privilege not hampered by worry over the end of oil, the rising cost of electricity, nor the weakening dollar. His ultimate overcoming of prejudice (for humans and wolves) makes him a good fit for a world we like to consider post-racial. Further, his capacity to love with every ounce of his being functions as a comforting salve in our era of ubiquitous infidelity, divorce, dysfunctional relationships, and domestic violence.

Edward is also the perfect being for our youth- and body-obsessed era, signifying that we can indeed achieve corporeal perfection. Bella, his less-perfect human counterpart, desires to become a Cullen vampire not only so she can live eternally with Edward, but also so she can be as beautiful as he and his family. As a descendent to many 1980s vampire texts and their bodily concerns, *Twilight* shifts from the earlier "anguish of embodiment as well as the inability to control the body and maintain its boundaries" to a celebration of the hard body and its imperviousness to time, age, weather, and attack (Abbott 137). With bodies like statues, the Cullens are walking Greek gods who are classically beautiful as well as ageless, impossibly strong, and perfectly chiseled. They do not need to sleep or breathe or eat. In effect, they are dream bodies for the 21st century — thin, beautiful, young, and hard to kill. If, as Abbott argues, the vampire body can be read as "the site upon which our concerns and anxieties about the body in the 1980s were projected," the 21st-century Cullen vampires might be similarly read as emobodying contemporary corporeal concerns (124). Bella's fear of aging, her constant clumsiness, her near-death experiences and brushes with serious bodily harm, the way her body is stalked by James, Victoria, and the Volturi speak not only to our cultural obsession with young, strong bodies but also to our cultural fears surrounding "terrorist attacks" and the global shadow of endless wars and escalating natural disasters. What better way to stave off aging, weight gain, and bodily harm than to become a living (not-breathing) statue?

The vampire, as a figure "who confounds corporeality itself," explores the boundaries not only of life, but also of the body (Winnubst 7). As Williamson asserts, the vampire expresses alienation from the body as well as a transcendence of bodily limitations (183). Estranged from bodily needs such as sleep and transcending bodily limitations in regards to aging/death, the vampire body is impervious (as are the statue-like bodies of the Cullens) but also infecting — able to breech the boundaries of other bodies and "turn" them — as Edward does with Bella. Just as *Dracula* revealed an obsession with the female corpse — a timely obsession given the context of grave robbing and the rise of the medicalized body — so, too, does *Twilight* reveal an obsession with the body beautiful — a timely obsession given our cultural context of bodily discipline and "improvement."

And, while we might read the staking of Lucy as "an erotically-charged corpse mutilation" that mirrors Victorian-era dissections of the female corpse, we might read Bella's turn to supermodel-like vampire as mirroring our current era's obsession with corporeal perfection (Williamson 19). Just as Lucy's death needs to be considered in the context of corpse mutilation as a fate worse than death, so, too, must Bella's turn to vampire, and the accompanying marriage and pregnancy this turn entails, be read in cultural context (Williamson 27). Like a fictional Madonna or Angelina Jolie, Bella both embraces the pursuit of fame/beauty and frames motherhood as a primary female accomplishment — one that de-sexualizes her body, making it "safe" for Edward to be around.

In addition to framing the female body *as* maternal body (to be explored further in chapter 3), the saga also allows for a vicarious experience of living the body beautiful without all the pain and maintenance such a goal requires. Or, as Charlaine Harris puts it, "Vampires don't have to go to the gym.... They don't have to go on nutri-system."[23] Likewise, they don't have to control their eating, watch their cholesterol, or yo-yo diet. They don't need cosmetic surgery or botox, don't require the nipping, tucking, or implanting so ubiquitous in our current cultural moment. And, as is particularly true of the Cullen vampires, they need not worry about their skin color or bodily sexual inclinations — they are *pure* in their white heterosexuality with bodies able to afford all that money can buy. A consumer capitalist dream family, the Cullens are not so much dead bodies as perfect bodies.

The Vampire — Werewolf Divide: Powerful Gentlemen verses Beastly Wolf-Boys

Though the wolf bodies of the texts (particularly Jacob's) also speak to contemporary bodily concerns (and particularly the "six-pack" vogue), their differing bodily realities are in keeping with the other ways in which the saga focuses on the white Cullen vampires as "devastatingly, inhumanly beautiful" and the Quileute as "russet-colored" and "beautiful in an exotic way" (*T* 19, 119; *NM* 149). Jacob, in comparison to Edward's "too perfect face," has "altogether, a very pretty face" (*T* 74, 119). Allying with the typical fictional representation of the alluring, seductive vampire and the semi-repulsive, dark werewolf that we encounter in so many other narratives, Edward is the gorgeous vampire gentleman and Jacob the more animalistic wolf-boy. If Edward is Bella's upstanding (and pale) Edward Rochester or Edgar Linton, Jacob is more of her Heathcliff — the darker, more temperamental male whose *savage* sexuality threatens her safety. As when he forces her to kiss him, Jacob exudes a sexual-beast-within meme — far from Edward's virginity warrior status, Jacob is more in keeping with how werewolves have been typically represented in lore and in popular culture — as primitive beasts. His hulking body, in a perpetual state of partial undress and relative immaturity, make him more Mr. Hyde than Dr. Jekyll — more irrational body than logical mind. The way his character contrasts with Edward's accords with popular conceptions of vampires and werewolves, wherein vampires are the aristocratic undead (as in, for example, *Fright Night*) and werewolves are the uncontrollable youths (as in *Teen Wolf* and *An American Werewolf in London*) or the uber-masculine sexual predators (as in *The Wolf Man* and *Wolf*).[24]

Popular culture has long had a fascination with both vampires and werewolves, and the two beings often populate the same texts. According to lore, vampires had the power to make wolves do their bidding and could also assume wolf form if they desired.[25] In fact, the story "Dracula's Guest," presumed to be the intended first chapter of *Dracula,* details Jonathon Harker's travels toward the Count's home, where he encounters a female vampire and is saved by a wolf. During the night, Harker sees "a beautiful woman, with rounded cheeks and red lips" and notes the air is "reverberant with the howling of wolves" (215). The story suggests Harker is attacked by the female vampire, who leaves wounds on his neck, but is saved by large wolf acting on Dracula's behalf. Harker wakes up with the wolf lying over him, protecting his body, and declares, "I was certainly under some form of mysterious protection" (220). Over a century later, the *Twilight* wolves are similarly depicted as protectors, though this time *not* at the beck and call of vampires, but as their enemies.

In European folklore, werewolves pre–date vampires. The 16th century was the height of the werewolf era, with thirty thousand cases of wolf transformations reported in France alone (Twitchell 210). The preponderance of wolves in Europe accounts for their presence in lore and fairy tales, and the wolves' predatory, aggressive nature of course lends itself to stories of beasts intent on attacking humans. The eradication of wolves (England, for example, was wolfless by 1530), explains the relative decline in werewolf tales. Vampires, on the other hand, had their historical heyday later, in the 17th and 18th centuries, and functioned in European folklore as a way to explain the spread of fatal illness (Day 12). Though the concept of vampires pre–dates this, the vampire as part of the Western popular imagination grew along with the spread of plagues and other fatal illnesses, with the burning of plague victims sometimes being termed "vampire disposal" (Twitchell 106). Werewolves, on the other hand, are associated with the "beast within," the animal nature of humans, which threatens to overtake their more rational, civilized side. King, in accordance with this line of thought, argues "the face of the *real* Werewolf" is Edward Hyde of *Jekyll and Hyde* — the crazy, beast that lurks within, the id to Jekyll's super–ego (78).

Maintaining that Stevenson's text explores the split between the Apollonian and the Dionysian, King contends that the this "werewolf" side of humanity horrifies us, suggesting that the potential monsters within us are far scarier than those without (82). This reading of the werewolf as a "Dionysian madness" also accounts for the relative paucity of werewolf tales in comparison to the vast popularity of vampire narratives (368). Like Dr. Jekyll, we seem to wish to be creatures of reason and intellect, often denying our more irrational, needy sides. The vampire, as an immortal creature of great strength, is those things many of us long to be — powerful, alluring, aristocratic, and good-looking. Alas, as King suggests, werewolves represent "something vicious in the human makeup that has not yet been bred out" — this is, as he contends, "what really frightens us in the myth of the Werewolf" (81).

Twilight, however, tames the werewolf just as much as it tames the vampire, presenting us with a breed of Quileute wolves that are an admixture of werewolf and shape shifter, part bestial attacker, part noble protector.

Werewolves were traditionally depicted as an embodiment of evil, or, as Frost puts it in his study, werewolves are "the most terrible of all Satan's bond slaves," who were the "emblem of treachery, savagery, and bloodthirstiness" (35). Yet, Meyer transforms them into dignified savages, combining stereotypical representations of indigenous peoples with werewolf lore (3). This admixture is quite fitting, if disturbing from an anti–racist, post–colonial perspective, as it builds upon imperial, white supremacist notions of native people as animalistic others and perpetuates the notion of white humans as *more human*, more civilized, than people of color. Given that the werewolf has long represented the "bestial instincts lurking beneath our civilized exteriors," it is not surprising that they have been associated with the non–white and the working class — with those members of society historically deemed Other and lesser (Frost x).

While the vampire is a "predatory, strangely thrilling aristocrat," the werewolf is more beastly attacker (Spooner 172). Or, as Nicholls puts it, "Vampires are aristocratic, drinking only the most refined substances, usually blood" while the werewolf lives in the lower classes in "a dog-eat-dog world" (10). Werewolves are further associated with wild teens (as in *Blood and Chocolate* and *Teen Wolf*), with the criminally insane (as in *The Wolfman* and *The Howling*), with the racially Other (as in *Skin Walkers* and *Wolfen* and Michael Jackson's *Thriller* video), and with working-class populations (as in *Underworld* or Charlaine Harris' Sookie Stackhouse series).[26] Further, while vampires are often capitalists extraordinaire (even lately forming what Abbott terms "vampire conglomerates" in films and series such as *Blade*, *Daybreakers*, *True Blood*, and *The Vampire Chronicles*), werewolves are drug addicts (*True Blood*), disaffected youth (*Ginger Snaps*), or — as in *Twilight* — Native Americans who "live on the res" in barn-like homes (217).

Whereas vampires are usually associated with wealth and capital mobility, werewolves are often presented as primitive. The term *werewolf* connotes beastliness and irrationality, attributes that were also associated with those "in need" of colonization. The word, literally meaning "man wolf" indicates this, as does the notion that turning wolf involves "regression to a lower or more primitive state" (Frost 5, 28). Lycanthropy and shape shifting has historically been associated with witchcraft and the devil, and werewolves were assumed to have two-sided skin, human on the outside and furry within (Frost 13). This "animal within" meme lends itself to racialized depictions (as well as to socioeconomically based ones) where those who are considered "less civilized" are more often depicted as werewolves—that is, the working class, people of color, and women. This aspect of werewolf lore can be read in relation to the racial and class divide that the *Twilight* series enacts. Just as werewolves are traditionally depicted as cunning, swift, ferocious, and cruel, so, too, have native peoples been associated with primitivism.

In *Twilight*, the wolves are depicted as less civilized than the vampires; they live in the more economically depressed La Push. Not much work focusing on the racial/class implications of the Quileute wolves of *Twilight* has yet been published, an omission that is itself telling. Though "Team Jacob" has legions of aficionados, the fandom seems to be generally far more vampire focused than werewolf obsessed. Likewise, most existing writing (both in print and online), does not interrogate the Quileute wolves in relation to werewolf and vampire lore, but focuses instead on the love triangle aspect.

For example, neither Sara Worley's "Love and Authority among Wolves" nor Rebecca Housel's "The Tao of Jacob," both articles from *Twilight and Philosophy*, examine Meyer's depiction of the Quileute from a sociocultural perspective. Worley's piece focuses on free will, arguing that the werewolves have limited ability to make decisions based on free will, a postulation that is problematically put forth without any considerations of the racial or class implications of this representation. Housel's article touches on social difference but only in order to examine Jacob's "emotional intelligence" (238). Reading Jacob as the "classic underdog," Housel does not mention race, instead focusing on the "unlimited possibilities" that Jacob's Taoist existence (as she reads it) offers (245). Offering an even fluffier, less analytical reading, Lois Gresh, in *The Twilight Companion: The Unauthorized Guide to the Series*, gushes over the desirability of vampires and jokes about the comparative loutishness of the wolves— "Given that a werewolf like Jacob is going to explode — at any moment — into anger and violence, his lover or wife had better learn, as quickly as possible, to (a) keep her distance and (b) run fast"— Gresh fails to consider the race/class ramifications of her own arguments as well as those of the saga itself (88). Noting that "these guys sound like human abusive men, don't they? They maim, attack, and otherwise hurt their women, yet later, they're sorry about it, and their girlfriends stay with them anyway," Gresh's comments are in line with the "brown men hurt white women" mindset (99). Similarly, when Gresh claims that "it's possible that werewolves hate vampires because the vampires are sexier and more appealing to young, beautiful girls," she might as well be saying that *whites* are sexier and more appealing (107). Reading the werewolf as "the school bully" and the vampire as "the boy every girl wants in high school," Gresh's work uncritically accepts the idea that "a godlike boy with golden eyes" is naturally preferable to a russet-skinned boy (107). Explaining "whereas the vampire tantalizes us romantically, the wolf attacks us, pins us to the ground in beast form, and then feasts upon us, usually to the point of death," Gresh unapologetically champions the vampire as romantic hero and castigates the werewolf as uncivilized beasty (80). Though the vampire as alluring and the werewolf as repugnant has historical precedence, the failure to examine this precedent in terms of race and class, especially in relation to a text so heavily laden with such implications, is scholarly unsound.

*   *   *

Though, as Twitchell writes of horror, "we rarely — if ever — think it worthy of careful observation. After all, it's kids stuff," *Twilight* is certainly worthy of careful observation (4). It introduces us to a new breed of sympathetic vampire and lusty wolf, one that promotes particularly conservative notions about gender, race, class, and sexuality. Through Bella's desire to become a vampire, we are encouraged to also desire the wealth, beauty, and privilege of the Cullen lifestyle. Simultaneously, we are told that abstinence is the best policy, that true love can indeed conquer all. We learn that we need to tame our bodily desires (and ignore the lustful advances of wolf-like boys), focusing instead on creating eternal families with the right (white) kind of men. Duly reminded that the feminine body is dangerously sexual, we are schooled to embrace our goodly Eve sides and denounce our malevolent Medusa or lusty Lilith. We should, as Meyer informs us, "be safe" — should follow the straight and narrow path — and, like Red Riding Hood, avoid the wolf. We should wait instead for the mighty woodsman, the man who will slay sexual danger and safely ensconce us back in the family home — much like Edward, who staves off various threats — James, Victoria, the Volturi, Jacob — and allows Bella to keep her "little red cap" until, that is, she can safely remove it once she resides in the marital bed — a bed that will keep her forever young, forever beautiful, and forever beholden to a sparkling vampire knight.

Chapter 2

Bitten by Romance
Happy Twilight-*Ever-After*

At *Twilight* events around the world, masses of "Team Edward" and "Team Jacob" fans don t-shirts, jackets, buttons, and bags, oozing with devotion for either Edward Cullen or Jacob Black. Their loud shrieks and squeals, their giggling and crying, and their thunderous clapping at the mere mention of the name "Edward" testifies, like their *Twilight*-clad bodies, their dedication to the male characters at the series' romantic core. Bella, the heroine, has no such following.

When I traveled to Forks during the summer of 2009 to attend the *Summer School in Forks Symposium*, I expected to find giddy fans, cars spray painted with *Twilight* quotes, and girls starry eyed for vampires. I also expected the tiny town to be populated with stores hawking *Twilight* gear. What I didn't expect was to find virtually no Bella paraphernalia. I thought she was the heroine, the protagonist girls wanted to be, the Buffy for the abstinence generation. After much searching, I found one location with Team Bella T-shirts (in baby girl pink). When I wore this T-shirt at *Twi-Con 2009* a few months later, I further discovered my sympathies for Bella are not widely shared. I noticed not one other attendee in any sort of Bella attire. In fact, a young woman I encountered in an elevator (wearing a Team Jacob T-shirt) sneered "Team Bella?!?" and proceeded to put her hands in claw-like formation and emit a threatening hiss. With more ire than a Volturi, she told me, "There is NO team Bella!" At *Twi-Con*, I felt decidedly out of place as I perused the vendor hall in my "Team Bella" shirt. Amongst the vampire candies, the scents to make Edward love how you smell, and the many smoldery-eyed photo stills of the male actors, there was very little Bella merchandise. At one booth, which sold team badges for virtually ever other character, there was no "Team Bella" badge. When I asked the vendor why, she replied, "Bella never sells." Why is this?

One popular explanation is that readers identify with her. They thus do not root for Bella, but *become* Bella. As one eager-faced, young 13-year-old explained as she clutched a stuffed wolf to her chest, "I *am* Bella." She looked like she believed it. Her mother, by her side, nodded in agreement. This identification seems particularly effortless for young fans. Bella represents the very same insecurities they face — she feels awkward, out of place, clumsy, unattractive, and unlovable. She is brooding and insular, worried about revealing herself to others less she be rejected. Yet, other characters *cannot* leave her alone in the texts. In her first few days at her new high school, she becomes the "it girl" that every male is drooling over. Wallflower Bella quickly takes root in everyone's imagination, including, of course, the "it boy" on campus, Edward Cullen.

This trajectory is appealing to female readers still raised on Disney fairy tales and Barbie movies. *Twilight*, a newfangled Disney-esque fairy tale, swaps vampires and werewolves for talking tea-cups, depicting the male protagonist as the beauty, the BFF as the beast. A modern-day bedtime story, it encourages female readers to identify with Bella — to be modest (as good girls *should*), to feel insecure, and to spend hours focused on males. It rewards them with the message, "You really are beautiful, smart, loved ... and by the hottest guy at school!" Given the way popular culture and feminine norms encourage girls to doubt themselves, to feign modesty even if they feel confident, it is no surprise that Bella provides the perfect conduit.

Carmen D. Siering in her *Ms. Magazine* piece claims, "Even though Bella is ostensibly a hero, in truth she is merely an object in the *Twilight* world" (51). I would counter that Bella is not so much an object as a means of expression. Through her, readers channel their desires and frustrations, sometimes hating her and sometimes loving her, just as we readers sometimes love and sometimes hate ourselves. Bella is objectified in the series, no doubt, but she also ultimately triumphs. Granted, her triumph largely accords with traditional notions of female achievement — she becomes a wife and mother — but it also presents her as empowered and immortal. By the series' end, she is instrumental in the battle against the dreaded Volturi. She is, as Alice puts it, "the superhero of the day" (*BD* 747). Her trajectory from a teenage nobody to a gorgeous and powerful vampire heroine is certainly alluring to female readers who have been schooled to doubt themselves, to hate their bodies, and to believe that only males can be heroes.

A Fork in the Road: To Be or Not To Be a Good Girl

Bella's path is appealing because it speaks directly to the reality of female's lives. We, like her, live in a complex prison-house of feminine norms and expectations. We still grow up in a society that keeps a good-girl paradigm firmly in place (as the recent book *Curse of the Good Girl*, by Rachel Simmons, so cogently makes clear). Yet, confusingly, we are also encouraged by the mass media and social expectations to be smart (but not too smart), athletic (but in a feminine way), successful (but not by becoming "bitches" or "ball-breakers"), and sexy (but not slutty). We, like Bella, are supposed to be modest, well-behaved, and demure.

However, also like Bella, we desire to rebel, to be uber-confident, and to throw off the shackles of femininity. The only way to do so, at least according to the *Twilight* universe, is to become a vampire — which for Bella means also becoming an *eternal* wife and mother. Hence, the series straddles conflicting visions of femininity — one that calls for dismantling feminine norms, and another that romanticizes the traditional message that a woman *needs* a man in order to be complete. At the same time, *Twilight* confirms that the vision of females as perfect Susie-homemakers is too confining. Bella's insecurities, her longings for a life of passion and adventure, her profound sense of need and emotional frustration all suggest that the patriarchal world she lives in is more dreadful than becoming a midday snack for the Volturi. Yet, it in the end, it also celebrates Bella's rise to vampire-housewife extraordinaire. Readers are thus able to simultaneously bemoan and celebrate Bella's lot.

The dangers females disproportionately face in our world, such as sexual assault, abusive partners, and rape, as well as the beauty imperatives they must live up to, are also addressed and then laid to rest in the *Twilight* universe. Jacob may sexually assault Bella, but he is redeemed via his later actions where he proves to be an invaluable and loyal friend while Edward's obsessive control is really just a sign of his undying love. And Rosalie's mirror worship can be excused due to the abuses she suffered in the past. *Twilight* characters thus suffer many of the injustices people face in the real world, yet love, both romantic and familial, allows them to triumph. Who wouldn't be seduced by such a message?

Yet, by suggesting the ultimate happy ending is only possible (especially for women) via the traditional path of love, marriage, and motherhood, the saga offers the same "happy ending" as the millions of Harlequin romances that precede it. By championing females for their private, domestic skills and men for their public roles and brave heroism, the saga upholds traditional gender roles. By depicting Edward's love for Bella as what at first sustains her and then as what allows for her transformation into female savior at the series' close, *Twilight* tells the same story females have been told for centuries — that someday our prince will come, and when he does all our dreams will come true.

Get Out the Smelling Salts: Twilight *Romance Online and Off*

Many fans are critical of the more conservative messages of the series, arguing that Edward is too controlling, or condemning Bella's failure to rebel against her framing as cook, wife, and mother. Many are downright angry and spew ire at Bella for being simpering, or berate Edward for being a domineering jerk. Fans are thus not the empty-headed *Twilight* lovers they are often made out to be. Rather, they are active readers who often reject and/or transform the saga's more delimiting undertones. True, these more critical reactions seem to go by the wayside when fans gather en masse at *Twilight* events, where they swoon at the mere mention of male characters or stars. This was certainly true at *Twi-Con*, where it seemed many would need smelling salts if they heard Edward's name one more time. The *Twi*-net, functioning as an online gathering of fans, is similarly dominated by such swooning. With pictures of the male actors dominating the virtual landscape, the *Twi*-net world often functions as a sort of *Playgirl* for *Twilight* fans (sans the full-frontal nudity but with plenty of bare chests and bulging muscles). This online world promotes the romantic message driving the series, albeit in a more "sexed up" form. While in the series, Edward is the chaste romantic hero; online, Pattinson is framed as a smoldering sex-god.

In both the virtual world and the real world, love, romance, and desire are held up as *the* meaning behind *Twilight*. As such, the series and the fandom surrounding it carry on a long tradition of rendering romantic love appealing and exciting. Like the romance narratives that precede it, *Twilight* (at least partly) conditions females to actively pursue the very types of relationships that have resulted in our social and cultural subordination. And, in the same way the websites position Pattinson and Lautner as demi-gods, so too do the texts position the male characters as rightful recipients of female worship. We are exhorted by the *Twi*-net, as well as by the texts, to focus all our desires on Edward or Jacob, to imagine losing our virginity (coded as our mortality), to picture, again and again, being the sole object of hot male attention. Given that the real world promotes similar desires, is it any wonder that we are eating *Twilight* like candy?

As humans (or even as vampires or werewolves) we want to feel important, powerful, smart, talented, etc. In our still-male-privileged world, males have many modes in which to have such feelings validated. Females, on the other hand, have far fewer validating opportunities. We may dream of being president, but like Hillary, we are likely judged by how we look. We may want to be a tennis pro, but like Serena Williams, will have fury rained down upon us if we show anger or have a fondness for swear words. We may picture ourselves as the next Miley Cyrus or Madonna, but we will be judged by how much cleavage we have and show, how much time we spend with our kids, and how many wrinkles we have. To escape the harsh light our media-saturated world shines upon us, it's no wonder we turn to romance. Romance allows us to partake in a narrative that is universally accepted for females—that of "true love" leading to marriage and family. At the same time, it allows us to escape from the realities of female inequality by escaping into a fantasy world. Females are in love with love not because it's wired into our DNA, but because it is the one path to happiness we are universally encouraged to follow.

Happy Twilight-*Ever-After*

Twilight is particularly appealing because it riddles the path of true love with roadblocks and potholes that echo impediments that real-world females currently face. Bella is a child of divorce, she is not wealthy, she lacks confidence, she is harassed by males, she is threatened with rape, she is assumed to be stupid, she is treated like a child, and she is positioned as pawn between competing males. No wonder so many, like the wolf-clutching tween mentioned earlier, feel they *are* Bella. It's not just because they love Edward, it's also because Bella's life echoes their own experiences in a male-privileged world. This appeal is then ramped up by rendering Bella's problems null and void, by turning her tribulations into triumphs.

While in the real world the desires Bella harbors for Edward and Jacob would label her a slut by many, in the *Twilight* world her desires result in no such shaming. Readers, who undoubtedly will either be the victim of such shaming or enact it upon others, surely find welcome relief in a text that fails to even once call women sluts, bitches, hoes, ball-breakers or any of the other misogynistic terms that are the virus of daily life. In the real world, Bella would likely be treated as lesser by her male high school teachers and professors, she would make less money for the same work, she would be denied reproductive choices, and she would judged by how she looks rather than by what she thinks or does. In the *Twilight* world, she is instead allowed to be a "typical female," but to triumph just the same. But the catch is that, just like in the real world, the way for her to prevail is by attaching herself to a male.

Given that being showered with love, attention, and affection from another human being is a surefire way to feel better about oneself and one's lot, is it any wonder readers the world over are so anxious to project themselves into the *Twilight* universe? It allows escape at the same time as it offers the comforting message that escape is not necessary — it really will be okay, *Twilight* tells us; don't worry about your problems; (vampire) love will find a way.

Radway's study of romance reading exemplifies that females read romance not only to escape into a fantasy world of desire, but also to resist "their situation *as women*" and "to cope with the features of the system that oppress them" (12). The system Radway refers to is patriarchy, and it is her contention that women read romance in order to escape the very roles patriarchy imprisons them within, namely that of wife and mother. Yet, paradoxically, romance reading ultimately bolsters the very system females are trying to escape by presenting heterosexual monogamy as *the* happy ending. *Twilight* reading, following this formula, allows females to escape our real-world positioning as sluts, as incompetent, as weak. It launches us into a world where we can be just as strong or smart as any man. But, it also tells us that the best way toward empowerment is via wedding oneself to a sparkly vampire or a brawny wolf.

Though Radway's study focused on married mothers living in the Midwest in the early 1980s, her findings can be used to extrapolate similar explanations for the immense popularity of *Twilight*. Although the social contexts are different, much about being female within society remains the same. As contemporary females, we still experience the deleterious effects of being constructed as what Simone de Beauvoir calls the second sex. And, creatures of survival that we are, we often turn to stories that romanticize our second-class status so as to render it exciting and fulfilling. Such a "fantasy resolution," as Radway calls it, can supply us with the happily ever after that real life often does not (14).

The Uber-Hotness of Edward's Icy Lips

Depicting Bella's obsessive love for Edward as exciting, rather than dangerous, the series suggests that life with an attentive, caring mate (even if that mate is over-protective, controlling, and arrogant) leads to a life of love and adventure. In the saga, Edward acts as a vampire knight in shining armor who repeatedly asks Bella if she is okay, scoops her up, throws her on his back, and uses his arms, tellingly, as a protective cage. While we might read this as promoting typical gendered norms, we might also consider how this representation reflects reality. Real-world romances, particularly those experienced by young, heterosexual women, often involve such inequality. This is largely a result of gender socialization — females are to be smittenly gaga, males to be protectively aloof. In real-world romances, females often get hurt, either as a result of the trash-talk encouraged amongst males or via the fact that males are conditioned not to love as much (or for as long) as females. We females are taught by our media-saturated culture to desire romance and true love, while males are taught to desire hot bodies and what Erica Jong infamously termed "zipless fucks." But *Twilight* rewrites this script to an extent, offering readers a relationship where Bella's devotion does not result in rejection or abandonment, where she too can desire head board-busting sexual encounters. No wonder females become addicted to all things *Twilight*.

The series' more modern messages, namely, that motorcycle riding, cliff jumping, and world travel are far preferable to cooking for your dad or shopping for prom dresses, furthers this appeal. Suggesting that being a good girl is rather boring, *Twilight* departs in key ways from the traditional romance formula in which "most heroines demonstrate passionate motherliness, good cooking, patience in adversity, efficient planning, and a good clothes sense" (Snitow 136). Except for the fashion sense (which is Alice's domain), Bella accords in many ways with a traditional romance heroine, especially when she sets up house in a Snow White–like cottage and takes to motherhood like a fish to water. Yet, the texts offer enough rebellion to keep contemporary readers appeased. In other aspects, though, the traditional romance formula is strictly adhered to. One of the most obvious of these is in the depiction of Edward. He, like most romantic leads, has a dark edge to go along with his irresistible good looks. He is set up as the prize both readers and Bella yearn for, and the delayed gratification structure of the narrative keeps readers (and Bella) in a heightened sense of anticipation. The expectations surrounding romance and relationships—the first touch, kiss, embrace, etc.—that readers experience (or desire to experience in real life) are there on the page, waiting to be discovered. Further, unlike first kisses in the real world, the fictional depiction of such kisses can be experienced again and again, through multiple reads. And this is exactly what many readers do—return to the texts to experience again the excitement and anticipation of falling in love. Many fans share they have read the texts 5, 10, even 20 times; surely these repeated reads cannot be to wallow in the splendor of Meyer's fondness for the word "glowered"—rather they allow for obsessive return to the image of those icy Edward lips.

Here is one of the scenes that results in return customers:

> Edward hesitated to test himself, to see if this was safe, to make sure he was still in control of his need.
> And then his cold, marble lips pressed very softly against mine.
> What neither of us was prepared for was my response.
> Blood boiled under my skin, burned in my lips. My breath came in a wild gasp. My fingers knotted in his hair, clutching him to me. My lips parted as I breathed in his heady scent.
> Immediately I felt him turn to unresponsive stone beneath my lips. His hands gently, but with irresistible force, pushed my face back. I opened my eyes and saw his guarded expression. "Oops," I breathed.
> "That's an understatement." His eyes were wild, his jaw clenched in acute restraint [*T* 282].

In what has been named the "abstinence porn" style of the book, Bella continues the description of their first kiss as follows:

> His hands refused to let me move so much as an inch.
> "No, it's tolerable. Wait for a moment, please." His voice was polite, controlled.
> I kept my eyes on his, watched as the excitement in them faded and gentled.
> Then he smiled a surprisingly impish grin.
> "There," he said, obviously pleased with himself.
> "Tolerable?" I asked.
> He laughed aloud. "I'm stronger than I thought. It's nice to know."
> "I wish I could say the same. I'm sorry."
> "You are only human, after all" [*T* 283].[1]

Here, in Harlequin fashion, Edward initiates the kiss and sets the rules; he is in control; Bella is not. Contemporary culture trains us to react with a "how hot is that?!?" and to ignore the fact that Bella is supposed to be a passive object in this exchange. She is to remain still so that *his* desire will not lead him to hurt her — she is given the burden of curbing his "vampire" nature by restraining her passion. Simultaneously, she is also framed as "only human" (which might as well be read as "only female"). Here, the novel departs significantly from many romance novels by disallowing her enjoyment of the passionate embraces and lip-lockings that are the cornerstone of such texts. Instead, the pro-abstinence, "virgins rock" message transforms the steamy into the chaste. While it might seem that this change would turn readers away, it has had quite the opposite effect. So, why is the "good girls don't" motif so appealing to modern readers? While this question will be more thoroughly answered in chapter 5, suffice it to say, for now, that our cultural fixation on virginity and abstinence allows readers to identify with Bella's predicament. Further, the fact Edward "saves" her from her own besmirching desires frees Bella from the burden of policing her own sexuality. By extension, readers are likewise released from such responsibility. Readers can safely lust after Edward (and Pattinson by extension) because his virtue metaphorically guarantees and substantiates their own.

The Second Shift Twilight *Style: Or, How to Be a Vampire Wife*

Thanks to the achievements of the women's movement and various other cultural shifts, women now have far more career opportunities, and to go along with these, more expectations surrounding their ability to earn money, obtain degrees, and excel in the public sector. In general, though, these strides have not been accompanied by sharing the work women have typically been assigned in relation to home and family. Whether we work outside the home as (one of the few) female CEOs or as (one of the many) part-time cashiers, we are expected to pull a double shift. This second shift, widely discussed in both feminist circles and women's magazines, translates into many females having more responsibilities than ever. As one woman lamented during the *Female Roles* panel at *Twi-Con 2009*, much higher demands are now being placed on females. *Twilight*, by metaphorically returning Bella to an earlier time through her old-fashioned romance with a man born in 1901, also returns readers to an era when men were expected to be providers and protectors foremost, and women to be wives and mothers. In the same vein, the series does not focus on the pressing world of work and career (and, when it does, everyone with careers is male, from high school teachers to sheriffs to doctors). Rather, it romanticizes domesticity, depicting Bella cooking for Charlie, Esme decorating the home, and Emily nurturing her wolf brood. Bella, more Rachael Ray than Rosie the

Riveter, *enjoys* cooking for Charlie. At the series' close, she has morphed into a Snow White, exultant in her cottage. She is also the perfect mom so idealized in our world, shaping her life around her baby and carefully selecting Renesmee's outfits down to the finest detail. Can't you just envision her chirping away to forest animals as she runs with vampire speed toward her fairy tale future (an image reinforced in the *New Moon* movie when a sparkling Bella frolics in the forest in a princess-type dress).

The framing of Meyer, who is perennially referred to as a "happily married mother of three," also suggests that wife/mother duties trump all else. This context of domestic utopia that the texts celebrate and the author exudes certainly must come as a welcome relief to varying types of readers. Girls and tweens are allowed to desire romance and are freed from the burden of worrying about exams, future career paths, or if/when they should hook up with their current crush of choice. Teens and twenty-somethings are given the opportunity to picture themselves free from college tuition, rent worries, or drunken regrets. Wives, mothers, and grandmas are allowed to revel in a "simpler time," when females were not expected to be do-it-all superwomen. All ages can appreciate the perfect family life of the Cullens, the doting noninvasive father, Charlie, the mom who is a best friend rather than a dictatorial enemy. While most of these projections are based on false notions of how families and relationships function, not to mention on a nostalgic past that never really existed, they nevertheless cocoon us in a seductive narrative that appeals to today's over-burdened, underpaid, and anxious-about-the-future females.

Although the series, via Bella's story, suggests that women should be happy cooking for men, should remain virgins until married, and, once married, should have children as soon as possible, female readers have not turned away. To the contrary, rather than balking at such traditional messages, fans revel in it. Wearing T-shirts proclaiming "Mrs. Cullen" and "I have OECD: Obsessive Edward Compulsive Disorder," the female fandom seems to *desire* such a message. Given that the series sugar-coats love and desire, making it seem like the most important aspect of existence, and given that a large part of the fandom is of the age when crushes/first love are a major concern, it is predictable that such a message resonates. Like Bella and Edward, readers can envision love as bringing about a "tidal wave of happiness." As the title of the closing chapter of the series, "The Happily Ever After," promises, readers can rest assured that they, too, can find such a fairy tale ending. Yet, alluring though they are, how might some of the messages of the series be problematic?

Given that more women are in college, more have successful careers, and more work outside the home than at any other time in history, how might such a glorification of romance promote readers to wish for a "simpler time" when marriage and motherhood were all that could be hoped for? While the depictions of love the books offer are captivating, the realities of marriage and motherhood are not as blissful as Bella and Edward's relationship makes them seem.

However, this disconnect is precisely what makes the message so attractive. At a time when females have extraordinary pressure put upon them to succeed in *all* arenas, from education to sports to career to politics, the notion that one could be loved just for being "clumsy old me" is captivating. By suggesting that the highest achievement for a female is to be a wife and mother, that love is more important than college, that sex before marriage is a no-no, *but* that violent, physically damaging sex after marriage is hot, the text echoes many of the messages females receive from mainstream culture. Further, by putting these messages in such pleasant wrapping, *Twilight* is able to render them desirable. To, in effect, make those who are oppressed by such parameters *hunger* for their own oppression.

Utilizing two of the defining characteristics of Harlequin romances, where "brutal male sexuality is magically converted to romance" and "stereotyped female roles are charged with an unlikely glamour," the series is able to deliver long-standing conceptions about gender and romance in an enticing new package replete with sexy vampires and hot wolf-men (Snitow 139). As such, the saga ultimately presents patriarchy as benign — as a social system that allows someone like Bella to triumph.

Does Your Gender Sparkle?

Along these same lines, Bella's relative plainness assures us that being ordinary is okay — that average girls can get their romantic cake and eat it, too. As Snitow notes, this is typical for the romance heroine: "She values being an ordinary woman and acting like one. (Indeed, for women, being ordinary and being attractive are equated in these novels") (137). This representation appeals to us, as we exist in a world where being ordinary is unacceptable, where instead, one is supposed to have a perfect face, perfect boobs, designer clothes, and an all-around "bootylicious" body. Yet, in the saga, Bella, who is represented as rather plain, nabs the hottest guy. Such a message is indeed addicting for a society of girls and women raised on the message they will never be hot enough.

According to gender norms, in addition to being nice, females should be (or at least aspire to be) beautiful. Especially in contemporary western culture, "the goal of hotness," as M. Gigi Durham terms it, "is pervasive in girl culture" (63). Yet, being "hot" is not to be confused with being "slutty" — one should be uber-attractive and desirable, but should *not* act upon these desires — there should be no slippage from pretty to promiscuous. "Walking the line between acceptable hotness and unacceptable sluttiness is the almost impossible challenge presented to today's girls," according to Durham (67). Bella (thanks to her chaste vampire boyfriend) traverses this challenge — maintaining her ideal thinness (she weighs a slight 102!) *and* her virginity. She also accords to female modesty standards, insisting she is not "all that" despite the fact every male —

from human to vamp to were — lusts after her. Despite her humility about her appearance, her size 2 jeans are quite hard to fill for many females. And, as Rosalind Wiseman points out, even though "girls know they're manipulated by the media to hold themselves to an impossible standard of beauty ... that doesn't stop them from holding themselves to it anyway" (77). Or, in other words, the female *Twi*-hards who read the books multiple times and who pour over the ubiquitous pictures of Kristen Stewart as Bella in magazines and on the web *know* that Bella and Stewart represent an impossible standard, *yet* this doesn't stop them from idealizing and believing in this standard.

As Wiseman's extensive interviews for her book reveal, girls' thoughts on their own appearance are overwhelmingly negative (80). According to her, "Adolescence is a beauty pageant.... In Girl World, everyone is automatically entered. How does a girl win? By being the best at appropriating our culture's definition of femininity" (77). In the books, Bella "wins" because she conforms to the ideal definition not only of how a female should act (modest, submissive, self-effacing) but also of how one should *look*. And, with her turn to vamp, she can win for eternity by not aging, not eating, heck, by not *breathing*. As in Sylvia Plath's poem, she "is perfected/Her dead/Body wears the smile of accomplishment." Or, as less elegantly and more affirmatively put by Lois Gresh, readers should aspire to be vampires like Bella because then "you won't have to worry about diets anymore, because you'll live on blood and remain thin and young forever" (37).

However, though her name literally means "beauty," Bella is not obsessed with her looks — as such, she at first glance serves as a positive female role model in our beauty-obsessed culture. Yet, when we pierce her modest façade, we see that she accords with the rules of modesty, unlike, say, Rosalie. Bella does not balk at her status as an object of the male gaze — in fact, she quite revels in Edward's topaz stare. And, in stereotypical female fashion, Bella is depicted as being age-obsessed. *New Moon* opens with Bella dreaming of herself in a mirror as an old woman next to an ageless, perfect Edward. What this dream leaves out is that Edward's age does not matter — even if he were to lose his 17-year-old looks he would be debonair, a gentleman, a silver fox even, while she will become a cougar, an old biddy, a crone. Repeatedly depicted as fearing getting old, Bella bemoans, "I get older every stinking day!" and admits, "Age is a touchy subject for me" (*E* 119, 121). While her fears of aging are understandable given the vampire context, they are not textually grounded in a way that highlights this; rather, the obsession with youth comes across as entirely normal, as something *every female* should desire — even Bella's mom, Renee, is depicted as young looking and thus able to attract a young husband, further equating the link between youth, beauty, and desirable femininity.

In Meyer's fictional world, female beauty and its accompanying attributes are more valued than female strength. All the key female villains, Victoria, Jane, Maria, and even the lesser mean girl high school friends, Jessica Stanley and

Lauren Mallory, are beautiful. Given the widespread analysis of how beauty ideals are harmful to both women and men, this unquestioned championing of beauty as female necessity seems remiss in *Twilight*, especially if we consider Meyer's own experience of falling short of America's beauty standards. As she relates at her website,

> I modeled Bella's move to Forks after my real life move from high school to college. (Personal story alert!) I mentioned in my bio that I went to a high school in Scottsdale, AZ, which is Arizona's version of Beverly Hills (picture the high school in the movie *Clueless*). In high school, I was a mousy, A-track wall-flower. I had a lot of incredible girlfriends, but I wasn't much sought after by the Y chromosomes, if you know what I mean. Then I went to college in Provo, Utah. Let me tell you, my stock went *through the roof*. See, beauty is a lot more subjective than you might think. In Scottsdale, surrounded by barbies, I was about a five. In Provo, surrounded by normal people, I was more like an eight. I had dates every weekend."[2]

Yet, despite not being sought after by "Y chromosomes" and realizing that beauty is "subjective," Meyer went on to pen a four-book saga wherein not only are her characters exceedingly beautiful, but also they do not question or rally against the normative conception of beauty. And, although the ever-astute Edward realizes the objectifying aspects of beauty standards in his musings in *Midnight Sun*, he, too, falls prey to appreciating Bella's beauty like all the other "sheep-like males":

> Today, all thoughts were consumed with the trivial drama of a new addition to the small student body here. It took so little to work them all up. I'd seen the new face repeated in thought after thought from every angle. Just an ordinary human girl. The excitement over her arrival was tiresomely predictable — like flashing a shiny object at a child. Half the sheep-like males were already imagining themselves in love with her, just because she was something new to look at."[3]

And, even though Bella is a "shiny object," her shine pales in comparison to the Cullen sparkle. But, thanks to Alice and her "thousand different products" that "beautify a person's surface," Bella is schooled in how to aspire to vampire beauty standards (*E* 580). Alice, after all, is not that different from Rosalie when it comes to beauty — she, too, is snobbish in regards to looks, chiding Bella for her lack of designer fashion know-how and continually encouraging her to make herself over. In fact, despite her representation as an "all that" snob, Rosalie resists the beauty paradigm far more than Alice. For example, when Rosalie notes, "The man named John was dark-haired and suntanned. He looked me over like I was a horse he was buying," she implicitly condemns these men for treating her as an attractive animal whom they can abuse as they please (*E* 159). The text then goes on to condemn the men for treating women as interchangeable objects. Yet, some of this more positive critique is lessened by the fact that Rosalie's shallowness returns in full force once she is a vampire. As she relates, "Shallow as I was, I felt better when I saw my reflection in the mirror the first time.... I was the most beautiful thing I'd ever seen" (*E* 162). This meme is echoed in her jealousy over Bella. Yet, to her credit, Rosalie realizes beauty can be a curse. In fact, the book frames her beauty as the possible cause she was attacked by Royce and his gang. When she relates that "men's eyes watched me everywhere I went, from the year I turned twelve," she offers a clue to her assault — men, it seems, cannot keep their eyes (or hands) off of her (*E* 155). Confessing to Bella that "I wanted to be loved, to be adored," Rosalie admits that "admiration was like air to me" (*E* 155). However, these textual hints that Rosalie's attraction to her own image result in her gang rape and death (where she is doomed to a life without what she wanted most —children) remain nascent — the texts never explicitly condemn the beauty myth.

Burning the Twi-Training Bra

We don't need to burn our tattered copies of *Twilight* nor drive a stake through the nearest *Twi*-fan despite the series' championing of traditional gender roles. Yet, just like the women who used bras as a metaphor for patriarchal control in their infamous attempts to burn their boob-holders at the Miss America pageant, so, too, might we think of *Twilight* as both pretty and constraining, both uplifting and confining, or, in other words, as like a bra. Just as most of us don't want to toss our supporting garments on the pyre, neither do we want to extinguish our love for *Twilight*. However, we can make this love more productive, more comfortable, if we question how the same conditions that have made Harlequin and other romances wildly popular since at least the 1970s are still at play in the *Twilight* saga. We may have much better bra choices now, but we are still taught that we should place primacy on love, romance, and family; we are still taught that men are the saviors, that heterosexual monogamous marriage complete with kids and a nice house is the end goal, that we should be pure, good girls who wait patiently for Mr. Right (and who keep our boobs and other bodily parts nicely packaged until our entry into marriage allows for their unpacking). And, precisely because the roles and lessons offered to us are still so staid (and relatively unchanging), the type of violent, passionate, irrational romance portrayed in the saga is still *very* desirable.

Like other romances, the saga serves as a "conservator of the social structure and its legitimizing ideology," functioning as a "cultural release valve" that permits us to address our frustrations and then lay them to rest (Radway 73, 158). Or, in other words, patriarchy creates our need for romantic escape in the first place, yet, in reading such texts, the tenets of patriarchy are reconfirmed and celebrated. Such texts are thus "compensatory literature"— part of an endless loop that provides emotional release via addressing dissatisfaction with prescribed gender roles only to ultimately offer happy endings (Radway 98). The mass appeal of such texts, as Tania Modleski argues, "suggests they speak to very real problems and tensions in women's lives" (14). According to Modleski, such narratives construct female readers not as mindless saps, but as angry about being done wrong. As she argues, "The very fact that the novels must go to such extremes to neutralize women's anger and to make masculine hostility bearable testifies to the depths of women's discontent" (58). As Ann Snitow similarly argues, such narratives fill a void created by the everyday realities and social conditions of our world:

> Harlequins fill a vacuum created by social conditions. When women try to picture excitement, the society offers them one vision, romance. When women try to imagine companionship, the society offers them one vision, male, sexual companionship. When women try to fantasize about success, mastery, the society offers them one vision, the power to attract a man. When women try to fantasize about sex, the society offers them taboos on most of its imaginable expression except those that deal directly with arousing and satisfying men. When women try to project a unique self, the society offers them very few attractive images. True completion for women is nearly always presented as social, domestic, sexual.... One of our culture's most intense myths, the ideal of an individual who is brave and complete in isolation, is for men only [138–39].

Given this, it is understandable why the constant return to imagining moments of courtship and love is so addictive for females. Romances "reinforce the prevailing cultural code: pleasure for women is men" and render this code desirable and sexy (Snitow 139). The texts render traditional masculinity desirable and sexy, championing strength, dominance, power, control, and virility. In a recent book-length analysis of the series, Ruth Felker Jones, a professor of theology, suggests that such a depiction is *naturally* desirable to females, who, according to her, all grow up watching *Snow White* and singing "Someday My Prince Will Come" (13). (I don't know what forest glen Felker grew up in, but I never sang that song or dreamed of a princess wedding; I was too busy complaining about the fact my brother had more freedoms and a later curfew than I did.)

So, I disagree with Felker that such desire is *natural*, but I see how the series itself is based on this premise. Grounded in a love-at-first-sight narrative, Edward is depicted as a modern dream-man who asks Bella about her deepest thoughts and feelings, listening as if his life depended on her answers.[4] Bella is also welcomed with open arms into his perfect family by everyone except the jealous, salad-bowl-smashing Rosalie. This trajectory of the tale takes Bella out of her mundane existence with her primeval computer and prehistoric truck while simultaneously disproving her claims of clumsy unattractiveness. A modern-day Wonder Woman, or Sidney Bristow, Bella is launched into a world of intrigue, adventure, and heightened emotion. Yet, the utopian world offered to Bella is ultimately not that much different from the world she is hoping to leave behind — this world still frames her primarily in relation to her role as future wife/mother and ensconces her safely within the domesticated world of the Cullen family.

Vamp Grrrl Power in a Patriarchal World

This is why, as critic Alison Light notes, romantic texts are often seen as "coercive and stereotyping narratives which invite the reader to identify with a passive heroine who only finds true happiness in submitting to a masterful male" (140). This strand of the *Twilight* narrative has indeed come under attack, with many detractors decrying the more antifeminist, conservative strands of the book. Yet, as various writers have addressed, romantic fiction not only works in delimiting ways—but also offers visions of a changed social structure, more egalitarian relationships, and transgressive messages about love, identity, and sexuality. Thus, as a particularly popular form of mass culture, the romance not only works to acculturate women into a male dominated society and make them desire their own submission, but also questions (albeit rather politely) the validity of patriarchy and the gender roles that patriarchal society perpetuates. Granted, many romance novel readers would never be caught dead uttering the word "patriarchy," or wearing a "This is what a feminist looks like" T-shirt. Yet, ask most women if they would like to be treated equally and have equal opportunities to men, and the answer will be a resounding yes. By showing that Bella has very limited choices within real-world Forks, and then revealing that a vampire/werewolf-inhabited world allows for excitement, adventure, and passion, the series offers the same resounding "yes." However, like the romance fiction genre, which Radway examines so closely in *Reading the Romance*, *Twilight* allows readers to envision the world otherwise, to revel in vamp-grrrl power, only to ultimately indicate that the dominant social order (and being dominated by a hot vampire or werewolf) leads to happy endings.

Yet, as Light notes, "Reading is never simply a linear con-job but a process of interaction, and not just between text and reader, but between reader and reader, text and text. It is a process which helps to query as well as endorse social meanings and one which therefore remains dynamic and open to change" (141). We *Twilight* readers take part, I argue, in such a dynamic, with our conversations and interactions with the text offering often transgressive re-imaginings of gender relations. The refusal to accept the claim that Bella is a typical damsel in distress is a particularly potent example of this re-imagining. Despite evidence to the contrary, many readers forge interpretations of Bella that focus on her independence, will, and ultimate triumph. In so doing, they enact what Radway argues is one of the primary pleasures of romance reading—the re-evaluation of femininity and the rewriting of traditional female identity.

As Light argues, romance is often most appealing to females at precisely the time "when the *impossibility* of being successfully feminine is felt, whether as a 'failure' to ever be feminine enough ... or whether in terms of the gap between fulfilling social expectations (as wife and mother) and what those roles mean in reality" (142). According to this reading, tweens and teens are drawn to *Twilight* as it navigates the impossibility of being the type of female our culture holds up as ideal and grapples with the social expectations heaved upon young women's shoulders. This not only accounts for the massive popularity of the series amongst young fans, but also reveals why women of all ages are drawn to the texts because the "impossibility of being successfully feminine" is felt, especially at this cultural moment, across all ages— women are now supposed to be beautiful, successful, and desirable from cradle to grave.

I'd Rather Be a Vampire Heroine than a Human Klutz

Meyer, when asked about whether she is a feminist, explains that Bella is weak because she is a human and not a vampire, not because she is a female. This human/vampire binary allows for a symbolic negotiation as well as a reaction to the ways females are kept in second place in the real world. However, as my feminist self noticed, this framing also justifies Bella's weakness, suggesting we females should be okay with our second fiddle status. In effect, the series rationalizes the male/female hierarchy, in which men are considered more capable and powerful, through its depiction of the irreducible difference between vampire Edward and human Bella. Yet, Bella and Edward ultimately end up as equals (some might even argue that Bella is stronger by the series' end), and this ending allows for a vicarious triumph for female readers— a triumph that is rarely echoed in the real world. Thus, the books simultaneously justify the imbalance of power between men and women by using the metaphor of vampire and human while also suggesting this imbalance can be overcome. But, significantly, the way to overcome such an imbalance (according to the series) is *through love and romance*— or, via partaking in what females are already socially conditioned to desire. Ah, what a way to have your quasi-feminist cake and add in some patriarchal frosting! In this way, the series accords to Radway's formulation of romance as speaking to women's desires to be seen as equals yet does so in a way that fails to subvert the very cultural dictums that construct them as unequal in the first place.

If we consider our love for *Twilight* as what Radway calls a "technique for survival," we can more readily understand the series' appeal (143). Rather than viewing girls, tween, teens, and adult women as being duped by an overly romantic message laden with male violence and female submission, we can see such reading as a type of resistance — as a way to question cultural norms. And what is, after all, more threatening to male rule than masses of females, declaring their opinions and desires matter? As much mainstream media coverage of the fandom reveals, this female-based movement scares the pants off male privilege. Why else would reporters be so insistent on mocking, criticizing, and attacking the fandom? As with Beatlemania, female fans are framed as mindless shrieking estrogen banks while their intellectual, passionate, entrepreneurial, and artistic engagements with the series go ignored. The promotion of feminine community is likewise ignored by the reports that frame fans as stupid girls (as will be explored further in chapter 8). To take my 11-year-old daughter as an example, reading the series made her part of a young group of female readers, many of whom question the characters' actions and choices in thought-provoking ways. For example, my daughter and her friends were aghast when Edward imprisoned Bella, and, though Edward is held up as someone they should desire, they nevertheless condemned his more domineering actions. In so doing, they take part in a female community of readers that engage with the texts in ways that allow them to interrogate social norms surrounding ideas about femininity, masculinity, and romance.

Just Say I Don't

The text also intriguingly sets Bella up as *not* desiring marriage — a rather unique move for a text so heavily steeped in heterosexual romance. In fact, Bella not only questions whether marriage is right for her, but also questions the entire institution of marriage, insinuating that it doesn't work for everyone, just as it did not for her parents. However, while Bella acts as a renegade here, Edward's position is in keeping with traditional masculinity — he wants to secure his right to Bella, his ownership of her in a sense, through marriage. While this impulse is read by many as proof of his love, this "you're mine and mine only" paradigm reads as rather selfish and old-fashioned. As Bella questions, are the ring and the ceremony necessary, or is the fact that they love each other more important? This emphasis placed on their feelings toward each other, rather than on the importance of marriage as a socially binding institution, speaks to modern readers' sensibilities. However, on this subject the series succeeds yet again in having it both ways. Readers can identify either with Bella's more modern stance or with Edward's traditional one. Comments on Meyer's website reveal the author's own vacillation regarding notions of true love. Meyer writes:

> First of all, let me say that I do believe in true love. But I also deeply believe in the complexity, variety, and downright insanity of love. A lucky person loves hundreds of people in their lives, all in different ways, family love, friendship love, romantic love, all in so many shades and depths. I don't think you lose your ability — or right — to have true love by loving more than one person. In part, this is true because you never love two people the same way. Another part is that, if you're lucky, you learn to love better with practice. The bottom line is that you have to choose who you are going to commit to — that's the foundation of true love, not a lack of other options.[5]

Here, Meyer uses the phrase *true love* repeatedly, a phrase that is traditionally used to indicate that each person has one soul mate that is the *true* love of their lives. Yet, she goes against this concept by also saying that "a lucky person loves hundreds of people in their lives" and that "you learn to love better with practice." Here again, she seems to be torn between traditional conceptions of love (and certainly ones held dear by her Mormon faith) and more modern, fluid conceptions of love. Bella similarly argues that loving more than one person is possible, even preferable, to loving one. Talking of how she "could stake a claim" on Jacob and referring to how her love for Jacob "wasn't the same love at all" as that for Edward, she even muses that Edward "wouldn't begrudge me this"(*NM* 375–76). Bella, via exploring rather than denying her feelings for both Jacob and Edward, questions the tenability of monogamy in a way that radically differs from the ultimate fairy tale ending the book upholds. Further, when Bella relates in the last book of the series that she has not forgotten Jacob, noting, "I wasn't sure exactly what to do about the leftover, unresolved character. Where was his happily ever after?" she belies the usual romantic set up where love of the hero supersedes all else (*NM* 550). And, even though this conflict is resolved in the text by having Jacob imprint on Renesmee (in a icky pedophilic narrative twist), the more subversive depictions of romance that come before this tidy, so-called happy ending cannot be denied. Further, fans' response to this triangulation of desire, including their Team Edward, Team Jacob, and Team Switzerland camps, frame readers as actively choosing their "hero" rather than letting the narrative do it for them.

This modern love triangle (which actually becomes even more multisided when one considers all the characters that fans desire) is particularly alluring to contemporary readers. Representing many different males and females as both desirable and desiring subjects accurately reflects our modern experiences of love and desire. Living as we do in a world where we are exhorted to immerse ourselves in romantic entanglements almost as soon as we are able to walk and talk, it is unrealistic to expect we will find our very own Edward from the get go. Watching the amorous plotlines that permeate everything from *Barbie* films to *Hanna Montana* as children, we are encouraged to desire romance at a very young age (especially if we are female). Continuing through to *Gossip Girl* and *Vampire Diaries* and graduating on to the likes of *True Blood* and *Sex and the City,* we learn that everyone from burgeoning pop divas to clairvoyant waitresses place primary importance on romantic desire. This cultural indoctrination into the "love is everything" mantra conditions us to fixate on heterosexual romance and to seek pleasure via imagining our (and others') romantic lives. The pleasure of such projections are heightened via the message that we can become different, better selves through successive relationships. This message is supplied in *Twilight* via the potential futures Bella's two different suitors offer.

Driving a Stake Through the Heart of Traditional Romance

While many critics have interpreted romance reading as evidence of female masochism or as a submission to patriarchal ideology, I would counter that romance appeals to females for complex, multilayered reasons. The loathsome view toward pulp romance and popular fiction that literary analysis has often upheld needs to be renegotiated if we are to understand and respond to what constitutes narrative pleasure and why. *Twilight*, offering pleasure to millions of fans around the globe, needs to be taken seriously. Though it has been derided as a poorly written, lightweight series, the reactions it has garnered prove that it resonates deeply with massive numbers of readers, most of them young and female.

I contend that the popularity of the series is due in part to the fact that, as Radway argues, such texts *do* in fact have the possibility to bring about social change. By encouraging analysis of the limited ways female pleasure and achievement is constructed in society, such books can support the formation of communities of females that engage with one another regarding the world they live in and the world as they wish it to be. Granted, while most *Twilight* communities are more often intent on drooling over Pattinson or discussing the latest shirtless image of Lautner, the fan culture also dissects the messages the texts and the phenomenon surrounding it uphold. Perhaps the most obvious reaction in this vein was the vocal disapproval for the trajectory of Bella's story in *Breaking Dawn* wherein many ardent "*Twilight*ers" criticized the book's representation of marriage, motherhood, and reproductive choice.

Moreover, the global community of *Twilighters* represents a thriving fandom that not only lusts after Edward and Jacob but also pens blogs, organizes conferences, and produces all sorts of creative work, from fan-fiction to videos to artwork (as discussed in chapter 8). Much of this work disdains the way females are framed as second-class citizens and gives voice to traditionally silenced female communities such as stay-at-home moms and tweens. Further, via its focus on humor, feminine desire, and the female voice, the fandom implicitly disproves and mitigates the mainstream construction of females as humorless, silenced, and/or hypersexualized objects. We thus should not assume that the readers of texts such as *Twilight* don't share anything with those fighting for gender equality. While *Twilight* fans may not be at the forefront of fighting for social justice, they nevertheless are participating in a subculture that demands that female voices and female desires matter.

We would do well not to ignore such voices and the popular trends and cultural zeitgeists they bring about. Rather, we should use the opportunity to engage in discussions about what the popularity of the series means and to forge ways to respond to the zeitgeist that promote analysis and critical discussion. In fact, many people are already seizing this opportunity — teachers are using the books in their classrooms to critique gender norms, scholars are writing about the series in relation to religion, philosophy, and history, mothers are capitalizing on their daughter's love for the series to initiate frank discussions about sexuality, and youth group leaders are discussing the texts in order to examine interpersonal violence and abusive relationships. Most significantly, though *Twilight* capitalizes on our culturally constructed tendency to desire romance narratives, the largely female fan base is not swallowing any one message of the saga. Rather, through their various *Twilight* blogs, parodies, and subcultures, many fans refuse to consume the abstinence-only, pro-life, love-is-everything messages. Like Meyer herself, who vacillates between traditional and subversive messages, fans question societal mores, suggesting that the good-girl paradigm is unrealistic. In so doing, they do not apathetically consume the messages *Twilight* offers, but rather use the narratives to create and examine their own conceptions of what it means to be bitten by romance.

Chapter 3

Vamping Femininity
Twilight *as (Anti?) Feminist Fairy Tale, Or, We Can't All Be Slayers*

The renowned feminist artist Judy Chicago notes that in the 1970s she was regularly given an ultimatum: she could be an artist *or* a woman. Chicago refused to make this choice, instead opting to be a *woman artist*. While the radical nature of her stance is likely lost on those born post–1970, the challenge Chicago was presented with some 40 years ago— that of being a woman (or, in other words, not fully human, not able to do all that men can do) *or* of being an artist (or, in other words, taking on a role reserved for men)— still plays itself out in various ways. Indeed, while the days of segregating life choices strictly by gender have waned, the concept that being a female somehow sets one apart from being fully human still permeates our culture. The 2008 presidential race, as a case in point, made this faulty assumption painfully clear. Hillary Clinton was constantly subjected to sexist critique, ranging from focusing on her appearance to making jokes about PMS. Sarah Palin, likewise, was focused on for her looks as well as her status as a mother. The larger question plaguing both of these candidates was "can a woman be president?" It was, of course, not so long ago that the question "can a woman be an author?" was common.

Though we have had female playwrights, poets, novelists, and philosophers right alongside men for as long as each of these categories have existed, women's authorship has long been questioned, maligned, belittled, and rendered invisible. Or, as the joke goes, "Anonymous was a woman." Today, however, some of our most beloved and well-respected authors are female— Toni Morrison, Maya Angelou, J.K. Rowling, and, of course, Stephenie Meyer. Yet, in the case of many female authors, and especially for those writing popular fiction, their female characters have not fared as well as they have. Often such authors create male heroes, depicting female characters as weaker, more submissive, or secondary. Typically, authors also create far fewer female characters, and they are often pigeonholed into a certain type. They can be beautiful or strong, good or bad, kind or evil, prudes or sluts. While this certainly does not account for

61

all female characters, it is far more common to come across flat, stereotypical female characters in fiction and film than it is to come across such one-dimensional males. In fact, it is less common to encounter female characters in general.[1]

To take J.K. Rowling as an example of a very popular female author who has created more (and more likeable) male characters than female ones, let's examine Hermione's character for a moment. First and most glaringly, Hermione is not the lead character in the *Harry Potter* series. Why couldn't we have had Hermione Potter or Henrietta Potter rather than Harry Potter? Likely, boys would not have been as eager to read a series with a female wizard at the helm — just that fact alone speaks volumes. I have no doubt an author as talented as Rowling could have made a success of a series with a female protagonist, but she chose not to. The secondary female character we are left with, Hermione, is a character focused on, at least in part, for big teeth and bossiness. Granted, there is more to her than this, but she is not the hero that Harry is. As Joanna Russ' famous essay makes clear, the role of hero is reserved for males.[2] Emma Watson, the actress who plays Hermione, calls her "bossy" and "horrible," while J.K. Rowling repeatedly describes her as "annoying" (Lamb and Brown 187). She is said to be whimpering, shrill, and panicky. She has no friends until Ron and Harry, and they are framed as making her nicer and more likeable. As one 12-year-old I interviewed about her character put it, "It's kind of like with *Twilight*, the female character is not complete without males." In contrast to Rowling, Stephenie Meyer has given us a female protagonist, and one that is arguably bright, brave, adventurous, and noble. Further, her series has a rather gender equitable character list, with the female characters just as well-rounded and key to the narrative as the males. Alice, Esme, Victoria, Leah, and Jane — to name some of these — exist in a fictional world far more gender balanced than most.

Meyer also pays homage to a number of female authors in her work, notably Jane Austen and the Bronte sisters. However, Meyer does not provide us with rebellious female protagonists who are confident and critical like Jane Eyre or determined like Catherine Earnshaw. On the contrary, Bella is portrayed as a "typical" female —clumsy, self-conscious, and lacking in confidence — until, that is, her vampire knight reveals her "true" self. Yet, Bella is not entirely lacking in rebellion either: she resists the shallow girl culture represented by characters such as Lauren, she rebels against the good-girl model by befriending (and then falling in love with) a vampire and a werewolf, and she insists the world is *not* too dangerous nor too sexual for a girl her age.

Thus, the texts are not the antifeminist rhetoric they are often accused of being, but teeter in between normative and transgressive representations of gender and sexuality. Admittedly, Jacob and Edward both treat Bella as child. Jacob calls her a "porcelain doll" while Edward carries, rocks, and cradles her through all four books (*NM* 179). Through such representations, readers are consistently encouraged to recognize Bella's frailty and to appreciate her protective, domineering mates. On the other hand, though, Bella rides motorcycles, jumps off a cliff, jets off to Italy, and doesn't balk at battles with vampires, werewolves, or other humans. She endures more injuries than seems humanly possible, and does so with a pronounced lack of complaint. Bella is thus both weak and strong, both independent and dependent, both unbreakable and frail. In other words, she is very much like real human females. While Meyer has been at pains to point out that Bella's weak, damsel-in-distress attributes in the text are due to a human/vampire distinction rather than a female/male one, I think the text can better be read as testament to the contradictory messages females receive about being "properly" feminine. Such messages, the trajectory of the series reveals, result in a rather schizoid female identity — one that is endlessly torn in different directions. This depiction undoubtedly speaks to the countless female readers who are likewise told to be good but daring, pure but sexy, confident but modest.

Given that the series is first and foremost a love story, it would be odd if a female were not the protagonist. However, as discussed in the previous chapter, though such stories are often told from a female character's perspective, most of the focus is nevertheless on males, and, in particular, on the male or males the female protagonist has romantic feelings for. It is also common for such protagonists to be ordinary. This allows for readers to identify with the character as she transforms from ordinary girl or woman to a romantic heroine. Bella accords with these traditions in ways, but she also departs from them. She starts out as a rather ordinary high school girl who many readers can no doubt identify with. She goes through a number of emotions and daily happenings that are also easily relatable to many readers, from being the new girl at a school to lusting over the hot guy on campus. But, by the series' end, she is far from ordinary.

So, how does the *Twilight* series depart from stereotypical representations of females as weaker or less important? Does Meyer's work champion strong, independent females? Is Bella's character too passive and too self-effacing to be a strong role model for young female fans of the series? Do these females identify with these strong female characters in self-empowering ways or only in order to vicariously desire the strong males the series sets up as necessary to female happiness? Finally, does the infamous feminist condemnation of the series have it right? I don't think these questions have definitive answers, and, like with all fiction, the answers to such questions are largely determined by the individual reader. However one answers these questions, though, one thing is sure: the series and reactions to it serve as a fascinating testament to our cultural ambivalence about females. On the one hand, the females in the series are interesting, smart, brave, and multidimensional. On the other, they are valued for their beauty, mothering capabilities, and fashion know-how.

Twilight *Through a Disneyfied Lens*

Due to the rabid popularity of the series, and especially given the series' extreme popularity with the 9- to 29-year-old age group, the messages and lessons it offers about femininity beg examination. Calling the media a "relentless dispenser of psychic Spackle," Susan Douglas notes that children in particular "have all these cracks and crevices in their puttylike psychological edifices" (*Where the Girls Are* 13). Currently, the *Twilight* series is a massive dispenser of "psychic Spackle," teaching girls what it means to be female as well as indicating what they should feel about males. Douglas, a baby boomer, notes, "My generation grew up internalizing an endless film loop of fairy-tale princesses, beach bunnies, witches, flying nuns, bionic women, and beauty queens" (*Where the Girls Are* 18). Douglas reveals that our era has not changed in this regard. We still have plenty of princesses, sexually objectified females, beauty queens, and monstrous women populating media representation. Indeed, we need look no further than Disney to prove this claim, or as Douglas puts it, "No one more powerfully or more regularly reaffirmed the importance of the doormat as a role model for little girls than Walt Disney" (*Where the Girls Are* 27). Disney princesses, like the female characters represented as good today, are beautiful yet not vain, industrious yet require male saviors, yearn for marriage and motherhood but not sex. They happily cleaned up after grumpy dwarves and vowed to change their beasts into princes, much the way Bella cooks for Charlie without complaint and works to civilize her vampire and wolf mates. The Little Mermaid, like Bella, marries extremely young and is willing to give up anything for Prince Eric; just as she gives up her voice for him, so does Bella give up her life for Edward.

Yet, *Twilight* is certainly an improvement on Disney. While Bella might be reminiscent of various Disney princesses—not only Ariel from *The Little Mermaid* but also Belle from *Beauty and the Beast* (particularly in relation to her attraction for abusive males), Snow White (in her domestic capacities), and Cinderella (in her rags-to-riches rise)—she is a far less dependent, less stereotypical character than your typical Disney princess. Other female characters are similarly strong and nonstereotypical, from Alice's role as savior to Leah's fierce ability to defy the wolf patriarchy. Rosalie, as we learn in *Midnight Sun*, is perhaps an even better mechanic than Jacob, and Bella's friend Angela is neither jealous, catty, nor overly emotional. The fact that females are represented in such strong, complex ways—and as humans, vampires, and werewolves—is still fairly unique in a world where most texts *still* sideline female characters and present them in stereotypical ways. Yet, while females in the *Twilight* series have many positive, empowering attributes, they are far from feminist heroines who champion egalitarianism and balk at gender norms. Most glaringly, they ultimately do not reject the notion that women should primarily focus on men, love, marriage, and motherhood.

However, despite the overarching obeisance to patriarchal norms, the series also slides in various critiques of male dominance. For example, practically all of the female characters have been abused, endangered, exploited, or abandoned by men. Bella, our romantic apologist, is nearly killed by Tyler and James in the first book, abandoned by Edward in the second, assaulted by Jacob in the third, and forced to fight for her life in the fourth due to the Volturi's virtual fatwa against her. The world of *Twilight* (which reflects modern reality in many regards) is a dangerous place for women, especially women who do not have vampire powers or werewolf strength. This dangerous world is in fact what Meyer claims justifies and explains her representation of Bella. She argues that Bella's choices should not be read as antifeminist *because* "she lives in a fantasy world."[3] Her use of this fictional world that reformulates male privilege as vampire/werewolf privilege allows Meyer (and readers) to account for Bella's damsel-in-distress attributes as logical given that she is *only human*. By eliding her femaleness with humanness, the text is able to at least partially complicate what seems like a radically antifeminist message — or, that a weak, passive, beautiful female's only hope for adventure, love, and triumph comes at the hands of domineering, violent, and controlling alpha males. Given that the two lead males are presented as vampire/wolf first and male second, the author (and readers) are able to make this retrograde message more palatable.

Yet, given the overarching romantic emphasis of the series, the claim that Edward and Jacob represent super-hero otherness rather than typical ideal male suitors rings false. While Bella has become a vampire super-heroine of sorts by the saga's culmination, her strength has been granted by Edward (via his vampire venom) and cemented through her entry into that most hallowed of female roles— wife and mother. Yes, Bella is tough by the close of *Breaking Dawn*, and she even exudes a certain amount of toughness throughout the series, but her strength, as is typical of female heroines, comes through her attachment to men and her acceptance of the patriarchal norms of family. Thus, although Sherrie Inness noted in her 1999 book *Tough Women* that the last three decades of the 20th century witnessed an increasing prevalence of "tough girls," it seems that the first decade of the 21st century — if *Twilight* is any indication — is keen to emphasize that a tough girl must be *girl* first and *tough* second (5). Or, in other words, Bella's vampire toughness is secondary to those things that mark her as an "ideal" girl — her beauty, her desire for men, her capitulation to marriage and motherhood. As Inness notes, we still connect males with toughness, and "tough women are still commonly portrayed as less strong and less effectual than tough men" (4). This lack of tough women perpetuates traditional gender binaries where tough males are to be expected but tough females (such as Rosalie, Victoria, and Leah) become virtual she-devils. As Inness further argues, "The toughest of tough women is limited, confined, reduced, and regulated in a number of ways" via over-emphasizing her femininity, her maternal role, her sexuality, and/or her "less tough" status in comparison to males (178). Women are usually made tough by some chance occurrence or modification, rather than being represented as "naturally tough"—just as Bella is made strong by her association with Edward, Jacob, and her ultimate turn to vampire. This assumption that females are not naturally tough "binds women to the cult of femininity and separates them from authority and power," Inness asserts (181).

At least since the 1960s, tough, powerful females have become more commonplace in media. From Samantha in *Bewitched* to Ripley of the *Alien* films, females have increasingly been characterized as potentially as tough (or even tougher) than males. Buffy Summers, one of the most iconic of tough heroines, was not rendered smitten by male vamps and weres à la Bella but instead used her strength to slay (usually) male villains (while delivering sarcastic verbal attacks alongside kung-fu kicks). Unlike Bella, who happily does the laundry and cooks for her father, Buffy, as Jowett argues, is "a woman resisting patriarchy" (24). Yet, as Jowett further notes, "A common strategy used to neutralize female action heroes' transgressive masculine behavior is to balance it with recognizable femininity," a strategy that is certainly used in both Buffy's and Bella's cases (23). Though Buffy is admittedly hyperfeminized in ways, she is certainly no Bella—Buffy is far stronger, wittier, and rebellious. She has far more agency—sexual and otherwise—than Bella, and does not frame her entire existence around love (nor marriage and motherhood).

Twilight, *Where Nice Girl Vampires Finish First*

Bella and Alice, arguably the two most prominent heroines of the *Twilight* series, are traditionally feminine. Both are hopelessly devoted to their male loves, both are nice, caring, and nurturing in the extreme, and neither questions nor attempts to subvert white male privilege. Alice, though represented as adept in vampire battles, is characterized by her extensive fashion know-how and undying desire to make-over Bella. Bella and Alice also accord to the so-called "nice girl syndrome"—no ironic verbal comebacks for them, let alone any buttkicking of the patriarchy.

According to Rachel Simmons' study of the so-called "Hidden Culture of Aggression in Girls," one enduring and highly regulated norm of femininity is the pressure to be "nice." Simmons argues, "The message that modesty and restraint are the essence of femininity persists. Contemporary feminist research shows that our culture continues to pressure girls to be chaste, quiet, thin, and giving, denying the desire for sexual pleasure, voice, food, and self-interest" (106). Girls cannot be openly confident, or they risk being labeled "all that"—a negative descriptor intimating that a girl is too assertive, snobby, and self-centered (115). Girls who come off as "all that" are rendered the villains—like

Rosalie in *Twilight*. On the other hand, girls that are modest, that deny their own attractiveness or accomplishment, or that wear self-effacement as their mask are held up as ideal, like Bella, who tellingly shares, "After eighteen years of mediocrity, I was pretty used to being average. I realized now that I'd long ago given up any aspirations of shining at anything" (*BD* 523). Bella's nice-girl status is rendered more obvious through the many mean girls that populate the saga-not only via the jealous Lauren Mallory, Jessica Stanley, and Rosalie Hale, but also via the vengeful Victoria, the masochistic Jane, the over-sexed Tanya.[4] Here, the saga seems to echo what Simmons names "the hidden culture of aggression in girls" (8) and Wiseman's documentation of "girl world" as a profoundly mean place (2). This culture may indeed *cause* girls and women to turn to books like *Twilight*, where Bella is profoundly *nice* and finds a nice boyfriend, nice family, and very nice sister/BFF (in the form of Alice). In comparison to "mean girls" and other societal celebrations of violent, cruel, catty femininity, the series does not represent females in the main as petty and vindictive — in fact, Bella develops good relationships with many females in the series — many who were first seen as "enemies" or threats to her. In so doing, her character is far different from the "femme fatale" and "mean girl" types that populate popular TV, film, and fiction.

In contrast, we might read the female villains of the texts — Rosalie, Victoria, Jane, Leah — in accordance with the stereotype of the cold, assertive bitch — a stereotype that Simmons argues "communicates to girls their worst fear: that to become assertive in any way will terminate their relationships and disqualify them from the primary social currency in their lives, tenderness and nurturing" (127). Bella serves as partial anecdote to this nice girl/mean girl dichotomy, allowing readers to vicariously become strong and powerful while simultaneously suggesting they will not be disqualified from the "good girl category." Not only does Bella comply to the patriarchal rules of her fictional world, but so too are readers encouraged to comply with the message her character arc offers — you can be strong, smart, and capable, but you still need to be nice, you still need to look good, and you still need to marry and procreate. Perhaps no other line better captures Bella's "nice girl" status than when she thinks about what kind of vampire she will make and muses, "I would probably never be able to do anything interesting or special like Edward, Alice, and Jasper could do. Maybe I would just love Edward more than anyone in the history of the world had ever loved anyone else" (*BD* 426–27). Wow, how nice, she can be the world's most devoted vampire mate.

Indeed, Bella is like a contemporary descendent of Mina Harker from *Dracula* — her goodness in effect proving that the society that produced her must also be good.[5] As noted by Griffin, Mina is the archetypal good girl who is obsessed with her duty as wife ("Your Girls" 145). Van Helsing, Mr. Patriarchy himself, likens Mina to an angel that gives him hope, noting thankfully that "there are good women still left to make life happy" (Stoker 211). Like *Dracula's*

Lucy Westenra of the same canonical text, Bella is similarly desired by many men, and becomes "the common ideal to which they pledge themselves" (Griffin, "Your Girls" 140). Yet, unlike Lucy, Bella does not become evil once courted by a monster — rather, she goes from human to angel, becoming the perfect mother and wife. This ideal, which Griffin links to Mina most prominently in *Dracula*, reveals that the underlying misogyny of Stoker's novel is alive and well in *Twilight*, *Dracula's* 21st century literary descendent (148). How pleased Van Helsing would be to know that a good woman such as Bella still exists to make men happy.

Bella is often described as ordinary and average, with an emphasis on her clumsy, awkward nature. While this representation undoubtedly appeals to young female fans who can identify with such feelings, it also serves to uphold the message that females are, by their very *nature*, less capable. This echoes the patriarchal messages of gender that construct men as the norm and women as the Other, males as extraordinary and females as sub-par. Bella has internalized such messages, referring to herself as "a curiosity, a freak" (*T* 147). As the following quote reveals, she chastises herself for not fitting into the norms of femininity:

> Physically, I'd never fit in anywhere. I should be tan, sporty, blond — a volleyball player, or a cheerleader, perhaps — all the things that go with living in the valley of the sun. Instead, I was ivory-skinned, without even the excuse of blue eyes or red hair, despite the constant sunshine. I had always been slender, but soft somehow, obviously not an athlete; I didn't have the necessary hand-eye coordination to play sports without humiliating myself... [*T* 10].

She then goes on to relate that she does not fit in anywhere, ending with the suggestion she is crazy:

> If I couldn't find a niche in a school with three thousand people, what were my chances here? ... I didn't relate well to people my age. Maybe the truth was that I didn't relate well to people, period. Even my mother, who I was closer to than anyone else on the planet, was never in harmony with me, never on exactly the same page. Sometimes I wondered if I was seeing the same things through my eyes that the rest of the world was seeing through theirs. Maybe there was a glitch in my brain [*T* 10–11].

A surface analysis of these quotes reveals Bella as a typical self-effacing female. However, further consideration of the constant references Bella makes throughout the series about not being capable, about her feelings of estrangement, and of her sense of inferiority can be read as her internalization of the negative messages that our patriarchal culture offers to women. Her only outlet in such a culture, as the series reveals, is to ally herself with a more perfect, more powerful specimen, a male. Thus, while the books seem to indicate that self-effacement is a necessary and normal component of being a "good" female, reading against the grain suggests that the texts perhaps represent such norms in order to condemn them. The fact that male characters are shown to require no such self-deprecation to be perceived as likeable furthers this claim. Edward's self-assurance, Jacob's cocky confidence, and Emmett's jocular ultra-masculinity are not presented as overtly problematic, but as appealing. In contrast, assertive females, such as Rosalie, Leah, and Jane, are all demonized. While such characterizations have been used as proof of the series' antifeminism, I suggest that they can also be read as representations of the gender binaries that bind. While the texts celebrate these bindings in ways, they also can be said to represent them as problematically compulsory.

In fact, Bella's accordance with many of the traditional attributes of romantic heroines can be read in light of arguments put forth by critics such as Radway and Modleski. As discussed in the previous chapter, romance heroines offer women ways to resist patriarchal conceptions of gender in a "safe" way. Bella, in accordance with this read, is a good daughter who follows the patriarchal path. Yet, she is also an intellectual, a rule-breaker, and a thrill-seeker who acts on her desires, sexual and otherwise. As the series' representation of man as hunter and woman as prey reveals, she ultimately must capitulate to patriarchal rules, or she will be destroyed. In terms of the narrative, this destruction is threatened through the various male "hunters" that keep her in her good-girl place: Edward, Jacob, James, Laurent, Charlie, etc. Reading this same meme in relation to the role of the author, we can surmise that the rebellious Meyer, writing vampire stories when she *should* be tending to her children or teaching Bible study, is similarly "hunted" by the male codes of her religion and kept in her place by the strictures of patriarchy.

The representations the texts offer of Bella as prey substantiate this reading, suggesting that females have no choice but to be preyed upon by males. They must accept this role, as Bella does at the very beginning of the series, as "a good way to die" (*T* 1). Given what the texts suggest is the inevitability of this paradigm, Bella (and Meyer by extension) may as well make the best of this status. Thus, as in the first reference to herself as prey, Bella depicts the hunter as looking at her "pleasantly," noting he "smiled in a friendly way as he sauntered forward to kill me" (*T* 1). Later, when a different hunter (Jacob) tells her "I bet you'd taste good," she thanks him (*NM* 200). Here and elsewhere, there is no sense that Bella is insulted by being viewed as prey; rather, she seems to quite like it, referring to herself as "helpless and delicious" (*E* 269). Yet, might we see her reaction as making the best of a bad situation? Might we read Meyer's depiction as suggesting (even if unconsciously) that patriarchy cannot result in equal relationships between men and women, that, instead, it results in a society of the hunter and the hunted?

The fact that Bella is represented as a pawn or prize for various males—not only Edward and Jacob, but also Mike, James, Tyler, and Laurent — suggests she is indeed the hunted. This status is particularly apparent when Bella sits between two "hunters" at the movie theater in *New Moon*, noting their hands are "like steel bear traps, open and ready" (210). When Jacob later shares that she is "a classic martyr.... She should have lived back when she could have gotten herself fed to some lions for a good cause," the predator/prey symbol is furthered (*BD* 187). As she seems to have no choice but to be treated like a conquest, Bella acquiesces to it, and particularly with her most handsome hunter, Edward. Yet, even this pairing is continually referred to in hunter/hunted terminology, with many references to him as lion and her as lamb. This dyad explored in the series is particularly relished by fans, who proudly wear lion and lamb pendants.

If we read this appreciation for Bella's "lamb status" as indicative of fan's desires to be viewed as comparatively weak, we might surmise that their identification with Bella is predicated on valuing such weakness. However, as evidenced by the tendency for fans to insist that Bella is a strong character, they also admire her strength. What, then, does this fondness for the lion and lamb metaphor indicate? In the text, Edward says, "And so the lion fell in love with the lamb," just after Bella says, "I would rather die than stay away from you" (*T* 274). Here, building on Bella's suggestion that he is a dangerous predator but she loves him nonetheless, Edward can be read as suggesting that his love allows him to overcome his predatory nature — or, in other words, he loves the lamb rather than wanting to eat her. Referring to himself as a "sick, masochistic lion," Edward constructs himself as the one who is endangered by the relationship, as one who hazardously takes pleasure in his own pain. This reading reveals that is not only Bella that puts herself in a precarious position by loving him, but that Edward is also sticking his neck out, so to speak. The fact that shortly hereafter Bella asks Edward to reveal why he ran from her earlier strengthens this interpretation, showing as it does that he runs from her, rather than vice versa. However, while this scene emphasizes Bella's bravery, many others highlight her weakness. Edward is continually depicted as lifting her, carrying her, and moving her about. Even Bella notices this tendency in him, as when in *Eclipse* she relates, "Edward insisted again on delivering me to the border line like a child being exchanged by custodial guardians" (*E* 318). Of course, we have to take into account that part of this comes from the human/vampire dynamic, but we cannot deny that this very dynamic allows for a typically sexist representation where the male is strong and the female is fragile and dependent. As I've asked before, why not make Bella the vampire from the outset? Couldn't that be a story to inspire fans as well?

Yet, in keeping with the largely old-fashioned representation of women in the series, Bella uses words like *obedient*, *belong*, and *addicted* to characterize herself and her relationship to Edward. Her desperate need for Edward results in a catatonic breakdown in *New Moon*, a breakdown that leads her to undertake various death-defying antics as way to hear Edward's voice. Her desperate cliff-jump positions death as preferable to a life without Edward. These deliberate echoes of *Romeo and Juliet* go against some of the more positive depictions of love and romance the series offers. Rather than allowing Bella the option of being strong when Edward leaves her, she is first placed in a depressive state and then represented as trying to placate her loss via Jacob — both of these storylines indicate that she cannot be complete without a man, that, as prey, she must capitulate to being hunted. Until, that is, she becomes a vampire.

Are All Vampires Created Equal?

As the back stories of Esme, Rosalie, and Alice reveal, female mortal existence is extremely dangerous, leading to abuse, rape, and confinement. Contemporary descendents of Bertha Rochester, Jane Eyre's more oppressed double, these females reveal that women —figuratively and too often literally — are locked within a patriarchal prison-house that puts their lives and their sanity at risk. Yet, by turning vampire, they escape the male/female divide, moving into a realm where they have as much strength (and sparkle) as their male counterparts. If we read the vampire/human binary in relation to the male/female one, we could argue that being a vampire is similar to having male privilege — it gives one strength, power, intellect, and, of course, makes one sparkle. When Bella transitions into her vampire role with ease, noting, "It was like I had been born to be a vampire," we might read her shift as placing her on equal footing in a male-dominated world (*BD* 524). However, given that the vampires most lionized in the series— Edward and Carlisle — are male, and that female vampires are not nearly as sparklingly heroic — they are either vain (Rosalie), evil (Victoria), cruel (Jane), or tend to serve as flat, background characters (Esme)— we must ask: are all vampires created equal? It seems, indeed, they are not. Rather, male vampires are born into a world of patriarchal privilege that echoes the male privilege of human society — they are doctors (Carlisle and Edward), leaders (Aro), military heroes (Jasper), and composers (Edward). Even Alice, the most positive and well-rounded of the female vampires, is not as glorified as her male counterparts. Likewise, the female villains are either at the beck and call of their male overlords (as with Jane) or are heartbroken over the loss of their male loves (Victoria/Tanya).

Thus, while the series can be lauded for its inclusion of many female vampire characters, many of which break with traditional representation, a closer look reveals that the texts actually uphold a strict gender binary, suggesting that males are the "superior" vampire sex. This representation is in keeping with longstanding depictions of women as monstrous, as documented in texts such as Auerbach's *Woman and the Demon.* As Auerbach notes, females are often presented as most dangerous when they break the boundaries of the patriarchal family (1). Using Lucy of *Dracula* as a prime example of this depiction, Auerbach contends that females are portrayed as more threatening than monsters. Indeed, in "Dracula's Guest," Stoker's short-story that is the presumed opening segment omitted from the novel, Jonathon Harker's life is threatened by a "a beautiful woman, with rounded cheeks and red lips" (215). Harker is saved by a wolf, who protects him from this presumed female vampire and her dangerous sexuality (as indicted by her round cheeks and red lips, which echo the lustful female vampires Harker will later encounter once he arrives at Dracula's castle). Over one hundred years later, a wolf will also play a prime role in saving a human — this time the female Bella, from the dangerous Victoria, whose red hair bespeaks of her wanton female nature.

Twilight *as Modern Fairy Tale*

In addition to popular fictional narratives wherein women are most often "disfigured, dead, or at the very least, domesticated," we have an entire genre devoted to teaching about the dangers of female sexuality and the necessity of not only killing the witch (or bitch) but also "taming" females via marriage and motherhood: the fairy tale (Modleski, *Loving* 12). *Twilight*, with its red apples, dark forests, dangerous wolves, deathlike sleeps, and magical transformations, has echoes of *Red Riding Hood, Snow White, The Ugly Duckling,* and *Sleeping Beauty,* to name but a few. These tales often are framed around the angel/whore binary. Bella, our fairy tale heroine, does Snow White one better — she refuses to bite the apple both figuratively (she is not duped by evil — be it the allure of defying the patriarchal order à la Victoria/Leah, or simply allowing her female sexuality to sully her Red Riding Hood innocence) and literally (as on the infamous *Twilight* cover or in the cafeteria scene where her apple remains unbitten).

Fairy tales, like romances, often end with a marriage — so, too, does the *Twilight* saga. Bella enters the dark wood (*Twilight*), emerges from her Sleeping Beauty state (*New Moon*), manages to ward off both witch and wolf (*Eclipse*), and is transformed from clumsy Swan to beautiful, married vampire (*Breaking Dawn*). Her body quite literally becomes, to put it in the terms of Adrienne Rich, "the terrain on which patriarchy is erected" (55). But, this is not any patriarchy — this is vampire patriarchy. With its fairy tale trappings of wealth, magic, and happily ever after immortality, the saga offers readers an enticing story — yet, like the witch's red apple, this story only *looks* good. Once bitten, once the surface gloss of the tale is penetrated, we can see that Bella is, like many female fairy tale heroines before her, trapped in a deathlike state. But this is not the story Meyer seems to want to tell — instead, she offers a Cinderella marriage complete with upward mobility, a perfect prince, and then she throws in a perfect baby to boot. It's as if all those parents desperately seeking a baby in so many tales (*Rapunzel, Tom Thumb, Sleeping Beauty*) have morphed into the poster family. In keeping with the dictates of romance, which often serves to render patriarchy enticing, Meyer's story ends with the message "that men and marriage really do mean good things for women" (Radway 184).

Of course, it is not only fairy tales and romances that offer this message. As Douglas argues in her book *Where the Girls Are*, the mainstream media is also "a dangerous and all too powerful enforcer of suffocating sex-role stereotypes" (6). In ways, *Twilight* acts as such a dangerous and all-too-powerful enforcer. For example, Bella's cooking is focused on repeatedly — a factor that does nothing to further the plot but seems to only serve to prove she is a "proper female" who knows her way around the kitchen. Other females in the series are stereotypically defined via their looks, their relationships to men, and/or their "feminine" know how. Renee is the deadbeat mom smitten with her younger ball-playing man. Alice excels at party and wardrobe planning while Esme thrives at home decorating. Rosalie is your typically mirror-obsessed beauty, while Leah is a classically bitter scorned woman. Fire-haired Victoria and evil Jane are the emblematic cold-hearted bitches of the series. While such depictions might seem to indicate that Meyer dehumanizes her females by turning them into mere character types, it can also be argued that such representations reveal the suffocating roles women are offered in our culture. As the above quote from Douglas indicates, acceptable feminine roles are smothering and don't allow for alternative avenues of female accomplishment. In the texts, many females balk at such strangulation, shirking their prescribed roles as doting wives, nurturing mothers, and dutiful daughters.

Bella, in fact, is particularly resistant to Edward's demands that they marry as soon as possible. Here, in opposition to the stereotype that females want to rush headlong down the aisle, Bella insists marriage is not the right choice. Shortly after sharing her distrust of marriage as an institution, she emphasizes, "The bond forged between us was not one that could be broken by absence, distance, or time.... As I would always belong to him, so would he always be mine" (527). Although the representation of love as ownership raises the feminist hackles, her emphasis on their equal ownership of each other is significant. Then, when Edward insists they get married before she become a vampire, she, with "an edge of hysteria" to her voice, replies, "I'm only eighteen." (540). Her panic here can be read symbolically: she is terrified not only of following the failed footsteps of Charlie and Renee, but also of the institution of marriage itself. Edward, naively assuming perhaps she has declined his ultimatum because he forgot a ring, is conversely depicted as romanticizing marriage, as buying into the notion that marriage will secure their love for eternity. Bella, insisting, "No! No rings!" reveals that she is not interested in displaying their love via diamonds and ceremonies; a woman of her time, she does not seem to believe in what theorist Chris Ingraham dubs "the wedding industrial complex" (26). Her stance comes at least partly from the supposedly "hare-brained" mother, who, Bella shares, "drilled it into me over and over — smart people took marriage seriously. Mature people went to college and started careers before they got deeply involved in a relationship" (*E* 45–46). Noting that Renee "knew I would never be as thoughtless and goofy and small-town as she'd been," Bella reveals that Renee may not be that hare-brained after all — that, in fact, she has given her daughter quasi-feminist sensibilities (46). Bella shares these sensibilities with Edward when she tells him, "I'm not that girl, Edward. The one who gets married right out of high school like some small-town hick who got knocked up by her boyfriend! Do you know what people would think? Do you realize what century this is? People don't just get married at eighteen! Not smart people, not responsible, mature people! I wasn't going to be that girl! That's not who I am" (*E* 275). Bella continues, "In my mind, marriage and eternity are not mutually exclusive or mutually inclusive concepts. And since we're living in my world for the moment, maybe we should go with the times, if you know what I mean." Yet, Edward's sensibilities come from another century, one where he would have "gotten down on one knee and endeavored to secure [Bella's] hand" as soon as possible (*E* 277).

Later, in the chapter fittingly entitled "Compromise," Bella finally agrees to compromise her own standing on marriage. Telling Edward that she wants to talk about "that whole ridiculous marriage condition thing" in order to negotiate, Bella reveals her fear that once she becomes a vampire, she will no longer sexually desire Edward in the same way, that all she will be interested in "is slaughtering everyone in town" (440). Noting that "there's something I want to do before I am not human anymore," Bella relates that she feels "awkward and idiotic," that she doesn't "have the faintest idea how to be seductive" (442). Then, as she tries to undo the buttons on his shirt, he pushes her away, "his face heavily disapproving," telling her to "be reasonable" (443). When she reminds him, "You promised," he tells her, "We're not having this discussion" (443). She retorts, "I say we are," as she unbuttons her blouse. Edward then grabs her wrists, pinning them to her side (443).

Here, Bella is depicted as actively resisting Edward's marriage demands while making sexual claims of her own. Though she alleges she is not apt at the art of seduction, she is (as shown early in the series when she knowingly seduces Jacob into telling her the legend of the Cold Ones). Bella refuses to be silenced, not bowing to Edward's domineering attempts. When he physically restrains her (symbolic of the ways in which women are restrained within patriarchy), Bella rejoins, "So you can ask for any stupid, ridiculous thing you want — like getting *married* — but *I'm* not allowed to even *discuss* what I —" (443). Here, Bella is cut off, as Edward puts his hand over her mouth, physically preventing her from speaking, or symbolically revealing that she is not allowed (within patriarchy) to discuss or act on her needs. Interpreting his actions as rejection, she tries to "banish the reflex reaction that told me I was unwanted and unwantable" (444).

While the above interactions might be read as evidence of an antifeminist message, they can also be interpreted as symbolizing the restrictions placed on females via patriarchy and its normalization of heterosexual, monogamous marriage. Bella, though she tries to resist Edward's demands, is silenced by his paternalistic rhetoric and physically constrained via his vampire strength. Here, the vampire/human dyad that the novel circulates around is revealed to represent not only immortal/mortal and strong/weak binaries, but also that of male/female.

Edward's status as a vampire can be read as encapsulating the male privileges that patriarchal society affords—he is the one, as the above negotiations indicate, who has all the power. His word is law; hers is only request. However, Bella (and perhaps Meyer by extension) does not seem to have the critical skill set (or perhaps the desire) to critique the patriarchal ties that bind. Rather, she interprets his acts as rejection, responding to his rebuttal as evidence of her undesirability, just as her culture teaches her to do. Whether her ultimate acceptance of the wilting flower role is meant to suggest that patriarchy has it right, or, on the contrary, whether these scenes are meant to reveal that Bella has no other choice given the world of male privilege in which she resides, is open for dispute. Yet, the above interactions undoubtedly prove that Bella does not agree with rules regarding marriage, abstinence, and female chastity. Thus, I disagree with Siering's contention that Bella "is merely an object in the *Twilight* world ... a prize, not a person, someone to whom things happen, not an active participant in the unfolding story" (51). As the above scenes reveal, Bella *is* an active participant. She is objectified *via patriarchy*, and couldn't this be Meyer's point?

Siering asks, "If Meyer hopes that readers see themselves as Bella, what is it she is suggesting to them about the significance of their own lives?" (51). It can certainly be argued that Meyer suggests that abstinence is the best policy, and that marriage and motherhood are the primary means to attain power as a woman. However, it can also be argued that she implies that patriarchy (and religion) circumscribes female agency, giving women limited choices and thus forcing them to align with male partners in order to gain power. Such alignment with males is no doubt represented as desirable in the series, but mightn't we also read this alignment as the only way to *survive* patriarchy? The saga does tend to suggest that patriarchy is inevitable, but, coming from a devout Mormon, who would surely be excommunicated should she promote feminist impulses too strongly, this is hardly surprising. In fact, couldn't we argue that Bella's survival stories that dominate each of the texts (from being targeted by James, Laurent, Victoria, and the Volturi to being abandoned by Edward), are not only supernatural survival narratives but also coded representations of how difficult it is for your average female to survive and thrive within a patriarchal society? Let's consider this possibility in light of Siering's claim that

> in *Breaking Dawn*, Meyer finally allows Bella's subordination to end as she takes her proper place: in the patriarchal structure. When Bella becomes a wife and mother, Meyer allows her to receive her heart's desire — to live forever by Edward's side, to be preternaturally beautiful and graceful, to be strong and be able to defend herself. Being a wife and mothers is the choice Meyer has made for herself, for Bella, and by

extension, for her readers as well. It is she, after all, who wrote she hoped readers could step into Bella's shoes [52].

As Siering rightly points out, Bella only achieves power once she "properly" aligns herself within the vampire/patriarchal structure. However, I would argue that she is not given beauty through this alignment, but that she is *required* to be beautiful as part of admission. Once she agrees to yoke her beauty to Edward in marriage, she is allowed to become ultra-attractive, her female beauty no longer the threat it was when she was a free agent (Edward reveals his awareness of her power in this arena, noting, "I feel like there's a line behind me, jockeying for positions.... You're too desirable for your own good") (*E* 445). The fact that marriage, motherhood, and vampirism give her super powers is also true of the text — but, lest we forget, marriage and motherhood as traditional paths to power is also true in real life (especially when combined with beauty and wealth). Further, contemporary society champions these roles (via the celebrity mom and what Susan Douglas and Meredith Williams call the "new momism"), suggesting to females that such power is both fulfilling and attainable.

Yet Meyer, a married mother of three, does not present marriage and motherhood in a wholly uncritical light. It is true she forces Bella to make the same choices she herself has, but not without consequences. In fact, Bella's travels from single, independent teen to married mother exact numerous costs— she loses her independence, she becomes more self-conscious and insecure, she exhibits rash behavior and obsessive thinking, she is nearly raped and then sexually assaulted by her best friend, and so on. These, we could argue, are the consequences of entering into the patriarchal world of romance. Only by becoming a vampire, the saga suggests, can she escape her status as weak, dependent female (and, as a bonus, she won't have to cook anymore either!). Thus, by suggesting that she hoped readers could step into Bella's shoes, couldn't Meyer be indicating a hope that females could be given the power and strength Bella has by the series' end *without* having to become vampires? By extension, as the Cullen vampires represent patriarchy, religion, wealth, and power, might she be hoping (even if only subconsciously) that female readers might be able to step into some nonpatriarchally binding shoes without giving up their humanity *or* their femininity?

As Radway argues, "American society is still remarkably successful at exacting the necessary compliance from its female members" (208). This claim applies to *Twilight* on multiple levels. First, the series reveals how contemporary U.S. society offers women limited options. Second, the series is remarkably good at allowing readers to dally in noncompliance while nevertheless complying to traditional cultural (and religious) mores. Third, U.S. readers, raised as they are in capitalist patriarchy, are apt to buy the message that this society wants to sell them — that they are only valuable for their beauty and their willingness to be dutiful wives/mothers. Fourth, I would contend that this claim similarly relates to Meyer — as a Mormon mother situated within the United

States, she has undoubtedly been inundated with the notion that her compliance to norms of femininity are binding.

Thus the saga, like traditional romance narratives, has a complex relationship to the mores of femininity. On the one hand, it resists them through various narrative threads, proving that readers desire alternatives to patriarchy and strict gender roles; on the other, via its "happy ending," it reifies the status quo. As Radway points out, the fact such fiction appeals to so many readers *proves* "the failure of patriarchal culture to satisfy its female members" (151). Or, in other words, we wouldn't love *Twilight* so much if we loved our own real-life options as women living under patriarchy more. Just like Bella, who notes that she "had been raised to cringe at the very thought of poufy white dresses and bouquets," we are seduced by a narrative that refuses to associate Edward with "a staid, respectable, dull concept like *husband*"—rather we are given an ultra-hot vampire extraordinaire. This, it seems, is our compensation for playing by the patriarchal rules (*BD* 6).

Of Vampire Born: Motherhood in Twilight

Human female mothers in *Twilight*, like those in many fairy tales, are either negligent (Renee) or dead and gone (Jacob's, Carlisle's, and Edward's mothers). In contrast, fathers are elevated into the better parents (Charlie and Carlisle), and women become uber-mothers through vampiric mothering (Esme, Bella). Might we read the championing of these perfect vampire moms (and the mother of three who created them, Stephenie Meyer) as indicative of the fact that the category "woman" is largely "womb dependent"?[26] While feminism has undoubtedly made inroads into the delimiting conflation of *woman* equals *womb*, we are now, at the beginning of the 21st century, seemingly moving backward rather than forward in regards to women's rights, especially in relation to reproductive freedom. In fact, we seem to be making a decided U-turn. From the new momism ideology in which women's "worth" is tied to their capacity to be "perfect mothers," to the increasingly restrictive legislation regarding a woman's right to choose, it seems the triumphs of feminism and women's rights in relation to reproductive issues and maternal subjecthood are eroding at an alarming rate.[7] Though a unique corpus of women's fiction has emerged over the past several decades that challenges the conception of woman as womb, *Twilight* instead seems to be in line with the neoconservative, fundamentalist, antifeminist fast track that is currently permeating the globe. Motherhood has become a more publicly visible goal for women over the past several decades, creating a "hypernatalism" in which magazines enact "bump patrol," surveying the (possibly) pregnant bodies of female celebrities (Douglas, *Enlightened Feminism* 260). The "monster stories" of the 1980s that warned of "women's potential as aborters and child abusers" have morphed into a media machine characterized by super nannies (Jo Frost), overzealous moms (Octomom, Kate Gosselin), and celebrity adoption (Madonna, Angelina Jolie) (Tsing 282). *Twilight* speaks to this intense focus on mothers and mothering, framing motherhood as a key goal for Esme and Rosalie and warning of Bella's potential to become a "bad mother" (like Renee) who puts her own desires above that of her daughter. Thankfully, Bella's "natural" (?!) love for her fetus kicks in even though, as she shares, "I'd never imagined myself a mother, never wanted that. It had been a piece of cake to promise Edward that I didn't care about giving up children for him, because I truly didn't. Children, in the abstract, had never appealed to me" (*BD* 132).

Even though Bella supposedly had *no* interest in marriage or motherhood pre–Edward, once she finds her vampire soulmate, she catapults down the aisle and then quickly embraces her unplanned pregnancy. Here, the texts seem to indicate that females who eschew marriage and motherhood need to "just wait"—that they too, will likely recognize their "true vocation" once the time is right—just as Bella recognizes that "this child, Edward's child, was a whole different story. I wanted him like I wanted air to breathe. Not a choice—a necessity" (*BD* 132). Bella's belief that her "little nudger" is male is also significant here—not only because she seems to be projecting her love for Edward onto their future child through her picturing of an Edward-clone baby but also as she uncritically perpetuates the patriarchal notion that *male* children are more desirable (*BD* 133). When Renesmee is born, Bella refers to her birth as "the most natural of patterns," sharing, "Something in me clicked into place at that moment" (*BD* 444). Given that Jacob imprints on Renesmee, effectively joining the Cullen clan, this "natural pattern" might be read as allowing Renesmee to have the relationship with Jacob that Bella was never able to—or, in other words, Renesmee and Jacob become the double to Bella and Edward, replicating the heterosexual pairing model the saga so champions.

In the texts, when females cannot successfully reproduce this "natural pattern" either through pregnancy/birth or through the adoption/creation of vampire children, they are presented as unfulfilled and bitter. Rosalie, for example, places motherhood as the prime purpose in a female's life, regretfully noting that she will never sit with Emmett "with him gray-haired by my side, surrounded by our grandchildren" (*E* 167). Yet, her regret at her childlessness, as well as her eventual protective mothering stance toward Renesmee, resuscitates her from the fate that plagues other "barren" females in the text—females such as Leah. While Meyer could have left open the option of Leah imprinting with a male and having wolf babies, instead Leah is rendered infertile, which is framed as one of the worst fates a female can suffer. As Leah puts it, "*There's something wrong with me. I don't have the ability to pass on the gene, apparently, despite my stellar bloodlines. So I become a freak—the girlie-wolf—good for nothing else. I'm a genetic dead end*" (*BD* 318, emphasis in original). This "genetic dead-endedness," as Meyer terms it, is problematically accompanied by Leah's supreme bitchiness. She is represented as purposefully making life "exceedingly unpleasant" for her fellow wolves and as being "deliberately malicious"— if read as a warning of what happens to motherless females, Leah is the stereotypical bitter old maid, unloved and unlovable (*E* 417–18). She, along with the characters Rosalie, Emily, Tanya, and other childless females, conforms to what Rich names the "suspect status of women who are not mothers" (34).

Despite what seems to be an overarching message that *woman* does (or at least should) equal *womb*, *Twilight* partially repudiates the idea that mothering is easy or "natural." In contrast to the message given to us by celebrity moms that motherhood is always a joy, Bella's pregnancy grotesquely presents the horror of motherhood and birth. As Edward relates to Jacob, "The fetus isn't compatible with her body.... It won't allow her to get the sustenance she needs," and thus he has to watch her "starve to death by the hour" (*BD* 235). Putting the notion that starving to death seems to be a goal for Bella throughout the series given her continued refusal of food and supposed lack of hunger, this representation can be read as positive — that is via pregnancy, Bella becomes the "model" woman, a virtual anorexic. Yet, this depiction can also be more ominously linked to the idea of the fetus as cannibal — a dangerous intruder that threatens to consume the mother. As Jacob relates, "Whatever was inside her was taking her life to feed its own" (*BD* 174). True to the martyr aspects of her character, Bella doesn't seem to care that her vampire-in-utero is destroying her. As readers, though, through the horrifying descriptions of her bruised pregnant belly, followed by the blood-drenched birth scenes, we are warned against celebrating her turn to mama-wanna-be. Her agonizing shrieks, her broken spine (!), the exorcist-style fountain-of-blood vomiting (more in keeping with a horror film than a nice Mormon romance), and the crunching and snapping of "the newborn monster" tearing its way out of her womb (more *Alien* than *Look Who's Talking*) — these graphic depictions indicate the cost that motherhood extracts on the female body and the female person, a cost that the author surely knows intimately.

Meyer as "Just" a Mother

Meyer, who had a miscarriage scare during her first pregnancy and then suffered a fall during her third pregnancy (which resulted in a badly broken arm), admits in various interviews that motherhood is no cakewalk (Shapiro 5, 38, 40). Talking with the *Phoenix New Times*, Meyer says of her third pregnancy, "It wasn't a great time.... I'd put on so much weight with the last two babies. My thirtieth birthday was coming up and I was so not ready to face being thirty" (qtd. in Shapiro 40). Here, we might link Meyer's concern with her pregnancy-induced weight gain to Bella's textual fear of both eating and aging — activities that are strongly connected in the cultural imagination to pregnancy. Further, given that Isabella was the name Meyer had planned for a daughter, we might further read Bella not only as a Mary-Sue version of Meyer herself but also as the wished-for daughter that Meyer never had. Renesmee's birth can be read as an incarnation of this wish fulfillment, one that not only provides Meyer/Bella with a daughter but also presents motherhood as the easy, natural state that it is so often claimed to be. Due to Renesmee's rapid growth rate, and superior intelligence, she is the perfect baby.

Though I do not wish to limit textual reads by focusing too much on the biography of the author, I think Meyer's life as wife and mother is an important part of teasing out the textual/cultural puzzle of why *Twilight* speaks to so many (and so many mothers and women). As the mother of three boys as well as iconic mother of the *Twilight* fan-pire, Meyer is a celebrity mom in her own right. She (at least if we are to believe interviews) sees motherhood as her real vocation and writing as a fun diversion that just happened to turn her into a millionaire. Given that motherhood has been historically framed as impeding career aspirations and artistic endeavors, with many famous authors lamenting the seeming incompatibility of "mother" and "writer" (i.e., Virginia Woolf, Tillie Olsen), Meyer's insistence that her "real" identity is mother is not surprising, especially given her Mormon belief system, which places a high priority on mothering. Yet, as Meyer shared in an interview with the *Arizona Republic*, "I loved my kids but I needed something extra, my way to be me.... I did feel like something was missing" (qtd. in Shapiro 42). Might we read Esme as also having "something missing"? Though a vampire-mom extraordinaire, she is not a key player in any of the narrative threads—rather, she hovers in the background, spending her time redecorating and staring lovingly at her undead brood. Renee serves as another unfulfilled mother, who leaves Charlie (and eventually Bella). Though her road-tripping with her new baseball-playing love is presented rather derisively, her story indicates that young marriage/motherhood is not for everyone (as Bella herself believes but ultimately repudiates). These depictions of mothers reveal that Meyer's presentation of mothering is more complex than the oft-focused-on ending where Bella becomes "perfect mom."

Though I don't put stock in over-reading the biography of the author in order to pin down the meanings of their textual productions, I do think it's important to take into account that becoming a mother often can be very politicizing, putting in stark relief the hurdles that mothers face as well as making one care about the injustices and dangers of the world that one's children inhabit. Thus, we might presume that Meyer's nine years as a "stay-at-home mom" (and six years of not writing anything) left some of her feathers ruffled.[8] And, though she admits to having "mom nightmares" about her brothers, whom she served as a quasi-mom to while growing up in her Brady Bunch-style family, we might assume these fears became more pronounced once she had three sons (Shapiro 22). Indeed, in her oft-told story about the dream that spawned *Twi-*

light, Meyer reveals her Bella/Edward sleep-time vision occurred the night before her sons were scheduled to start summer swim lessons, an anxiety-producing event due to her fear of her children drowning. Might we thus read her "vivid dream"—where an "average girl" and a "fantastically beautiful, sparkly" vampire were discussing the problem of falling in love given that he "was particularly attracted to the scent of her blood, and was having a difficult time restraining himself from killing her immediately"—as a subconscious way to allieve both her stay-at-home mom doldrums and her fears for her children's safety? As she admits in mom-guilt fashion, "Though I had a million things to do (i.e. making breakfast for hungry children, dressing and changing the diapers of said children, finding the swimsuits that no one ever puts away in the right place, etc.), I stayed in bed, thinking about the dream"—of course she did— for it offered the mechanism from which to find that "something missing" as well as to address the inextricable links between all-consuming love and fearing that those we love might die (and/or be harmed by us).[9] As an added bonus, her saga ultimately resolves the dilemma that women cannot "have it all" by allowing Bella, as a vampire mom, to have just that. Yet, along the way to her "happy ending," Bella encounters many other females who lack power and/or fulfillment due to their relationship to motherhood, or, like Rosalie and Leah, who are rather warped and bitter due to their childless futures. In this vein, the texts show mothering as *smothering* other female aspirations and/or resulting in lives compromised by the imperative to reproduce. The answer Meyer offers is to become a vampire—a condition that not only allows for perfect, ageless beauty for all eternity but also produces the uber-baby—Renesmee.

To Be or Not to Be a Feminist: Slaying the Patriarchal Beast

To speak to the overarching question posed at the outset — does the feminist condemnation of the series get it right — my answer would be yes *and* no. The series raises my feminist hackles in its steering of female readers to desire strong males and to work to attract them via the traditional standards of beauty and youth rather than to desire strength and independence in their own right. As for Bella, I do think she is ultimately too passive and self-effacing to serve as a strong role model, and her ultimate capitulation to Edward's demand that he marry her, followed by her decision to carry out a pregnancy at age 18, one that literally ends her life, are, in my book, far from empowering material. I certainly would not want my own daughter to emulate Bella's path — not only because I don't particularly want her to become a vampire, but also more prosaically because I don't want her to choose marriage and motherhood over college. I hope she won't value her beauty over her brains. I hope she will see that there is more to life than hot sex with a hot guy.... I hope she will choose to feed her own desires rather than cook for no-count Charlies.

While Bella may not be an antifeminist heroine, I would say she is most certainly not a feminist one either, nor is Meyer. The wider representations of femininity in the books, where females are scatterbrained, klutzy, good with fashion, great decorators, and able to cook/launder for the men in their lives, accords with my claim that the series does not ultimately hold up strong females as role models—rather, readers are encouraged to pine after men, cook for their dads, marry and have babies out of high school, and to "just say no" before the wedding ring is on their finger. However, Meyer, responding to the accusation that her writing is misogynistic and relies on the damsel-in-distress paradigm, "emphatically rejects" this type of reading, arguing, "I am all about girl power—look at Alice and Jane if you doubt that."[10] Ok, fair enough, but Alice gets her "power" through her vampireness—her femaleness, on the other hand, makes her love fashion, make-overs, and wedding planning. Hardly revolutionary stuff. As for Jane, is power through the infliction of severe pain/fear really the type of "you go girl" power we are aiming for? And who would want to shack up with all those musty Volturi dudes, anyhow?

Meyer notes, "We can't all be slayers"—and I agree—but we can work to expand the limiting gender parameters that still work to keep females in general and mothers in particular culturally disenfranchised. We may not yet be able to slay the patriarchal beast entirely, but at least we can weaken it through our critical reading and response to this latest and hugely influential female-driven narrative.

Chapter 4

The Dawning of New Men

Hegemonic Masculinity,
Sparkly White Male Vampires,
and Ab-tastic Wolves of Color

Twilight is most exhaustively examined and discussed in relation to females and femininity. The common assumption is that, given that the vast majority of fans are female, the way this pop cultural phenomenon will affect society is most pertinent in relation to women and girls. However, it is crucial to consider males and masculinity in relation to *Twilight*. Many of the key protagonists of the series not only are male, but also exude a rather traditional, conservative conception of masculinity. Further, to claim that *all* readers/fans are female is faulty. Some of the best-known bloggers and *Twilight* critics are, in fact, male — take, for example, Kaleb Nation, who rose to *Twi*-fame thanks to his popular blog, *The Twilight Guy*. Many of the best-known stars of the films, some of the most popular *Twi*-bloggers and podcasters, and many of the speakers at conferences and conventions are male. In keeping with gender trends of wider society, men share a large "voice" in *Twilight* culture, one that is in fact disproportionately larger than their participation as readers. It is thus crucial to examine how *Twilight* is engaging with changing conceptions of masculinity.

Gender is a fluid construct, changing in response to sociocultural contexts, and this is no less true of masculinity than femininity. However, as masculinity is the "default" gender, with males and masculinity constructed as generic, universal, and unmarked in the same way that "white" is the default race, masculinity is more resistant to change than femininity. Masculinity is intricately bound up with patriarchy, heterosexuality, capitalism, and ideas of the nation-state, and is generally more strictly policed and guarded than femininity. Masculinity is a sort of citadel, a stronghold fortified by the notion that men (and especially white, wealthy, heterosexual men) are the best and brightest humanity has to offer. This notion is perpetuated particularly strongly in the mass media, where most representations of masculinity accord with traditional ideas of men being stronger, smarter, less emotional, more successful, and more capable. Yet, as noted by masculinities scholar Jackson Katz, "There is a glaring absence of a thorough body of research into the power of cultural images of masculinity. But this is not surprising. It is in fact consistent with the lack of attention paid to other dominant groups" ("Advertising" 113). By paying attention to the ways that male characters dominate the fictional landscape of *Twilight*, as well as to the way that male voices largely dominate the cultural response to *Twilight*, we can begin to redress this absence. Interrogating the predominate cultural images of masculinity in relation to *Twilight*'s depiction of males reveals that romantic heroes have not changed all that much, that what Michael Kimmel terms "guy-land" is a rather hostile place for females, and that male voices still dominate, even in supposedly "female narratives" and largely female fandoms.

The (Romantic) Men of Twilight

Twilight is, by Meyer's own admission, first and foremost a romance novel. Given this, it is hardly surprising that the narrative revolves around Bella's fixation on various males. As Radway argues, the romance genre has had a huge impact on the way we conceive of gender (as discussed in chapter 2). Radway reads romance novels as putting masculinity to the test and toying with just how strong, violent, sexy, etc., romance heroes can be. In her study, she finds that traditional conceptions of masculinity are ultimately presented as benign — as something that produces rather than hinders female happiness. As Radway notes, even when male characters are extremely violent or misogynistic, even when they rape the heroine or constantly belittle her, the majority of romance texts still ultimately imply that traditional masculinity is good for women (168). *Twilight* accords with this claim, presenting as it does a domineering, condescending boyfriend (Edward) as irresistible and a violent, hypermasculine aggressor as best-friend material (Jacob). These two characters are what bring Bella the most happiness in the text — yes, she may love Alice, but Edward and Jacob are her North and South, the twin planets she orbits around.[1]

According to Radway, traditional romantic heroes have "spectacularly masculine phallic power" accompanied by a "capacity for tenderness and attentive concern" (14). Edward, with his hard-as-marble body is, to put it bluntly, a walking erection — always hard, always ready. Yet, he is often very tender with Bella and extremely protective, denying his lust for her blood and ever concerned for her safety. He is a considerate mate, asking her questions, letting her do most of the talking, attending to her needs and desires (though not, of course, meeting her desires for sex, being the good virginity warrior that he is). Jacob, her second (and second-class) suitor is also a bastion of phallic power, his half-naked wolf body rippling with strength. He, too, has "attentive concern"— he and Bella take long walks on the beach, fix motorbikes, and do homework together.

Females readers of romance, according to Radway, are looking for a male hero "who is capable of the same attentive observation and intuitive 'understanding' that they believe women regularly accord to men"— or, in other words, they want an uber-hot macho man who is also nurturing, caring, and can fulfill the role of friend; they want, in short, Edward and Jacob types—males who exude masculinity on the outside but are all soft and caring on the inside (83). As in most romances, *Twilight* suggests that masculinity may need a bit of tweaking, but overall, it is just fine as it is. Or, as Radway puts it, "The hero is permitted simply to graft tenderness onto his unaltered male character" (148). In so doing, such narratives fail to question current constructions of masculinity, instead suggesting that beneath the "tough guy" exterior lies a loving, tender, and affectionate male — it only requires the "right" woman to bring out the teddy bear lurking within the beast.[2] In *Twilight*, Bella is this woman — she is able to both humanize the vampire and civilize the wolf. This underlying message is one that has colored not only romance novels, but also general societal conceptions of gender. When males are "bad," female interest or influence can "fix" them. Conversely, if such "bad men" can't be "fixed," females, either lovers or mothers, are blamed. Why is this idea, that good masculinity is dependent on the "right" kind of woman, still so appealing here in 2011? To address this question, we need to take a closer look at the current cultural landscape of masculinity — or what Kimmel calls "guyland."

Destination Guyland

In many respects, the terrain of contemporary masculinity that Kimmel documents reads like a heterosexual female nightmare. In guyland, it's "bro's before ho's"— a homosocial mantra that reveals that masculinity is most about proving one is a "real man." In this game, women are used as pawns to prove one's sexual viability, as objects who males masturbate over, belittle, and make fun of, and as scapegoats blamed for the lack of power and opportunity many males face as individuals (as opposed to that granted them as a group via male privilege). The type of guy Kimmel depicts as all too common in guyland is a macho, porn-obsessed, emotionally stunted walking pillar of testosterone. To be fair, this is a gross simplification of real men — but it is what our culture presents as *desirable* masculinity. Boys and men who are not traditionally masculine, or who fall too far outside "the man box," risk being labeled in one or both of the two key ways males are insulted — as female or gay, as either pussy or faggot. Yet, while males are schooled in how to be "real men," the very rules that make up the "man box" are in opposition to what many females (and indeed males) want in a relationship. And, given that heterosexual monogamy is still framed as the end goal (especially for women and certainly within the narrative framework of the *Twilight* saga), females must find ways to make these macho men seem desirable. Enter *Twilight*.

Hitting shelves in a "hook up" culture where changing views of sexuality, relationships, and family are widespread, *Twilight* offers protective, caring males interested more in talking than in booty calls. Further, it presents Bella as an "every girl" who, through no special powers of her own, is able to lure prized masculine attention. More significantly, Bella is able to tame dangerous masculinity into something far more female-friendly. As in romance novels, what seems to be dangerous, predatory male behavior is transformed by the "right woman"— a woman whose love and desire transforms "guyland" impulses into true love. In keeping with our hypersexualized culture, this love is not entirely chaste, though. Indeed, the sexual undercurrent of the series speaks to modern females' desire to be seen as sexual agents in their own right. Bella may love Edward's listening proficiency, but she is also hot for his marble body. She certainly appreciates Jacob's mad mechanic skills, but she doesn't fail to notice his hulking muscles either.

These two male protagonists are representative of the neither too macho nor too feminine male characters that the saga depicts. While Edward is traditionally masculine in many regards, he is also an emo-metrosexual, a queer boyfriend for the new millennium. And though Jacob seems to be a mega-hard body type, he is also quite the softy—a wolf man who is really just a puppy dog. Through these and other male characters, *Twilight* presents neither a subversive nor a conservative view of masculinity, but a contradictory mixture of both.

Forks-Style Masculinity

Though white heterosexual middle-class masculinity has lost its secure place in the hierarchy of social positions due to the achievements of the civil rights movement, feminism, and gay rights, in the world of *Twilight*, it seems as if these movements never happened. All the teachers at Forks High School are male. The chief of police is male. Doctors are male. No one is gay. Most people are white. Women love to cook, shop, and decorate. It's the nostalgic view of the 1950s all over, or *Leave it to Beaver* with vampires. In this Cleaveresque world, Charlie is the patriarch of the human world — the police chief who is also a doting dad. As a "real man" type, Charlie is not comfortable expressing emotions, instead treating the police station "as his wife and family" (*T* 11). He can't cook and has no food in the house because he feels "awkward" in the kitchen (*T* 35). Indeed, he is so inept at culinary arts that he puts a jar of spaghetti sauce in the microwave with the lid on. No wonder he misses Bella when she leaves— as he admits, "The food around here sucks when you're gone"

(*E* 70). Bella revels in this recognition rather than balking at it, joking at one point, "I feel just horrible, leaving you to cook for yourself — it's practically criminal negligence. You could arrest me" (*BD* 56). Here, Charlie's lack of kitchen skills and inability to express his emotions are portrayed as *natural* — as to be expected given that he is male. Moreover, his penchant for hunting and fishing, his love of televised sports, his fondness for weapons, and his policing of Bella's sexuality are all presented as both normal and benign. In fact, what some might read as negligent fathering is presented in a very positive light — he is the dream dad who doesn't hover, who is so oblivious that the vampire boyfriend can sneak into Bella's bedroom every night.

The other human males of Forks are depicted as similarly benign, if strikingly nonindividuated. They are "typical guys" interested in the new beauty on campus, or, as Edward puts it in *Midnight Sun*, these "sheep-like males" act like children with "a shiny object" (n.p.). In general, the saga presents males as beholden to their Y chromosomes, chromosomes that the book indicates makes them aggressive, competitive, and fond of girls and sports. Females are presented as outsiders to this guyland world. This becomes particularly apparent when Jacob, Embry, and Quill discuss motorbikes. As Bella notes, "Many of the words they used were unfamiliar to me, I figured I'd have to have a Y chromosome to really understand the excitement" (*NM* 139). In a similar vein, Angela tells Bella, "You're lucky Edward has his brothers for all the hiking and camping. I don't know what I'd do if Ben didn't have Austin for the guy stuff" (*E* 134). This so-called "guy stuff" is particularly linked to violence and fighting, as when Bella relates, "The urge to fight must be a defining characteristic of the Y chromosome. They were all the same" (E 463). Presenting masculinity as chromosomal destiny, the saga suggests that challenging norms of masculinity is fruitless — that patriarchy is here to stay.

Patriarchal Vampires and Predatory Sexuality

Like its predecessor *Dracula, Twilight* affirms the patriarchal order, suggesting that men are rightful rulers whose power comes from the supreme patriarch — God the Father.[3] With Carlisle as the vampire patriarch of the Cullens and Edward as his chosen son, we might read this father/son duo as a depiction of God the Father and Christ the Son (a theme that will be further explored in chapter 6). As a god, Carlisle is immortal and has the power to bestow life. He is able to overcome his bodily need for human blood to such an extent that not only did he become a "vegetarian" but he also became a doctor — a vampire who saves rather than kills humans. Creating his vampire family after rejecting life with the Volturi (the saga's evil patriarchs), Carlisle is the saga's good patriarch — the kind father who welcomes Bella into his vampire family and saves her life multiple times. At the saga's close, he summons his vampire connections from all over the world in preparation for the showdown with the Volturi. Associated with healing, restraint, and wisdom, Carlisle represents paternalistic care as a benevolent force. He is, as Charlie puts it, "an asset to the community" (*T* 36).

Edward, as a chip off the old block, is similarly good. Like Carlisle, he is framed as a gentleman via his vegetarian lifestyle and his dedication to chastity. Bella refers to him as a "godlike creature" with "the voice of an archangel" (*T* 292, 311). He is further described as "impossibly selfless" and "very old-fashioned" (*E* 49, 59). As Bella's "perpetual savior" he is "interesting ... and brilliant ... and mysterious ... and perfect ... and beautiful ... and possibly able to lift full-sized vans with one hand" (*NM* 166, 79). In the text, Edward is depicted as drop-dead gorgeous, as a good listener, as sensitive, as devoted — he seems to be, as so many T-shirt slogans claim, the perfect boyfriend. In the film, Robert Pattinson plays the part with smoldering, sensitive passion, his eyes transfixed on Bella as if she is the center of his universe.

But isn't Edward just a tad scary in the boyfriend department? From breaking into Bella's house and watching her sleep to sabotaging her car, restricting her movement, and policing her sexuality, Edward is hardly the model boyfriend for contemporary times. Instead, he is a throwback to another era — the one in which he was born (the early 1900s) — when women couldn't vote let alone wear pants. Yet, despite his old-fashioned views about gender and relationships, he has been welcomed with open arms by much of the fandom. Indeed, T-shirts that proclaim "Bite me, Edward," "Mrs. Cullen," and "Edward can bust my headboard, bite my pillows, and bruise my body any day" indicate that female fans LOVE not only his looks but also his actions. If we believe Suzy McKee Charnas, this love is actually a survival mechanism. She argues, "The predator-male identity is endowed with romantic trappings by women to make life in the real world that is run by and for this identity bearable — just as all people tend to romanticize our imaginary predators, our monsters" (62).

Bella certainly views the predatory male as desirable. Indeed, this view opens *Twilight*, with Bella dreaming about "the dark eyes of the hunter" as he saunters forward to kill her, something she views as "a good way to die" (*T* 1). Edward, as the world's best predator, looks at Bella as if she is "something to eat" (*T* 221). As he continues to stalk her throughout the series, we are encouraged as readers to view this as benevolent, as his attempt (and even sacrifice) to keep her safe. Bella at one point feels she should be bothered that he is following her but admits, "Instead I felt a strange surge of pleasure" (*T* 174). Likening their relationship to balancing "on the point of a knife," Bella wonders "if it would hurt *very* much ... if it ended badly" (*T* 248, 251). Here, Bella is particularly worried about their pending date, as indeed she should be, for Edward will reveal his vampire self, telling her, "I'm the world's best predator" and taunting her with "as if you could outrun me," "as if you could fight me off." (*T* 264–65) Bella, though frightened, feels he has never been "more beautiful" and sits "like a bird locked in the eyes of a snake" (*T* 265). Here, the depiction of their relationship as inherently dangerous (romance by knife point), as one of predator and prey, *should* be a turn-off to both Bella and readers. Instead, we are encouraged to see this dangerous romance as incredibly exciting, as addicting as heroin. And while Edward is framed as king of the jungle in all of this, as the lion, Bella is the weak lamb who is "incredibly *breakable*" (*T* 310).

As noted by Simmons in her book *Odd Girl Out*, "Aggression is the hallmark of masculinity.... The link begins early: the popularity of boys is in large part determined by their willingness to play rough" (17). While toughness is valued in boys, niceness is valued in girls. Being that we live in a heteronormative culture fixated on monogamous coupling, this leaves us in a situation where *nice girls* must like *tough boys*— or, in other words, where lambs need to fall in love with lions. Given the pervasiveness of the "tough guy" ideal, is it any wonder that so many female readers fall in love with a saga that romanticizes tough, violent masculinity? Indeed, as Radway argues, this is *the* function of romance — to make females desire that which is rendered as *naturally* masculine — the tough guy. As she writes, violent male behavior "may be incorporated into the romantic fantasy ... not because certain writers and readers enjoy it but because they cannot imagine it away.... Such behavior may seem so natural, permanent, and unassailable that they hunger even more for a fantasy that will contradict their suspicions and convince them that it can lead to female contentment and happiness" (169). Radway concludes that this romanticization of male violence allows women to suppress their fears about rape while promoting them to desire that which they fear (169). As Modleski similarly argues, "The transformation of brutal (or, indeed, murderous) men into tender lovers, the insistent denial of the reality of male hostility towards women, point to ideological conflicts so profound that readers must constantly return to the same text (to texts which are virtually the same) in order to be reconvinced" (*Loving* 111). Women's lives under patriarchy, according to Radway and Modleski, *promote* the need for texts that render violent masculinity romantic. In other words, women read the romance because women live in patriarchy. And, as is the case with the romance genre in general, *Twilight* renders certain types of controlling, violent masculinity as desirable (i.e., Edward) and otherizes violent physicality onto nonwhite males (Jacob, Sam, etc.).

Hegemonic Masculinity, White Male Vampires, and Wolves of Color

In contrast to Edward, Jacob is depicted as having a hard time controlling his anger. Though he is a leader, a wolf action hero of sorts, and becomes alpha wolf of his own pack by the series' end, he is, like most stock rivals in romance texts, "insufficiently masculine" in comparison to Edward (Radway 133). He can be read as a sort of villain who attempts to abduct the heroine from the hero. As a villain, he is both too masculine (and too violent) and, at the same time, not masculine enough. In contrast to prince-like Edward, Jacob is a temperamental boy — a point Edward is quite happy to point out. He warns Bella to "keep a safe distance" that "I can control myself, but I doubt he can. He's very young" (*NM* 551). Jacob, referring to himself as a "time bomb" and recounting the time he almost "ripped" his father's face off, confirms Edward's assessment, as when Bella asks him what is the hardest part about being a shape-shifter and he replies, "The hardest part is feeling ... out of control ... like I'm a monster who might hurt somebody" (*NM* 345). While these feelings of being unable to control one's emotions and actions are framed in relation to Jacob's turn to wolf, we might also think of them in relation to his turn from boy to man — or from teen to adult male. As masculinity scholars share, this shift is incredibly difficult and carries with it all sorts of unrealistic expectations.

In effect, Jacob is living in what Kimmel names "guyland," or the place "between the dependency and lack of autonomy of boyhood and the sacrifice and responsibility of manhood" (6). This state of "suspended animation" has many rules. One of the pressures is to "score" — or to prove your prowess with females, especially with "taken" females. In the saga, Jacob is fixated on Bella, intent on *making* her want him. While he seems to genuinely care for her, he also cares about besting Edward, or proving once and for all that wolves are better than vampires. Thus, his fight for Bella becomes as much an attempt to beat Edward as it is an attempt to win Bella's heart. When Bella informs him of her intent to soon become a vampire, he responds that this is "all the more reason to fight" (*E* 330). Just after stating his intent to "fight harder," he forces Bella to kiss him, which is described in the text as follows: "His lips crushed mine, stopping my protest. He kissed me angrily, roughly, his other hand gripping tight around the back of my neck, making escape impossible.... I grabbed at his face, trying to push it away" (*E* 330–31). Later, Bella refers to this as "an assault" and shares that she likes him better as a wolf because then he "*can't talk*" (or kiss, we might add) (*E* 476, 478). Jacob disagrees, telling her that "it's easier for you to be near me when I'm not human, because you don't have to pretend you're not attracted to me" (*E* 478). Talk about male ego! And, to worsen his macho bravado, Charlie even congratulates him, saying, "Good for you, kid," when Jacob tells him he kissed Bella (*E* 336). This strand of the narrative reveals not only that males feel entitled to act on their desires even when those desires are not reciprocated, but also that other males encourage and congratulate them for doing so. Indeed, males are so inundated with messages that couple violence with desire that many are turned on by violence, just as when Bella later asks Jacob to kiss her, and he reacts "with an eagerness that was not far from violence" (*E* 526).

But what does it mean that this Quileute teen, with his "russet-colored" skin, mechanic skills, ultra-hard body, and anger issues, is framed as the third wheel in the saga's romantic narrative? What cultural contexts are at play here, and why does Meyer not allow this "classic underdog" to be a textual hero in the same way that Bella and Edward are (Housel 242)? While Meyer certainly may not have intentionally or consciously considered the race, class, and belief contexts when placing the working-class wolf of color as the inferior rival, we, as astute readers, must take these contexts into account — especially as the males that populate the series are held up as ideal by legions of Team Edward and Team Jacob fans. *Twilight,* in effect, offers a certain ideology with which to view the world, a "Twilight Ideology," if you will. As Richard Dyer argues in his book, *White,* ideologies are best thought of as "a way of seeing the world that serves particular social interests" (83). The *masculine ideology of Twilight* serves to champion and bolster hegemonic white masculinity.

As Dyer puts it, "The white man has been the centre of attention for many centuries of Western culture" (*White* 146). This "phallicized whiteness," as Shannon Winnubst calls it, instigates an impossible ideal, one that "no living white straight man embodies," yet Edward, who is not living but is hyperwhite and straight, *does* embody this ideal (16). According to Dyer, the ideal white male body is "hard, achieved, wealthy, hairless and tanned" (150). Though Edward's vampire state excludes him from the "tanned" component of white male bodily perfection, he not only meets but also exceeds all the other expectations. He is a "perfect marble creature" with a body that is "white, cool, and polished as marble" (*E* 429; *BD* 25). He has a face that "any male model in the world would trade his soul for" and "perfect, ultrawhite teeth" (*E* 17; *NM* 50). His "magnificence" is "too beautiful to be real"; indeed, Bella can't imagine "how an angel could be any more glorious" (*NM* 241, 26). Overtly associated with angels and godliness throughout the *Twilight* texts, Edward is Christ incarnate — a white god who has died and come back to (vampire) life to save Bella, our white Virgin Mary.

As Dyer argues, the Christian concept of god has "been thought and felt in distinctly white ways for most of its history" with the accompanying "gentilising and whitening of the image of Christ and the Virgin in painting" serving to bolster doctrines of white racial superiority and imperialism (17). Though these ideas will be further explored in chapters 6 and 7 in relation to race and religion, they are also pertinent to the construction of ideal masculinity. While white female beauty is the paragon of virtue and chastity and can be thus linked to spirituality (and spirit *as* white), the white male body is linked to power and strength, to the body incarnate (or ideal materiality and wealth *as* white). This is why, according to Dyer, male bodies are less often nude in representation. As he writes, "There is a problem about the display of his body.... A naked body is a vulnerable body. This is so in the most fundamental sense — the bare body has no protection from the elements—but also in a social sense. Clothes are bearers of prestige, notably of wealth, status, and class: to be without them is to lose prestige" (146). Hence, in the *Twilight* texts we rarely see Edward's body without clothes, while Jacob's body is incessantly focused on and almost always without a shirt. When Edward takes off his shirt, it is to open himself up to extreme vulnerability — as when he shows his sparkly side to Bella in the meadow, or as when he plans to bring about his death by revealing himself as a vampire in the Italian public square. In contrast, for Jacob, it is presented as *natural* to be naked — he is, after all, an animal (both literally via the werewolf narrative and figuratively as a "savage" Native American). When he does wear clothes, he pays no attention to fashion, opting instead for "ragged, grease smeared jeans" (*E* 77). But for Edward, clothes makes the man (or the vampire), and his fashion choices reflect his wealth. The fact that his family is so fond of white clothing and white home décor also speaks to their wealth; white items take time and money to keep clean; or, as Dyer puts it, there is much symbolic power "carried by clothes and grooming" (*White* 146).

There is also symbolic power in muscles, though the way that muscular bodies are represented often differs depending on race/ethnicity. Ideal white male bodies are often clearly what Dyer names "gym products" whose "cut" bodies represent armor (*White* 152). This built body is also a wealthy body, which has had "enormous amounts of leisure time ... devoted to it" (*White* 155). Such bodies are showered with attention and praise, or, as Housel puts it, "Edward is given undeserved consideration; similar to other beautiful 'sparkly' people in society, like celebrities" (241). Perhaps this is what allows him to feel entitled to his wealth, which he flaunts, as Housel argues, "by driving expensive cars, wearing designer clothing, and looking down on humble possessions like Bella's truck. On the other hand, when Bella brings two discarded motorcycles to Jacob, enticing him to help her fix them by offering him one, Jacob is delighted" (239). This "delight" can be read in relation to race and class privilege, neither of which Jacob has.

His racialized, working-class body is not linked to mansions and private islands, but to labor and sweat — to the messiness of materiality. Jacob works not at composing melodies or getting degrees from Harvard, but at fixing cars and motorcycles. In such depictions, the *Twilight* texts uphold traditional notions of ideal masculinity that associate white males with mind, culture, and wealth, and nonwhite, nonwealthy males with the body, nature, and labor. As a *mind*, Edward has various graduate degrees, is well-spoken and well-read, and is distanced from his ice-cold (but perfect) body. As a mind reader, he lives not only through his own mind, but also by reading the thoughts of others. Jacob, on the contrary, is grounded in corporeality — his bodily size, color, and temperature are constantly focused on in the books. For working-class, wolves of color like Jacob (like working-class men of color in the real world), masculine power has to be enacted through the physical body. As Katz argues, "For working class males, who have less access to more abstract forms of masculinity-validating power (economic power, workplace authority), the physical body and its potential for violence provide a concrete means of achieving and asserting manhood" (135).

In fact, we might argue that the Quileute are *forced* to become wolves in order to access power. Their shape-shifting not only allows them to assert power, but also provides the opportunity for them to legitimate their identities as "properly masculine"—an assertion that is necessary because powerful white males (who are the vampires of *Twilight*) render their identities as Other, as lesser. In keeping with the colonial viewpoint that the text proffers (and our world still labors under), "the manly white qualities of expansiveness, enterprise, courage and control (of self and others) ... are in the foreground," and Others—both females and nonwhites, are in the background (*White* 184). As with Tarzan, who is "a friend to good natives" but also "physically, mentally and morally their superior," Edward is framed as friendly to Jacob (and as fatherly by the series' end), but undoubtedly as also the superior *man*—the one Bella (and readers) should choose—just as Jane chose Tarzan. Like the Tarzan narratives, *Twilight* serves as a justification for colonialism. Just as Tarzan proves that the "ape men" are in need of civilizing, so does *Twilight* reveal that "wolf men" benefit from what we might call "vampire colonization." This is particularly evident at the series' close when the wolfy Jacob is slowly civilized by the Cullen clan, invited into their home, and even clothed in their designer duds. Even more problematically, Jacob is depicted as a happy subject/slave, telling Bella, "I offered eternal servitude, remember. I'm your slave for life" (*E* 321).

The differing focus on white versus nonwhite males in the texts also furthers this colonial viewpoint. Edward, Carlisle, and Jasper are variously championed for their degrees and "special powers." While all of them are described as exceedingly good-looking, their bodies are not fetishized in the way the bodies of the wolf pack are. In short, they keep their clothes on and their anger in check. Emmett is perhaps an exception here, and perhaps we can put this down to his working-class background.[4] However, none of the white vampires (or white humans for that matter) are presented as almost always half-naked—this is reserved for the wolves of color (and, in the *New Moon* film, for the vampire of color, Laurent). Interestingly, James (the evil vampire) is depicted as shirtless in the *Twilight* movie—perhaps this can be read as indicating he is "less civilized" (i.e., less white) than the Cullens? The fact that the wolves are never fully clothed doesn't escape Bella's attention (nor the fan's). At one point, she asks Jacob, "Is it really so impossible to wear clothes Jacob?"(*E* 215). While the explanation that the text offers—that shape-shifting makes wearing clothes difficult—seems plausible, the films' obsessive focus on the nudity of the "wolf pack" smacks of objectification. Though it is still relatively rare to see semi-naked white males in film, this is not the case for nonwhite males—a trend with a long history, as noted by Dyer: "In the Western, the plantation drama and the jungle adventure film, the non-white body is routinely on display" (*White* 146).

But I Don't Want to Be a Monster: Edward's Bad Macho

Though white masculinity is certainly idealized in the text, especially in relation to Edward, it is not depicted as entirely problem free. Edward is routinely shown to be arrogant, harshly sarcastic, and domineering. As he admits, he has a problem with his temper. Throughout the series, he drives like a lunatic, routinely orders Bella around, rolls his eyes at her, physically grabs/restrains her, enjoys making her jealous, and regularly makes his condescension apparent. He calls her a coward and "silly Bella," making rules she is expected to follow without question, such as "no werewolf friends" (*E* 32). He sabotages her car, follows/watches her without her permission, and even marks her with his scent! When Jacob comes on the scene, he treats Bella as his property, telling him, "She *is* mine" (*E* 341). Though Jacob is far from perfect in the potential boyfriend department, he at least recognizes Edward's behavior as abusive, asking Bella, "Is he your warden, now, too? You know, I saw this story on the news last week about controlling, abusive teenage relationships" (*E* 224). Indeed, Bella's relationships with both Edward and Jacob can be considered "abusive teenage relationships." Commonly cited indicators of an abusive (or potentially abusive partner) include excessive jealousy, inability to control anger, making threats to do harm to self or others, and a tendency to criticize, humiliate, and belittle.[5] Abusive partners also often try to control their partner's whereabouts, with a tendency to try and isolate their partners from friends and family. Jacob, and especially Edward, exhibit these tendencies, as has been well documented elsewhere.

Problematically, the books do not encourage readers to condemn these abusive actions, but rather actively encourage viewing Edward as a perfect boyfriend. He is not framed as a monster, but as an uber-masculine god. In *Midnight Sun*, he reveals he is the Cullen "lookout" in charge of protecting his family from discovery. He extends this "protective instinct" to Bella, seeing it as that natural the strong should take care of the weak. Emphasizing her "frail-looking shoulders" and that she seems more "vulnerable" than most humans, he imagines the best ways to kill her upon their meeting. This is not surprising given he is a vampire and Bella has "the sweetest blood" he has smelled in eighty years (*MS* n.p.). What is surprising is the way his murderous desire is rendered as sexy rather than sick — much the same way that violence against women is depicted as a turn-on in the majority of mainstream pornography. In addition to being problematically prone to violence, Edward's bad macho reveals him to feel superior to just about everyone and to flaunt his two graduate degrees in medicine. Though he seems to recognize that some of his behaviors are wrong (for example, he notes he is much worse than a "sick peeping Tom" for watching Bella sleep), he assigns himself to be Bella's lord and protector, her male vampire savior — an act that ultimately puts Bella in a great amount of danger (*MS* n.p.). So, how does the saga rectify this conundrum wherein our hero is revealed to be a monster? It does so by making Edward into not only a desirable macho lover, but also a caring father figure.

The Fathers of Forks

As with the majority of mainstream narratives, the mothers in the series are sidelined and put on a pedestal. The mothers in the *Twilight* universe are not as key to the narrative as the fathers, yet, at the same time, they are championed when they are good mothers (Esme), castigated when they are not (Renee) — and, smacking of Disney, they are largely dead (the mothers of Edward, Jacob, Leah). Further, women who are unable to have children are portrayed as damaged goods (Rosalie and Leah), but the male characters are not presented as "needing" to be fathers. In keeping with the ideas of Aristotle, in the saga "the principle of life is carried exclusively by the sperm, the female genital apparatus providing only the passive receptacle for human life" (Braidotti 79). Alas, generative "life" becomes vampiric immortality, with males (such as Edward and Carlisle) creating new vampires with their venom. Similarly, wolves are "made" via the male line. Females, in contrast, are either "passive receptacles" (as with Bella's bruised and waiting womb) or barren (as with Leah). The championing of males (and their generative capability) is all the more surprising given this is a vampire narrative. Vampires, traditionally considered "sterile," create and produce quite a bit of "life" in *Twilight*. Carlisle creates a vampire brood with his "venom," and Edward impregnates Bella on their honeymoon. These offspring are the texts heroes, while the "newborn army" created by Victoria is volatile and dangerous. These representations of male creations as good and female creation as flawed link back not only to Aristotle, but also to the Christian notion of God as creator and, as in Genesis, females as evil. As argued by Lindsey Averill in the essay "Un-biting the Apple and Killing the Womb: *Genesis*, Gender and Gynocide in Stephenie Meyer's *Twilight* Series," *Twilight* furthers the notion of male creation and female subordination, rendering Bella as a new and better Eve, one who does *not* bite the apple, but who chooses to submit (to God/Edward) (n.p.). In the Bible, as in many religious and mythological texts, males are the creators — so, too, in *Twilight*. As Averill argues, "Much like *Genesis*, Meyer's construct of the vampire eliminates the procreative and creative powers of the female body, gifting creative powers to the male sex" (n.p.). Indeed, the male vampires can impregnate human females supposedly because their fertility is not based on bodily "change" (*BD* 126). As Averill notes, this representation renders "fertility as not of the living body, much like the male-god's spoken powers of creativity" (n.p.).

In addition to penning infertile female vampires, Meyer also seems quite fond of matricide/gynocide — not only does she kill off Jacob's mom and Edward's mom, but she also kills the storyline of Bella's mother, Renee. While we learn lots about Charlie, Renee is "off-screen," or off-page, almost entirely. In the case of the human-vampire hybrids, they kill their mothers during birth, tearing their way out of the womb. Bella is rescued from this fate, of course, by Edward, the texts' ultimate father/god. As "vivid red spouted" from her womb, "like a bucket being turned over, a faucet twisted to full," Edward uses his tongue to "sweep along the bleeding gashes" of Bella's body, using his tongue to wash "venom over her skin" and seal her wounds shut (*BD* 350). While Rosalie loses control so that "her lips pull back from her teeth and her black eyes glint with thirst" (a sign she is about to "eat" Bella), Carlisle and Edward are the fathers/saviors of the scene — saving not only Bella but also Renesmee (*BD* 350).

Not only does Edward father and birth Renesmee, though, but he is also depicted as fathering Bella throughout the text. From the outset of the first novel in the saga, Bella is portrayed as more of a child than a woman — for example, when her mom drives her to the airport, she wears "white eyelet lace," a fabric often used for female children's clothing (*T* 3). She is presented as "putting her foot down" to express dismay, an action redolent of an angry toddler stomp (*T* 4). Once at Forks, she stumbles off the plain into the protective care of her dad, Charlie (this constant clumsiness that continues throughout all four texts also symbolizes being childlike and unable to "walk" in the world — indeed she is often described as skipping, an action reminiscent of childhood) (*T* 6). Bella shares she is not adept at expressing emotions, finding it difficult to show her appreciation for the armor-like protective truck Charlie has purchased for her (*T* 7). Retreating to her bedroom, still decorated as it was when she was a child, she notes, "The rocking chair from my baby days was still in the corner" (*T* 9). Though I don't place foreshadowing as part of Meyer's forte, rocking indeed becomes a recurrent symbol in the saga — as well as the cradling, nurturing, and care representative of the rocking chair. However, Bella is not "rocked" by a mother, but by her new father — Edward. Like a loving, protective mother, he is repeatedly presented as cradling her, carrying her, watching her sleep, kissing the top of her head, mussing her hair, even strapping her into her car seat (as he does after James et al. show up in the baseball scene). To illustrate, a small sampling of such representations follows:

> He pulled me around to face him, cradling me in his arms like a small child [*T* 280].

> He ... reached out with his long arms to pick me up, gripping the tops of my arms like I was a toddler [*T* 297].

> Sleep, my Bella. Dream happy dreams. He started to hum my lullaby.... I closed my eyes and snuggled closer to his chest [*E* 94].

> He opened my door for me, lifted me in, and buckled my seatbelt around me [*E* 262].

Jacob is also presented as a father of sorts, with his protective stance toward Bella and his towering figure. Bella notes when she embraces him, "I felt like I was a child hugging a grown up" (*NM* 178). In fact, Edward and Jacob can be read as quasi-fathers fighting for custody of Bella — as when Edward takes her to the vampire-werewolf treaty line and she shares, "I feel like a child being exchanged by custodial guardians" (*E* 318). In addition to being handed off from one "father" to another, Bella is frequently shown as a daughter figure excluded from male conversation. In *Eclipse*, when Jacob and Edward talk on the phone, Bella notes her feelings of exclusion —feelings she similarly links to being excluded to conversations held between Carlisle and Edward and Charlie and Edward (*NM* 212). She is like the daughter Eve as represented by Milton in *Paradise Lost*, who is either left out of conversations or forcefully put to sleep so she doesn't hear the conversations between Adam and the male angels.

Bella is further presented as childlike as she pouts, skips, and stumbles her way through the narratives. She is described as climbing into Edward's lap, crawling into his arms, and even standing on his feet so he can waltz her around the prom. Though Meyer is not known for carefully selecting her words, the excessive use of infantilizing words in association with Bella — such as cradle, crawl, skip — have the (unintentional?) effect of giving the saga a decidedly Oedipal spin. For example, Ruth O'Donnell reads Bella as a symbolically rejected and neglected child, arguing that her character is stuck in the oral needs phase, or the phase that Freud argues needs to be overcome in order for normal psychosexual development to occur.

The work of Nancy Chodorow is also relevant here. One of the many feminist scholars to offer a reworking of Freud, Chodorow argues that developing independence and agency is not easy for the female child due to her identification with the mother, who lacks the freedom/power of the father. At the same time, Chodorow suggests that females experience an unending longing for the unconditional love of a mother — something that Radway points out women often give but don't get in our culture (13). Radway, drawing on Chodorow, argues that women turn to romance (and romance narratives) in order to experience the type of unconditional mother-love they are seeking, displacing their desire for a mother onto a male romantic figure (94).[6] Radway asserts that romantic heroines equally desire to be the hero's lover as well as his child — that they seek not only heterosexual romance through their interaction with the hero, but also "the love of the mother and all that implies— erotic pleasure, symbiotic completion, and identity confirmation" (146). As she notes, many romances conclude with a union that represents not only that of a couple, but also that of parent/child — or, as she puts it, "original, blissful symbiotic union between mother and child ... is the goal of all romances despite their apparent preoccupation with heterosexual love and marriage" (156). However, as with *Twilight*, mothers are replaced by male figures in romance texts— males who act as both father and lover to the heroines. Fairy tales are similarly populated with such conclusions with daughters being saved by father figures—from Red Riding Hood's woodsman to Sleeping Beauty's prince. Perhaps Bella is most like Snow White, though—with her seven father figures—Charlie, Carlisle, Jacob, Jasper, Emmett, Billy, Seth—and her prince, Edward. This displacement of mothers is explored in Olga Silverstein's *The Courage to Raise Good Men*. Noting that fear and displacement of the mother gets "invoked with special urgency" during times of societal strife, Silverstein's text suggests that we might interpret *Twilight*'s championing of fathers within the context of our war-ridden, economic downturn, not to mention our societal concerns over "saving" marriage and keeping traditional gender norms firmly in place. Arguing that "we would all be so happy together, father and children, if only we could get rid of the woman (mother) in our lives" is "the story of our times," Silverstein asserts that "we still think that mothers get in the way of masculinity ... and the stories we tell reflect that belief as surely as the myths and fairy tales of earlier times" (13).

Thus, although some theorists have convincingly argued for *Twilight* as carrying on the gothic tradition, the saga departs from that genre in one key way—in its championing of fathers and husbands. As Modleski asserts, gothic fiction circulates around the forced confinement of females where the fear of fathers and husbands dominates. Offering a "paranoid sense of the world," such novels, Modleski argues, "help women come to terms with the mothers who ... seem to be responsible for passing on this paranoia to their daughters in a world ruled by men" (19). Bella inherits this gothic paranoia from her mother specifically in relation to love and marriage. Further, her mother's failure to fully nurture her results in Bella's general fear of the world—a world she views as a dangerous path that her klutzy self cannot navigate. Though Bella is shown to be scarred from lack of mother-love and other female characters are variously scarred (in keeping with the Gothic tradition), the series contrastingly shows fathers and husbands as mother-like nurturers and saviors—as, indeed, better at mothering than women. In fact, Edward quite literally replaces Bella's mother, Renee—he is the one who rocks and cradles her, the one who saves her from beasties, the one who soothes her fears and nourishes her (in fact, one of the few times she eats a meal in the saga is at Edward's insistence—the infamous mushroom ravioli).

Edward's mothering role is made particularly overt when Bella goes to his home for the first time. While there, she is mesmerized by the piano, recalling how she loved to watch her mother play as a child, relating, "She was happy, absorbed—she seemed like a new, mysterious being to me then" (*T* 324). Given that Bella repeatedly describes Edward as a mysterious being, and that he gladly steps into the piano-playing role her mother left vacant, we might read Edward as a new, improved mother—one that does not abandon her but instead pens her lullabies. We further see his displacement of Renee in the climactic battle scene with James in the first book. James lures Bella to her intended demise by claiming he plans to kill her mother—instead, he attempts to kill Bella while Renee's voice plays in the background. Though Bella has childhood visions of her mother as protector, it is Edward that saves her from James' murderous intent. Then, when she wakes up later in the hospital, Edward is by her side, and Renee is absent—having gone to get something to eat. Interestingly, the film version switches this—Bella wakes to a concerned Renee, and Edward is pretending to sleep off to the side of the room. While the film makes Renee's role more central in general, the texts continually efface her, putting Edward in her place. He is, in comparison to Renee's "erratic, harebrained" incompetence, the perfect parental figure, never needing sleep, ever watchful, ever at the beck and call of Bella's needs.

In addition to being presented as a good mother to Bella, Edward also takes on a disciplinarian, fatherly role. For example, when Bella expresses her *sexual* needs, Edward puts her in her place, firmly scolding, "No"—as in the scene in *Eclipse* where her attempts to "be seductive" result in Edward putting her in a decidedly baby-like hold, described as follows: "I was in his arms, my face cradled between his shoulder and his hand, while his thumb stroked reassuringly against my cheek" (*E* 444). So, not only is he the good, loving mother, but he is also the protector of her chastity, a role fathers held historically (and still do in some "abstinence only" circles and many religions—as will be discussed further in the next chapter).

But why, we might consider, is all of this parthenogenesis and male as *both* mother/father worship housed within a vampire narrative? As noted in chapter 1, vampires of legend and lore (as well as of early literature) were often female. However, the most well-known literary and screen vampires are male—from Dracula to Lestat to Angel. Further, many vampire texts have circulated around father figures and families. Van Helsing acts as the father to the "crew of light" in *Dracula*, attempting to save not only his figurative sons (Harker et al.) but also his daughters (Lucy and Mina). Where are the mothers in *Dracula*? The same place they are in *Twilight*—dead or gone. *Dracula* is, as Auerbach exemplifies, soaked in "paternalistic morality" (*Our Vampires* 187).

More recently, films such as *Near Dark* and *The Lost Boys* have reaffirmed the importance of paternal figures. In *Near Dark,* Caleb is turned back into a human by his father, rescued from the dangerous world of the lawless vampire family that allows—horror of horrors—its women a modicum of power. In *Lost Boys*, the ditzy single mom not only fails to protect her kids from the local vampire clan, but also falls for the vampire patriarch himself; in the end, thanks to her father, her son is saved from being lost to the vampire world. And, while *Buffy the Vampire Slayer* reworked the notion of family, offering a queer/chosen family alternative, *Twilight* has taken us back to the conventional family—married, monogamous, and intent on reproduction.[7]

According to Robert McElvaine, the myth of male mothering strengthens when male social roles are under threat (as they certainly are now). Perhaps the male mothering in *Twilight* is in response to females' (perceived) take-over and infiltration of the "man's world," of the much-circulated (but grossly false) claim that we are in a "post-feminist" moment where not only has female equality been achieved, but also male power is under attack. Such antifeminist, misogynist impulses lie at the heart of what Braidotti names "the recurring fantasy of a child born from man alone" (87). Reading the myth of male parthenogenesis in relation to our contemporary fascination with monsters and machines, Braidotti suggests that the fear of the monstrous feminine drives the turn toward reproductive technologies—or the ability to reproduce via science/mind rather than via the female body. *Twilight* certainly seems to speak to the underlying fear of the monstrous feminine (Victoria and Jane being two prime incarnations) and the horrors surrounding human female birth (as with Bella's blood-drenched birth scene in *Breaking Dawn*), but, rather than turning to technology to usurp female generative power, it turns to male vampires— and particularly male vampire doctors (Carlisle is a practicing doctor, and Edward has two medical degrees). These angelic men are the good fathers who resist nontraditional families (the Volturi, the newborn army, etc.), who create perfect nuclear families of their own, and who work to assimilate Others into the "proper" family model (via, in particular, assimilating Bella and Jacob into the Cullen clan). Far from the world of "guyland" they are not men acting like boys—rather, they are old, wise patriarchs who don't put "bros before hoes" and are responsible in the extreme. While many females understandably find such a depiction alluring, why does this representation appeal to a growing number of male fans?

Twilight *Guise*

Though much has been made of the predominantly female readership, the popularity of male bloggers and the vocality of male fans proves many *Twilighters* are male. Indeed, at *Summer School in Forks* I spotted a man, probably in his late 40s, with hair bleached Carlisle-blonde, wearing a "Real Men Read *Twilight*" t-shirt who was deeply absorbed in the hardback copy of *Breaking Dawn* he held in his lap. Though his vampire hairdo made me do a double-take, it was his T-shirt that intrigued me the most with its insistence that being a "real man" is defined via one's actions, and claiming, of all things, the reading of *Twilight* as one of these defining actions. The T-shirt is surely at least partly a joke, playing off the popularity of the book *Real Men Don't Eat Quiche*. Yet we can also read this as a statement of defiance — one that not only questions how we define "real men" but also suggests that such an idea is itself a joke, that, in other words, "real men" don't exist any more than vampires do; it is only our belief in them, our socially constructed ideas of what "real men" are, that allows for the allusion to seem a reality. This allusion — that gender exists outside of our social ideas about it — is precisely what necessitates its strict policing. For, if "real men" did exist, surely they would not have to wear T-shirts (or do anything else) to prove they were real. Rather, the very notion that what constitutes a real man is debatable reveals the category to be open to change, question, even destruction. This is why males adopt what Katz calls a "tough guise." "The myth of the "real man," he argues, "is linked intimately with the phenomenon of the 'tough guise,' wherein boys and men learn to show the world only those parts of themselves that the dominant culture has defined as manly" (n.p.). As *Twilight* has *not* been defined as manly, being a *Twilight* fan is not something most males are eager to show the world. This is at the heart of a question that circulates throughout the fandom — the question of whether males can like the series and still "keep their man card."

This very conundrum dominated much of Kaleb Nation's keynote address at the *Summer School in Forks* symposium. Otherwise known as *The Twilight Guy*, Nation infused his speech with fawning references to true love, inspiring the fans in attendance to swoon. So, perhaps a good place to begin a consideration of male fans of *Twilight* is with Nation — one of the saga's most well-known fans, now an author himself, and a sort of pseudo-celebrity in his own right. Nation's popular blog, *The Twilight Guy*, came about, as he explains, by accident. Nation happened to post a piece joking he had been cast as Edward Cullen for the upcoming *Twilight* film at the same time Summit announced the casting of Robert Pattinson. Within hours, as he explains, "girls ... stormed my website ... screaming in all caps" things like "SUMMIT HAS GONE MAD" and "DEAR GOD, NO!" This reaction prompted Nation to read the books in order to find out what all the fuss was about. As he shared during his *SSIF* keynote address, "I had to get a copy of *Twilight* and absolutely none of my friends could know." Joking that he "ordered it online, in secret," Nation told of opening the book hidden away in his bedroom and concealing his purchase by storing it on his bookshelf spine side in. Sharing that such secrecy for guys in the fandom is common, Nation suggested how reading *Twilight* results in shame, guilt, and embarrassment for males. His comments revealed he, too, shares these feelings, that when he himself was "bewitched" by the series, he "tried to fight it."

His choice of language here and elsewhere is telling. His use of a word that insinuates that his fascination and enchantment is the result of witchcraft is particularly revealing, speaking to the long-held historical idea that women "bewitch" or "seduce" men with their dangerous powers and, in so doing, threaten to annihilate their masculinity. In being "bewitched" by *Twilight*, he can place the blame for his "obsession" (a word he also uses liberally) on the female author, who he emphasized at the outset as having a very bewitching way with fans. Tellingly, he tries to "fight" his fascination with the saga, assuring the audience, "I had never once been inclined to read a romance." Or, in other words, his masculinity tries to "fight" his interest in something he should supposedly *not* be interested in — love and romance. He also went to pains to establish that he used to think *Twilight*ers were crazy, that he poked fun at fans, that he "avoided *Twilight* at all costs." Given that he receives numerous "male confessions" that disclose what lengths males go to hide their reading and/or enjoyment of the series, his reaction is certainly not unique. Nation noted that "like many guys, I read the books with some form of secrecy," and shared stories of one young man who confessed to stealing his sister's books and another who disguised the covers so he could read the saga in secret during class. Nation noted that many of the same males who make fun of others or mock the series are secretly reading it themselves. To illustrate this claim, he told the story of being in a group of male and female friends, all of whom were reading the saga, yet, when a guy pointed at a *Twilight* T-shirt one of the females in the group was wearing and mocked, "*Twilight*, what a stupid girls' book," no one said anything, including Nation.

However, what is particularly interesting is that in spite of the lengths Nation went to to joke about this macho stance in his speech, he never analyzed it. Indeed, he continued to *perform* a macho stance in a speech framed around deriding such macho-ness as silly. For example, he explains he felt he had to get to the bottom of the *Twilight* mystery "for all the guys asking questions like ... 'why is my girlfriend ignoring me for this book' and 'how can I be more like Edward Cullen.'" Here, he frames his endeavor in terms of "helping a brother out" — as a sort of way to help all the males struggling to understand not only the popularity of the saga, but also how it might help them "with the chicks." While this stance was underplayed in Nation's keynote, it occurs regularly in the blogosphere, with many blog posts discussing how *Twilight* knowledge can help males "score." However, given that Nation was speaking to a predominantly female audience, he wisely didn't choose this common route. Instead, he situated himself as a sort of male preacher, opening with repetitions of "we are gathered together" as if to frame his talk as a sermon for the female flock in attendance. As a preacher, he metaphorically alluded to nonbelievers, or those who don't appreciate the series, as missing the "true message" — that of true love. We might also view his speech as a born-again confessional, one that shares his "empty" life pre–*Twilight* and ends with the resounding message that he has found the (*Twi*)light. In this performance, Nation thus adopted the traditionally masculine role of preacher — a very fitting role given the predominance of religious fans in attendance. But he also played to the female audience by framing himself as a romantic champion of "true love." Indeed, the end of his speech served as an ode to true love where he testified the following:

> The deepest, most underlying message is the strength of Bella and Edward's love.
>
> *Twilight* is a story of love and even more so a story of how true love can break down any barrier.
>
> True love can defy all odds.
>
> There is one solid message ... true love is unbreakable.... Bella and Edward are unbreakable.

If this seems nauseatingly romantic, be aware that this is only a *sampling* of his platitudes on love. Indeed, he seemed to be attempting to perform the very dedication to love that his speech claimed is the reason fans love Edward. Closing with the line "maybe somewhere there still exists something as true and real as the love of Bella and Edward" to a round of thunderous applause, the young Nation's performance revealed that Edward's performance of masculinity, which is loved by so many fans, can easily be adopted by young men like Nation–all they need do is joke about the silliness of trying to be macho and swear on their *Twilight* Bible that they, too, believe in true love. However, what this adoption misses is the fact that many do *not* love this particular performance of masculinity, that they do not seek a mere performance of "the romantic male lead," but rather desire the alternative masculinities the *Twilight* series offers.

In relation to Nation's keynote, there were moments in his speech that hinted at an awareness of the masculine façade, what Katz calls the "tough guise." For example, Nation's observation that "for being tough males a lot of them seemed pretty afraid of this little book," suggested that he is aware of a performance of masculinity that depends on appearing tough on the outside in order to hide the fear/weakness many males feel on the inside. Further, his acknowledgment that Edward "makes human guys look dismally inadequate," reveals an awareness of the impossible standards males are held to. Yet, rather than fully disrobing his macho stance, Nation only hints at its removal, suggesting that he knows it's an uncomfortable garment to wear, but fully realizing at the same time its power to make some females swoon — as many did in the audience that day.

Others, such as the blogger "Constant Revision," argue that Edward's brand of macho ruins things for mere mortal men.[8] Framing Edward's actions as abusive and controlling, Constant Revision refers to his character as setting "sick standards" that not only provide an unrealistic picture of love but also suggest that such love justifies violence. This is exactly the point Katz makes in his critique of the "tough guise"— that it sets "sick standards" for masculinity, standards that render violence sexy, encouraging men to act tough and persuading women to find this tough guise attractive. Perhaps no story better illustrates how far-reaching the lesson that toughness is desirable is than the one Rob Pattinson tells of the seven-year-old girl who asked him to bite her. Absorbing the message that a vampire's phallic bite is desirable, this young girl's request is partly an understandable fan response, but it is also a worrying indication that the bite — the violence — is being successfully sold as attractive to a new generation — this young girl, oddly, wanted a bite, not an autograph or a photo. What does this say in regards to what *Twilight* is teaching us about desirable masculinity? More specifically, how is it shaping female desire for a new, sparkly tough guise?

In *The Unofficial Twilight Guide*, Gresh defines Edward as "the vampire any girl would want," noting, "True *Twilight* fans know that you can never talk enough about Edward or be too devoted to him. He's worth thinking about constantly, no matter where you are or what you're doing" (121, 127). Here, Gresh sets up Edward as *the* real man, framing female devotion to such a man as entirely natural and expected. Yet, as Gresh warns, this vampire lover is likely "sucking the necks of lots of other women," even though "he really loves you and only you," because "after all, he's a guy, and a thousand years is a long time to spend with just one woman" (36). Thus, though this vampire male deserves total and utter devotion from females, he cannot be expected to reciprocate that devotion. Here, Gresh is parroting a very old message, that "boys will be boys" and need to "spread their seed," while females are hopeless saps whose only care is "does he love me?" Though one would hope this message had died at least by the time we stepped into the 21st century, Gresh reveals that the message is alive and well, and hawked not only by the patriarchy makers but also by female authors claiming to have their fingers on the pulse of contemporary girl culture — like Gresh herself. She is correct in at least one regard, though — most females are caught in what Rosalind Wiseman calls "a cycle of craving boys' validation" (235). This craving leads them to only deem themselves worthy if males are attracted to them — and, since most males are busy putting on the tough guise, girls need to at least act like they like it. Vampires and werewolves fit perfectly into such a twisted performance of gender. Moreover, the fact that they are historic rivals (or at the very least, not equals) results in a tale revolving around who can out-macho the other — will it be the sparkly marble vampire-god or the hot-blooded abtacular wolf-boy? Meanwhile, Bella stands by in the wings, craving their validation. Back in the real world, male bloggers, podcasters, and authors vie for attention, dominating much of the cultural response to the supposedly all-female fandom. Yet, much of their response is extremely negative, framing *Twilight*ers as stupid, obsessive, screaming fans.[9]

What, we might ask, is the way out of this labyrinthian gender maze? How might we rethink both femininity and masculinity so that the tough guise and the violence it results in is neither desired by females nor enacted by males? One path, according to Suzy Mckee Charnas, author of *The Vampire Tapestry*, is to make those with privileges, the "tough guys," experience what it's like to play the victim, the oppressed. "The inference is that if you walk a mile in my high heels, you won't be so quick to trample me again with your societally-issued hobnailed men's boots afterward," Charnas insists (63). As she continues, "In other words, the only 'good' male is a feminized male; or, the only male with any likelihood of behaving like a decent human being is a male who has been deprived of his automatic swagger-privileges and so has some insight into what it means to live in the world without them, that is, to live like a woman" (63). Intriguingly — *Twilight* seems to have the makings of some of these good males. Jasper, while he hardly walks a mile in high heels, at least has empathy for those he murders-or, as he puts it, "I could feel everything my prey was feeling. And I lived their emotions as I killed them" (*E* 300). Indeed, when he shares, "I live every day in a climate of emotion," the females amongst us might be inclined to say, "Welcome to our world"(*E* 300). Yet, in Jasper's case, this emotion is not framed as making him a sap or a bitch (as it so often is with females), but as what gives him his humanity. Seth, Eric, and Mike can be similarly argued to represent alternative versions of masculinity. Even Edward, who is tougher than stone on the outside, is really a big softie, or, as hinted at in a Foxtrot comic, just a really nice guy in a cute J. Crew sweater.[10] Thus, as with its representation of femininity, *Twilight* offers conflicting messages about masculinity. As readers, we are encouraged to root for a white, wealthy, macho (vampire) hero, but we are also introduced to likeable wolves of color and tender-hearted father figures. In this regard, *Twilight* engages with changing conceptions of masculinity, suggesting that emo-vampires with great listening skills are perhaps even *hotter* than the traditional masculine tough guys, that BFF wolf-boys can be great friends, even with their shirts on.

Chapter 5

Sexuality Eclipsed

The Taming of Female Sexuality
via Vampire Abstinence

Unlike the dominant cultural message that sex is bad, the *Twilight* saga represents sexual activity as extremely desirable. In fact, the saga could be summed up as follows: Girl meets boy. Girl wants to sleep with boy. Boy says, "No sex until marriage." Girl considers other (wolfy) options. Girl gives in and marries boy. Headboard busting ensues.

In addition to sparking a debate about good versus bad mates, the series represents female sexuality with a twist. The saga is somewhat atypical in its representation of a young female protagonist who actively desires sexual activity. Unlike the dominant cultural message that sex is dangerous (and is for men only), the saga contends that sexual activity is enjoyable and natural for both males *and* females. While Edward chastises Bella for her desires, and while the series ultimately only condones sexual activity within the confines of heterosexual married monogamy, Bella is nevertheless represented as active in her desire. Given our sex-saturated culture, which tends to frame males as desiring subjects and females as desired objects, such representations of female sexual agency certainly make for a nice change. In a "sexophrenic culture," where purity balls, chastity rings, and vows of abstinence from celebrities are paradoxically accompanied by a media saturated with hypersexual imagery, *Twilight*'s representation of sexuality as a natural, joyful part of life is refreshing.[1] However, just as our culture is beset by rather contradictory messages about sex and sexuality, so, too, does the saga offer rather incongruous representations and ideas about sexuality.

Despite our supposedly sexually liberated society, sex still has to be largely *coded* as romance (especially for females) in order to be acceptable. In *Twilight*, Bella's desire to get into Edward's pants is thus depicted as "undying love." Sex also remains extremely *gendered*, with the onus of virginity placed squarely on female shoulders. In *Twilight*, this is reflected in the fact that no one cares how many times the male characters have sexed it up, but Bella's virginity is the *grail* the text protects. Sex is also rampantly *fetishized* in contemporary culture, with its erasure and denial resulting in *more* sexualized representations. Sex in the saga (as in real life) is simultaneously relegated to the realm of the sinful and functions as a key goal/motivator.

While we live in an abstinence-happy culture, one can turn on any television channel to find sex oozing from the screen. Our society largely buys into what Jessica Valenti calls "the purity myth," an ideology that fetishizes chastity and virginity. At the same time, the hypersexualization of girls and the commodification of sex results in a decidedly sex-obsessed society. Ours is society in which the cult of virginity is lauded in theory but not practiced in reality, in which we are supposed to pledge abstinence until marriage, but in which premarital sex is more common than ever, in which sex is supposed to be about love and commitment, but in which sexualized violence is presented both as normal and as a huge turn on. In what follows, *Twilight* will be read as at least partly renegotiating these messages, as putting the fun back in sexual desire and giving readers the world over the permission to luxuriate in lust. On the other hand, it will also be read as promoting rather problematic ideas about abstinence, sexualized violence, and rape culture.

Female Sexuality: Girls Just Want to Have Sex

As many contemporary books explore, girls and young women are being given a contradictory message — to be pure, virginal, abstinent, and "good," but to look hot, to desire boys and men, and to prioritize relationships with males. According to Douglas, "The legacy of the 1950s was that no 'nice' girl ever, ever, went all the way before marriage, and no nice woman every really liked sex" (*Where the Girls Are* 61). This message has certainly changed since the 1950s, but it is still rare to see female sexuality depicted in a positive light. This is not to say that females are not sexualized — quite the opposite.[2] As Ariel Levy's popular book, *Female Chauvinist Pigs: Women and the Rise of Raunch Culture*, details, girls and women are more sexualized than ever. Our media currently hypersexualizes girls and young women, for example, via its relentless focus on the female body as an object for male desire.

Being a sexual being is something that comes from within — something that is part of our shared humanity — yet the natural desire and curiosity surrounding sex is rendered as aberrant, as something that needs to be under lock and key until monogamous coupling is achieved, preferably with the benefit of marriage. This is not to say that sexuality exists in some "natural" space outside of culture — but, rather, that humans are sexual creatures. We certainly learn socially constructed ideas and norms of sexuality from our culture, but we are born into bodies that have the capacity to experience and pursue sexual pleasure. However, the longstanding message has been, as summarized by Douglas: "Girls, (don't) have much, if any, sexual desire (and need) to protect themselves from boys, who (are) completely governed by their crotches" (*Where the Girls Are* 63). When girls do have desire, it tends to be framed as monstrous and dangerous—as something that will harm boys specifically and society more generally. Yet, in *Twilight*, Bella's yearning for Edward is not used to chastise her or to depict her as a "bad girl." Further, the fact that she is often the sexual aggressor in the relationship counters earlier messages that only males care about sex. However, the saga ultimately leaves us with the message that female desire needs to be safely practiced only within the boundaries of marriage. It also, of course, presents this message in a context in which Bella might quite literally die if she has sex with Edward before she is a vampire.

This pro-abstinence message of the saga appeals to many modern readers, especially those whose religious beliefs frame pre-marital sex as sinful. However, reality proves that most teenagers do not wait until marriage — in fact 95 percent of people have sex before marriage (Valenti 58). The abstinence paradigm thus dooms the majority of people to fail — and since it focuses mainly on females, they are the failures. Constructing those females who have sexual desire and act on it before marriage as depraved, the abstinence agenda punishes females (such as Bella) who desire sex. How healthy is such an agenda? More to the point, why is this agenda, promoted in *Twilight*, not rejected by readers?

Safe Sex with a (Mormon) Vampire

I think the answer lies in the way the texts are able to act as if the story of Bella and Edward is a special case given the human/vampire framing. Meyer has even indicated as much, claiming that Bella's and Edward's sexual decisions are necessary because he is a vampire, and thus one wrong kiss could literally lead to death. Reading between the lines, one could argue that such strict adherence to the abstinence code would not be necessary if not for the vampire/human situation. Might this suggest that the series (intentionally or not) intimates that sexual mores are necessary when relationships are profoundly unequal (as is the relationship between Edward and Bella, but also between many real world male and female couples— and often in couples who are fundamentalist in their belief, Mormons included)? In other words, might Meyer be oh-so-slightly indicating that if the world were not dictated by gender norms that result in unequal male/female pairings, egalitarian, violence-free relationships would be far more likely? After all, when Bella and Edward are rendered equal at the saga's close they are allowed to revel in endless sex. In fact, we might read Bella's fear of the Volturi's wrath as fueled mainly by her concern that if she or Edward is destroyed they will no longer be able to have sex, as she indeed articulates in *Breaking Dawn*.

This focus on the joys of sex in the saga may stem from Meyer's experiences of relationships. Admitting that no-sex rules make relationships go faster,

Meyer shares that much of her time in high school "was about restraint" and that she went through a phase in college of "getting engaged a lot"—presumably *engaged* to the idea of being allowed to have sex (Shapiro 32–33, 28). The presumption that Mormons and others who believe in abstinence before marriage are preoccupied with getting married so they can have sex is explored in Deborah Laake's *Secret Ceremonies*. As Laake reveals, a key motivation for getting married among young Mormons is so they can partake in allowable sex. This Mormon practice admittedly spills into Meyer's fiction — she even refused to include scenes of pre-marital sex at the request of her publisher (Shapiro 63). Even her fictional creations have to practice abstinence! But, Meyer puts a new twist on the abstinence-only imperative, equating pre-vampire sex to pre-marital sex, eliding the real danger of the first (sex with a vampire) with the false danger touted in relation to the second (sex before marriage).

Fallen Vampire Women: From *Dracula* to Twilight

Vampirism has often been deployed as a metaphor for sexuality, so much so that it is hard now to envision the vampire without the penetrating, phallic bite. Dracula is the quintessential founding image here, his likeness duplicated across narratives that span generations, especially on the filmic screen. Many have argued that the "latent sexuality" of Stoker's novel is the reason for its enduring popularity.[3] Various critics interpret the repressed sexuality of the novel as speaking particularly to the notion of the dangers of female desire given that the count's bite wreaks the most enduring havoc on Mina and Lucy. As Weissman puts it, the novel represents "a very extreme version of the myth that there are two types of women, devils and angels" (72). The textual exploration of what Phyllis Roth names "the dark woman and the fair, the fallen and the idealized" certainly speaks to the era's concern with policing female sexuality, much like *Twilight*'s concern with regulating female desire (58).

While *Dracula* revolves around conventional character types of its era (the pure woman, the fallen woman, the rake or gothic villain), *Twilight* transplants these Victorian types to the modern United States and brings along with them the sexual mores of earlier time periods. However, while repressed sexuality is embodied and then released via a male vampire in *Dracula*, in *Twilight* the male vampire protagonist polices and "saves" the pure Bella from becoming a fallen woman. Unlike Lucy, who happily succumbs to the dark sexuality Dracula represents, or Mina, whose purity must be saved by a band of men, Bella is rescued from the dangers her own sexuality poses by a new form of vampire, a virginal vampire touting abstinence as the best policy. While *Dracula* can be read as "a man's vision of a noble band of men restoring a woman to purity and passivity, saving them from the horrors of vampirism," *Twilight* can be read as a single man — a Christ-like savior if you will — saving a female from her raging desire by turning her into a vampire (Weissman 70). Like Stoker's novel, it exudes "an extreme version of the stereotypically Victorian attitudes toward sexual roles," and directs its condemnation of sexuality toward females (Weissman 70). Instead of becoming a "fallen woman" and being doomed to literal death or else figurative death as an outcast or prostitute, Bella becomes the ultimate "pure woman," the new Virgin Mary, if you will. Though Bella indeed has sex before giving birth to the savior child Renesmee, she is duly punished for doing so (represented by her bruising). She might be read as a sort of virgin in that her impregnation comes not from a human sexual encounter but from sex with a superhuman, or godly, vampire. While sex with Jacob would certainly have defiled her (a topic to be considered later in the chapter), sex with Edward offers a sort of rebirth — a figurative transformation of the young, overly sexual Bella into a mother. While *Dracula* turned women into what Gail B. Griffin terms "sexual predators," Edward Cullen, like his vampire father, domesticates women, turning them into wife and mother.[4] Whereas the vampire women in *Dracula* fulfill the "worst nightmare and dearest fantasy" of the Victorian age, "the pure girl turned sexually ravenous beast," the vampire women in *Twilight* are conversely "fallen women" turned into "pure girls" via the blessed Cullen venom (Griffin 142).[5] This turn intriguingly releases them from the long-held curse of womanhood — menstruation — a curse historically linked to vampirism.

Menstrual Monsters

Menstruation is historically maligned and associated strongly with impurity. Griffin reads this denigration in relation to a male-dominated culture that frames females as beasts. Creed similarly reads the vampire legend as "a symbolic story about woman's menstrual flow," referring to the vampire as "menstrual monster" (62). Noting the vampire's association with "womb-like coffins" and the full moon, Creed (63) draws on the work of Julia Kristeva, who names blood as "a fascinating semantic crossroads" that threatens the stability of the symbolic order (59, 63, 70). Menstrual blood, Kristeva argues, represents a "danger issuing from within" the body, a danger that she allies to sexual difference — a difference that the symbolic order reifies, turning women into *the* sex of difference in the process— making man (or in *Twilight*'s case — male vampire) the center, the pureness from which meaning emanates (71). Kristeva traces the idea that (female) blood is impure to Leviticus, arguing that the Bible's framing of blood as defiling is utilized in order to frame woman, particularly in her role as "maternal body," as similarly impure (100).

This is partly why the myth of parthenogenesis (discussed in chapter 4) emerges, as Braidotti, like Kristeva, argues. Compared to the bloody and impure maternal body, God (or Edward!) is solid Logos — pure mind devoid of bloody emissions (and in *Twilight*, also devoid of sperm!).[6] While Meyer may not be conversant in French feminism, she is certainly familiar with the Bible, and we might presume that the simultaneous desire and disgust with blood that *Twilight* enacts issues at least in part from the teachings of Leviticus. In the texts, Edward lusts after Bella's blood, but he abstains from it; while the narrative frames this as his heroic refusal to kill Bella, we might also read it as a refusal to be defiled by her blood — a fluid that (as *Midnight Sun* makes especially clear) threatens to turn him into a ravenous monster. Bella, our heroine, also fears blood — unable to even stand the smell or look of even a drop of it as revealed early in *Twilight*. Unlike Lucy of *Dracula*, who becomes a blood-drinking "demonic mother-parody" as the child-murdering Bloofer Lady and is thus transformed from woman to monster, Bella's hatred and fear of blood frames her as not fully female, allowing her to be transformed from not-quite-monster to perfect mother (Griffin 143).

As many fans have noted, the text fails to address what happens when Bella menstruates given that Edward is inexorably drawn to her blood. Perhaps blood is so defiling in the *Twilight* universe that menstruation is not allowed to sully its pages. While Meyer shies away from dealing with the problem menstruating females would pose to her blood-addicted vampires, the link between menstruation and vampirism is historically resonant. As Dijkstra details in *Idols of Perversity*, women were believed to become vampires in order to replace the blood lost during menstruation. Or, as Sue-Ellen Case puts it, the vampire's "kiss of blood is a weakening device" that speaks to "male myths of menstruation, where a women's monthly loss of blood was associated with their pale, weak image" (386). Menstruation is also associated with another vampire symbol — the full moon. Griffin reads Lucy in *Dracula* as a representation of the supposed insanity that menstruation releases in women, of the notion that "under the light of the moon this raging, hungry female force is released" (142). Creed, noting that the Greek word for vampire is *sacromens*, meaning "flesh made by the moon," similarly argues that *Dracula* revolves around the horror of female sexuality, of which menstruation is a key symbol (64).

As Valenti explores in *The Purity Myth*, part of the fear and hatred of menstruation stems from the notion that females lose their "innocence" once they start menstruating — that it represents the dawn of their existence as sexual creatures (72). Asking "if being premenstrual is 'innocence,' does that make those of us with periods guilty?" Valenti's work suggests the same thing as many vampire tales — that, yes, bleeding women are guilty of being sexual. Part of the fetishizaton of purity, as Valenti notes, is about not wanting women to be adults. The onset of menstruation is read as the loss of girlhood, and menstrual blood is thus the defiling and dangerous fluid that turns women into beasts (i.e., sexual females). Perhaps this accounts for the turn of vampire from female to male. While early fiction and lore often represented the blood-sucker as female, the Victorian age cemented the vampire as male. Or, in an age particularly horrified by female sexuality, a male monster began to suck blood from females— draining them not only of their life blood, but also of their sexual power. Though Lucy and Mina are initially sexualized via Dracula's bite, ultimately his intervention leads to their control — Lucy through death and Mina (much like Bella) through being tamed into wife and mother.

The life-giving power of female blood is not lost in *Dracula* on another level — he, like so many of his vampire descendents, looks younger and healthier after drinking. This component of vampire tales has historical precedent in the case of Elisabeth Bathory, whose case, as Creed notes, was copiously noted in Stoker's unpublished papers (63). Brian Frost reads Bathory's "habit of bathing in the blood of slaughtered virgins" as an attempt to "stave off old age and keep her skin smooth and white" (16). Frost's study reveals that such activities predate Bathory, at least fictionally — as in La Morte D'Arthur's depiction of a lady whose life is sustained by dishfuls of virgin's blood (36). More of interest to the present study, though, is how such depictions are replicated in current vampire tales— particularly in Meyer's saga.

While her series has its share of murderous females (Victoria, Maria, The Cold Woman), it replicates, or rather transforms, the Bathory narrative on another level — via its pursuit of youth. Bella bemoans aging throughout the four texts, citing fears of crow's feet, for example, in *Breaking Dawn* and lamenting, "I get older every stinking day," in *Eclipse* (119). However, rather than framing virgin blood as the fountain of youth à la Bathory and La Morte D'Arthur, *Twilight* portrays (male) vampire venom as the means to stop aging. In yet another erasure of the female, Meyer rewrites the longstanding historical association of virgin blood with youth and instead impregnates male vampires with restorative and generative powers. Not only does Meyer put menstruation under erasure, but she also erases the very blood that gave birth to much vampire lore. In so doing, she echoes Stoker on two key levels—firstly, she renders female sexuality (which is so often linked to menstruation) as null and void by supplanting female birth with vampire parthenogenesis; secondly, she displays great enmity regarding female sexuality, suggesting its threat must be tamed via vampirism (which, in her saga, is also representative of religion and its emphasis on heterosexual reproductive married monogamy — as will be explored in the following chapter). Given the rampant popularity of the saga, we must concede that Roth is correct when she asserts that both "Victorian and twentieth-century readers" find "hostility toward female sexuality" hugely appealing (57). In fact, perhaps the enduring appeal of one of the texts that *Twilight* pays homage to—*Jane Eyre*—is linked to that novel's similar hostility toward female sexuality.

It seems, in fact, that we might consider Bella as a modern-day Jane Eyre — a female able to split off her dark side (her inner Bertha Rochester, if you will) thanks to her Edward (Rochester) savior. According to Weissman, Bertha Rochester represents "the one violently sexual woman in a major Victorian novel" (71). More to the point, not only does Jane "basically accept this idea that sexual women are monsters and the good ones are asexual," but also this monstrosity is linked to vampirism when, in chapter 25 of Bronte's novel, Jane notes that Bertha reminds her of a vampire (Weissman 72). *Twilight*, as a purposeful descendent of *Jane Eyre*, gives modern voice to the sexual fear that permeates Bronte's novel (and era). A modern-day Victorian text of sorts (at least in length and message if not in literary style), *Twilight* accords with that era's notion that female sexuality must be controlled. However, it gives this message a modern twist — one thoroughly in keeping with the current cultural moment — via fetishizing abstinence.

Throw Those Virginity Keys Away: Abstinance Twilight Style

By framing male sexual desire as beastly on the one hand (Jacob) and godly on the other (Edward), Meyer's text allows for a narrative in which females will be either physically harmed (as Emily is by her wolf lover) or killed (as Bella is by Edward). Even human male sexuality proves extremely dangerous in the *Twilight* world, as evidenced through the rape of Rosalie, the near-rape of Bella, and Esme's history with domestic violence. Yet, rather than suggesting that male sexuality needs to be tamed or changed, the saga *blames* females for this violence — Rosalie because she is vain, Bella because she walks down a dark alley, Emily for courting a wolf lover. Males (human and otherwise) cannot control themselves according to the saga, hence females need to police themselves so as to avoid becoming victim to rape culture. Sexual violence occurs in the text when females step outside the abstinence paradigm and the passive virgin model it promotes, when they want — whether it be sex, money, independence, etc. — violence ensues.

The solution, according to the saga, is to buy into the abstinent-until-married model — a solution that resonates with the current cultural moment, a milieu that has managed to turn virginity into a coveted prize. Yet, this prize would be far easier to attain if all partners pursued it. In the real world, the onus of virginity is put on females: they are to ward off males (who are framed as *always* wanting sex). This construction keeps traditional gender norms, to say nothing of heteronormativity, firmly in place. Yet many females recognize the unfairness here — why should girls and women be the keepers of the virginity keys? *Twilight*, through its depiction of Edward, allows females to throw these keys safely away and places the burden of virginity squarely on Edward's shoulders. His control allows them (and Bella) to revel in their desires — his chastity assures they will remain "pure" no matter how desirous they are. This is indeed a very compelling representation for contemporary female readers—Edward will keep Bella (and them) safe. Bella emphasizes this in *New Moon* when she relates:

> Edward had drawn many careful lines for our physical relationship, with the intent being to keep me alive. Though I respected the need for maintaining a safe distance between my skin and his razor-sharp, venom-coated teeth, I tended to forget about trivial things like that when he was kissing me [16].

And forget Bella can, because Edward intends to keep her alive (or, reading between the lines, to keep her a virgin). When read via this lens, Edward's more controlling nature (he grabs Bella's face numerous times, forces her to look at him, imprisons and isolates her, cuts her off, interrupts her, and gives her orders) becomes necessary and endearing—he is not so much the domineering boyfriend but the considerate knight, protecting Bella for the sake of her own chastity. This may be why Bella, a rather self-respecting, independent woman, does not balk at his overcontrolling and possessive tendencies. Like many contemporary readers, she seems to recognize that his control will keep her safe—or, in other words, that his influence will keep her a virgin.

This motif can only become seductive for readers in a culture that values abstinence and so-called sexual propriety—hence, novels with similar messages were extremely popular during the Victorian era. That era, like our own, allied female sexuality with monstrosity and deviance. For example, the allure of Dracula can be tied to the text's exploration of sexuality, or, as Roth argues, "for both the Victorian and twentieth-century readers, much of the novel's great appeal derives from its hostility toward female sexuality" (57). But can *Twilight* be read as similarly hostile toward female sexuality? Does part of its appeal derive from the way it chastises Bella for her desires and champions Edward for his devotion to chastity? And, why is the "good girls don't" motif at *Twilight*'s core so appealing to modern readers?

In many regards, *Twilight* does exude hostility toward female sexuality—Bella is castigated for her desires, desires that nearly lead to her rape and/or death. And, as is the case for many contemporary female readers, Bella is given contradictory messages—she is supposed to be a grown-up, to care for her father and not need her mother, yet she is not apparently grown-up enough to make decisions regarding sex. Charlie makes this patently clear when he tells her, "There are some things that you need to be careful about.... You're still young" (*E* 58). Bella responds by begging Charlie not to have a "sex talk" with her, referring to such a conversation as "beyond the seventh circle of Hades" (*E* 59). Surely, the cultural fixation on virginity and abstinence of our contemporary moment allows readers to identify with Bella's predicament.

On the one hand, Bella has physical desires; on the other, she is told these desires are wrong—just as readers are encouraged to physically desire Edward (and other male characters) and then are castigated by parents and the media for doing so. Likewise, females are inundated with sexualized messages yet live in a culture in which sex is not supposed to be openly discussed. As indicated in the text, talking about sex (especially with one's parents) is akin to burning in hell. Thus, although *Twilight* concedes that young women may want to have sex, which puts it a step above the virginity movement, it nevertheless indicates that such desires should be kept secret, under lock and key.

This depiction accords with what Valenti calls the "moral panic in America over young women's sexuality," a panic that uses the "myth of sexual purity" in order to fetishize virginity (9). As Valenti argues, "The lie of virginity-the idea that such a thing even exists-is ensuring that young women's perception of themselves is inextricable from their bodies, and that their ability to be moral actors is absolutely dependent on their sexuality" (9).Within this myth, "women are led to believe that our moral compass lies somewhere between our legs" (13). This "ethics of passivity," as Valenti calls it, defines females by what they don't do (25). Bella is good because she does not sleep around, because she waits until marriage. Though the book does not depict her attending any purity balls, she might as well — she, like the young females that are part of the virginity movement, is inundated with "fear and shame-based tactics" aimed at preventing her from having sex (Valenti 103). In particular, Edward suggests sex will lead to death and shames her for wanting to destroy her (and his) soul.

And, though Bella doesn't attend abstinence-only sex education classes at Forks high school, it seems she has absorbed the message about the "potential filthiness" of sexually promiscuous females (Valenti 33). Why else would she so readily accept Edward's ruling that sex is a no-no? Indeed, as others have argued, the saga works to eroticize abstinence, functioning as what Siering calls "abstinence porn." In her *Ms. Magazine* article, Siering contends that *Twilight* is "an allegorical tale about the dangers of unregulated female sexuality," a tale that castigates Bella for her desires and champions Edward for his control (51). This framing certainly rings true in the depiction of Bella and Edward's first kiss, where Bella's lack of control prompts Edward to stop kissing her. In contrast to what we might read as Bella's wantonness, "Edward hesitated to test himself, to see if this was safe, to make sure he was still in control of his need" (*T* 282). As the texts make clear, if Bella is unable to keep her desire in check, she is putting her life on the line. Yet, she throws caution to the wind, noting, "If I had my way, I would spend the majority of my time kissing Edward" (*E* 43). Due to Edward's superior self-control, she does not often get her way. Moreover, Charlie's protective stance, Jacob's worry, and Emmett's intrusive commentary about Bella's sex life reveal that her sexuality is routinely policed by males.

However, Bella, unlike the chaste heroine of many romances, is presented as full of desire — as the one whose blood boils, whose breathe deepens, who lustfully clutches Edward. Edward, in contrast, acts like an unresponsive statue. Here, the saga flips the cultural script regarding sexuality by representing the female as active and the male as passive. The text even nods to this flip when Bella says to Edward, "Traditionally, shouldn't you be arguing my side, and I yours?"(*E* 451). Then, when Bella tries to negotiate with Edward about his marriage ultimatum, she claims, "I didn't have the faintest idea how to be seductive," yet she is definitely the sexual aggressor in this scene and many others (*E* 442). Edward, with his "heavily disapproving" face, tells her to "be reasonable" and informs her, "We're not having this discussion." Unwilling to be ruled over by him, she retorts, "I say we are" (*E* 443). Edward then grabs her wrists, pinning them to her sides, and suggests her desire for sex before they marry is not even "faintly realistic," to which Bella retorts, "So you can ask for any, stupid, ridiculous thing you want — like getting married — but I'm not even allowed to discuss what I" — at which point Edward cuts her off and puts his hand over her mouth (*E* 443). In the ensuing discussion, Bella points out to him that he has placed many demands on her, while she has only one "lone, solitary, little demand." Her phrasing this as a demand and Edward's subsequent reactions are very telling — for, while he is demanding and ordering her about all the time, he does not appreciate it when she makes demands in return (*E* 445). These negotiations regarding their physical relationship no doubt appeal to readers who have to navigate the tricky, emotionally charged world of sexual activity. More often than not, such conversations do not take place in other media representations or in reality, with sex being perhaps the most represented but least talked-about subject there is. Thus, these conversations, though they problematically frame Bella as wanton and Edward as the morality police, are nevertheless preferable to not talking about sex at all.

Yet, the fact that Edward (and Meyer by extension) chides Bella for her stance, as when Edward laments, "Look what's become of you. Trying to seduce a vampire," is likely less pleasing to sexually liberated readers (*E* 455). However, the vampire/human framing of the saga works to excuse Edward's behavior. He is depicted as someone who is rightly concerned with her safety — as when he warns her he can't control himself in her presence and, in so doing, comes dangerously close to furthering the stereotype that men just can't help themselves. While such representations have led many to read Meyer as championing abstinence, it seems rather she goes back and forth on this topic, one moment representing sexuality as natural and desirable, the next moment linking it to danger, death, and damnation.

A (Mormon) Jab at Patriarchy

Most have read Meyer's purported promotion of abstinence as in relation to her Mormonism, assuming because she is Mormon she likely holds very strict views about sex before marriage. However, the text itself is not so clear-cut; perhaps instead of using the Mormon card as prescriptive, we might see

Meyer as questioning or working through ideas about sexuality and purity—ideas that are not stamped with a "this is sinful" label, but that are negotiated and examined by Bella and Edward, with Bella importantly being the character who most strongly questions sexual mores. This also allows Edward to play against type. *He* is the one encouraging abstinence, a move that likely appeals to readers who have been pressured into sexual activity by males. Our culture still frames males as sexually active and desirous and females as passive and chaste. Thus, Bella's active desire in the text contrasts to stereotypical representations of femininity just as Edward's chaste ways depict his as a "dream man"—as when Bella jokes she feels like a licentious villain in a melodrama trying to steal *his* virtue, and he replies, "No, silly girl.... I'm trying to protect yours. And you're making it shockingly difficult" (*E* 453). Further, if we read Edward as a representation of patriarchy, of male power within both society in general and Meyer's church more particularly, we can see that the text attempts to negotiate a mutually agreeable sexual contract given the limiting parameters of the vampire/human dyad. If we superimpose this dyad onto the real world, we can read males as representing the power both of the church and of patriarchy, and women representing the fallible, licentious humans.

Here, it is important to remember that as a practicing Mormon, Meyer does not have much choice in how to approach pre-marital sex if she wishes to remain a respected member of her faith. As Edwin B. Arnaudin writes in his thesis on the subject, "If she were to betray her faith in her writing, she would cease to comply with the strict adherence demanded by the Mormon Church" (n.p.). Thus, while Meyer ultimately capitulates to the doctrine of her church and advances the idea that sex before marriage is a dangerous no-no, we can see areas of the text where she questions this notion, even if only subconsciously. In effect, Meyer's hands are tied by the doctrine of her faith, and if she herself wants to be a "good girl," she cannot advance ideas about sex that are not in keeping with Mormonism.

Also, those who claim that Edward is the "good boy" saving the wanton harlot, Bella, from her dangerous desires fail to account for the fact that Bella is held up as a heroine and is *not* represented as a harlot. Thus, it can be argued that Meyer, through Bella, is questioning the mores of her religion, and particularly those mores that hold up a strict divide between good and bad girls—a questioning that many readers likely also negotiate. Just as we do a poor job in our culture of distinguishing between healthy sexuality and damaging or exploitive sexuality, so, too, does the *Twilight* saga traverse this dichotomy, suggesting on the one hand that sexual desire is normal and, on the other, that it is dangerous. Via this wavering presentation, Meyer does not promote a rigid abstinence-only line—in fact, I feel her representation of sexuality can at least partly be read as a jab at patriarchy.

Bella's lust is not condemned by the authorial voice nor by readers; rather, as fan sites such as *RavisHim* indicate, readers, like Bella, actively desire Edward (and his human counterpart, Rob Pattinson). What those who argue that the saga is "abstinence porn" (such as Siering) fail to note is that the only real condemnation regarding Bella's sexual appetite comes from Edward — he is the keeper of the chastity keys. She, like readers, hopes to grab those keys and smash them to the ground. Edward does chastise Bella, as Siering details, but this need not be read as indicating that his actions are lauded by either the author or readers. Siering's thesis that "the overriding message is that young women are incapable of understanding or controlling their own sexuality; it takes a man to keep them in check" is no doubt tenable, but I argue that we can also see Bella's sexuality as working to contest patriarchal norms while Edward's abstinence mantra is framed as *so* last century (51). I agree with Siering that *Twilight* can be read as "a cautionary tale for young women," but, in the same way that Radway frames traditional romance novels, such tales can be read as "cultural release valves" that address women's disgruntlements within patriarchy (51, 95).

Although Radway focused primarily on young married women in her study, we might surmise that the predominantly young female readers of *Twilight* experience similar discontent as they begin to navigate relationships and sexual attraction. While Radway attempted to answer "what it was about the romance heroine's experience that fostered the readers' ability to see her story as interesting and accounted for their willingness to seek their own pleasure through hers precisely at the moment when they were most directly confronting their dissatisfaction with traditionally structured heterosexual relationships," we might ask what it is about Bella's experience that so speaks to contemporary readers (12–13). Like earlier romances, hers is a story that suggests passive female sexuality leads to a happy ending, and, in so doing, suggests that patriarchal relationship models are beneficial. Bella's story also emphasizes the inevitability and endurance of "true love," focusing on romance instead of sexuality.

The Dark Side of Chivalry

After Bella views Edward for that first time in the Forks High School cafeteria, she is drawn to him like a magnet. Shortly thereafter, as she walks into biology, Edward's thirst for Bella's blood causes him to give her a "hostile, furious" look (23). While this anger may seem to counter claims of first love, the fact that he "suddenly went rigid" serves as an under-coded message that her presence is an excruciating turn-on (23). His "coal black" eyes indicate danger (which is so closely associated with sexual desire in romance fiction), and his physical actions convey that he cannot control his longing. Following these early charged scenes, Bella continues to obsess about Edward, unable to concentrate or sleep. As readers, we are unsure at this point if his actions speak of love or hate, and this heightens the exciting anticipation that keeps us turning the pages. Then, in one of the most potentially dangerous scenes in *Twilight*, Bella (and the readers who identify with her) experience a life-saving moment of release when Edward saves her from the probable rapists. Sweeping in on his horse, this time in the form of a shiny Volvo, Edward speeds her away to safety. Here, the text informs us that his claims of being "bad" and "dangerous" are a ruse, and we receive comforting verification that Edward is the good guy we have suspected all along. Further, the text promotes what Katz names the "chivalry trap," a paradigm that frames women as always in need of protection (*The Macho Paradox* 52).

From here on out, the romance throttles forward and does so, significantly, mainly through conversation rather than physical interaction. In so doing, it speaks to contemporary readers schooled in the virtues of abstinence, readers who nevertheless live in a hypersexualized culture where sexualized violence is particularly rampant. Bella's story negotiates these realities, conveying that true love is possible even when one lives within a violent, patriarchal culture. In fact, according to Radway, such narratives help assure readers that a bit of violence is a small price to pay for male protection. As Radway writes,

> By picturing the heroine in relative positions of weakness, romances are not necessarily endorsing her situation, but examining an all-too-common state of affairs in order to display possible strategies for coping with it. When a romance presents the story of a woman who is misunderstood by the hero, mistreated and manhandled as a consequence of his misreading, and then suddenly loved, protected, and cared for by him because he recognizes that he mistook the meaning of her behavior, the novel is informing its readers that the minor acts of violence they must contend with in their own lives can be similarly reinterpreted as the result of misunderstandings or of jealousy born of "true love." The readers are therefore assured that those acts do not warrant substantial changes or traumatic upheaval in a familiar way of life [75].

Twilight assures readers that "minor acts of violence" are to be expected in the course of true love and, further, that the threat of real violence exists outside of the monogamous pairing, an assurance that allies with the chivalry code. In so doing, it upholds traditional gender roles and the "normal" sexuality associated with them — or, girls should love boys and boys should want girls. By loving boys in the right way, the saga promises, girls will be rewarded with a (vampire) knight complete with sparkling armor.

Not a Girl and Not Yet a Woman

The saga also upholds traditional notions about age, suggesting that younger females are best paired with older males. Not only the pairing of Edward and Bella, but also that of Carlisle and Esme, Quil and Claire, and Jacob and Renesmee accord to this model. Further, many of the females are very young — so young as to be girls rather than women. In accordance with what

Durham calls the "pretty babies" syndrome, the sexualization of young females allows for a "regressive and oppressive gender politics" and "a version of sex that is disempowering and objectifying" (55, 118). The young females of *Twilight* don't have much choice in regards to sex — they are ordered not to desire it (by Edward, for example), have little or no choice whom they will mate with (as in the cases of Claire and Renesmee), and, in some cases, have their lives taken away from them and their mates chosen for them (Esme). The females in *Twilight*, in many regards, are more like little girls than women — they are ruled over by patriarchal father/mate figures. When they are not (as is the case with Victoria), they are represented as evil. We might interpret this depiction in relation to Durham's argument that patriarchal culture intentionally infantilizes women in order to keep them passive. As she writes, "Little girls fit more easily into a conventional mold of female sexuality: a perspective in which she lacks authority over her own body and is therefore less threatening than any adult woman today. Because of this, little girls epitomize a patriarchal society's ideal of compliant, docile sexuality" (129). In the saga, Bella most epitomizes patriarchal society's ideal female — she is not only compliant and docile, but also eternally young and exceedingly nonthreatening. Much like the Britney Spears song, "Not a Girl, Not Yet a Woman," *Twilight* females are *in between,* a space that, as the series reveals, is right where patriarchy wants them. This depiction is further in keeping with a sexual ideology that insists the female sexual role is that of pleaser, both in the fact that females are instructed that their role is to please men via their submission to male desire and in the fact that females are framed as objects of titillation for the male gaze.

Even within publications that are aimed at female readers, girls are framed according to this pervasive male gaze. Girls' magazines, for example, exude a "constant awareness of the critical male gaze," "of an invisible, phantom boy who is watching their every move" (Durham 165). In *Twilight*, Edward embodies this gaze, literally watching Bella even as she sleeps. *Twilight* has thus taken the controlling male gaze and rendered it both protective and erotic — Edward's watchful ways keep Bella safe — a safety that, according to blogger Neesha Meminger, allows girls a place to explore their "budding sexuality."[7] Meminger accounts for the popularity of *Twilight* due to its creation of a space that allows girls and women to "explore the wonder and excitement of their own sexuality" — an exploration that she argues is truncated by a hypersexualized culture where females "are bombarded with images of sexuality before they lose all of their baby teeth." As scholars like Durham and Valenti insist, female sexuality is constructed as taboo — as threatening purity — and thus it must be either excised or chained to male sexuality. This, in effect, is what Meyer's saga does — it eliminates the possibility of sexuality (i.e., Bella's forced virginity) until it can be safely controlled and monitored by a male. Like the teen magazines analyzed by Durham, *Twilight* promotes the message that a female should "focus on figuring out how best to appeal to the whims of these godlike beings" — to the male keepers of the chastity keys (159). In popular texts such as these magazines, and certainly in *Twilight*, sexuality for girls is framed as a matter of resisting and controlling male desires rather than having desire of one's own, and, if one should slip and tarnish one's purity, guilt and regret are framed as appropriate responses.

And They Fornicated Happily Ever After

Yet, at the same time that female sexuality is represented as a purity that must be protected, so, too, is it commodified and sold on the cultural marketplace. On the one hand, girls are told their pure bodies are sacred vessels; on the other, consumer culture encourages them to buy thong underwear, shorts with handprints on the butt, and T-shirts with slogans such as "Eye Candy" or "Scratch and Sniff" across the chest. At the same time, t-shirts for toddler boys read "Pimp Squad," and an energy drink called "Pimp Juice" promises those who drink it that "Pimp Juice is your mojo, your 'It' factor that works with women of every color, creed, or kind from 50 down to 9" (Levin and Kilbourne 140). Within this contradictory context, where girls are pure but sexy and boys are "pimps" who should hook up with as many females as they can, violence is also presented as exciting and alluring. Horror films, video games, advertisements, and music videos provide a constant onslaught of stylized depictions of violence. Stephen King, arguing that the media teaches that "successful sexual relationships are based in man's domination and women's submission," concludes that the popularity of the horror genre is based on its exaggeration of this message — a message that it often twists so that male domination is not dependent on sexual prowess, or, as King puts it, the vampire "doesn't have to get it up to do it," (77).

The insinuation that so many horror films offer that males can "penetrate" and dominate women without "getting it up" accounts for, according to King, the huge popularity of horror films with young males. "What better news to those on the threshold of the sexual sphere," he asks, noting that "most fourteen-year-old boys ... feel capable of dominating only the centerfold in Playboy with total success" (77). As he claims, "Sex makes young adolescent boys feel many things, but one of them quite frankly, is scared. The horror film in general and the vampire film in particular confirms this feeling. Yes, it says; sex is scary; sex is dangerous" (77). But what horror films also do is perpetuate the message that males are the ones who do the scaring and females are the ones who should be scared — as with pornography, such films frame the female body as something to be conquered and/or destroyed. Twitchell makes a similar claim, noting that "contemporary formulaic horror sequences" are "rife with misogyny, incest, rape, and aggressive antisocial behavior" (3–4). Yet, as Twitchell notes, these hyperviolent narratives often have lessons about sexuality at their core (90).

While he draws on Claude Levi-Strauss, interpreting horror films as imparting the message that incest is taboo, I would counter that the message of much horror is that female sexuality is monstrous. As Stephen Neale argues in his book *Genre*, female sexuality "constitutes the real problem that the horror cinema exists to explore, and which constitutes also and ultimately that which is really monstrous" (61). Or, as Creed identifies in *The Monstrous Feminine*, "All human societies have a conception of the monstrous-feminine, of what it is about women that is shocking, terrifying, horrifying, abject" (1). What is most often horrifying is the female, her body in particular, and the way it poses a threat to male rule. Or, as Creed puts it, "The horror film consistently places the monster in conflict with the family, the couple and the institutions of patriarchal capitalism" (61).

This is where *Twilight* is key — in its reclamation and revision of a key monster — the vampire. Rather than relating vampirism to aberrant sexuality, as has been the tradition, *Twilight* offers us a clan of abstinent vampires, who do not bite necks let alone feed off human blood. Rather than attacking the female body in order to subdue it, *Twilight* focuses on one potent female — a female who attracts all males in her vicinity — and turns her into a married, monogamous vampire — a patriarchal set piece in the Cullen family drama. In so doing, the saga renders Bella's sexuality both safe and pure — once married, her virginity does not threaten to destroy Edward's soul; once vampire, her irresistible beauty "belongs" to Edward for all eternity.

While the novel *Dracula* explored sexuality as a dangerous evil that must be controlled, *Twilight*, in contrast, reclaims sexuality, making it pure and purposeful — tying it to the creation of an eternal family, a concept surely dear to the heart of its Mormon author. Whereas, as King argues, it is likely the strong sexual undertones of the vampire that keep our love affair with this brand of monster alive, in *Twilight* the sexual undertones are laden with virginal, monogamous messages — messages more in keeping with romance than horror (75). Quite the opposite to Dracula's depiction of aberrant sexuality, *Twilight* offers a decidedly innocent version of sexuality — one in which kisses are a matter of life and death. While Dracula explores orality, contamination, and infidelity, *Twilight* focuses on what we might term *fairy tale sex* — or sex that promises a "happily ever after" of forever, happily fornicating the same partner. According to King,

> Dracula sure isn't a book about "normal" sex; there's no Missionary Position going on here. Count Dracula (and the weird sisters as well) are apparently dead from the waist down; they make love with their mouths alone. The sexual basis of Dracula is an infantile oralism coupled with a strong interest in necrophilia (and pedophilia, some would say, considering Lucy in her role as "bloofer lady"). It is also sex without responsibility [75].

Twilight, while it certainly has disturbing undertones of pedophilia and necrophilia, is obsessively focused on "normal" sex — on married sex, responsible sex, sex for the purpose of procreation. Yet, if the vampire myth is so popular, as King claims, due to its focus on an "infantile, retentive attitude toward sex" that says, "I will rape you with my mouth and you will love it; instead of contributing potent fluid to your body, I will remove it," why might *Twilight*'s version of vampire sex, which inseminates vampire venom into the virginal Bella, be so compelling to contemporary adolescents (75)? Part of its popularity stems from its eroticization of abstinence, as previously discussed. But another aspect of the saga that undoubtedly rings true is its representation of our society as a rape culture.

Living in (Vampire) Rape Culture

Like *Dracula*, *Twilight* certainly circulates around an underlying rape script. In fact, a rape script runs throughout the entire saga, with Bella and Edward's romance set in motion when Edward saves Bella from a group of rapists in Port Angeles. Other female characters, namely Rosalie and Esme, are raped and abused by men and similarly saved by vampires. Yet, while human males are coded as rapists (and even the human-wolf hybrid Jacob is guilty of sexual assault), vampires such as Edward and Carlisle are the heroes. This is in sharp contrast to many other vampire texts where the vampire is coded *as* rapist. However, even though Edward is depicted as husband rather than rapist, his romantic heroism certainly involves violent love that is variously represented as crushing and bruising Bella. In the series, the representation of Edward's dangerous desire for Bella, his crushing kisses and bruising love, as well as of Jacob's forced kissed and vice-like hugs, construct Bella as what Rosalind Coward refers to as "the ultimate expression of passive sexuality" (147). *Twilight* is colored particularly by what Coward calls the bruised-lip syndrome, or "an uncontrollable desire (that) has close resemblances with descriptions of rape" (147). Coward also refers to an untouchable syndrome in many male romantic heroes in which the hero is remote and "the heroine alone awakens his desire. The desire he feels for her is so great that he has to come off his pedestal, gather her in his arms and crush her to his chest" (147). In fact, as Coward argues, "the hero's desire is so great that it borders on the uncontrollable" (147). In many romance novels, this translates into either the threat of rape or the inclusion of rape/sexual assault scenes, as it does in *Twilight*.

On Edward's part, his romantic heroism certainly involves a violent type of love — a "bruised-lip syndrome" if you will — that is variously represented as restraining, containing, and hurting Bella. Problematically, the description of their honeymoon certainly has close resemblances with descriptions of rape. The suggestion is that the perennially calm and kind Edward turns fiend in the sack. Edward's transformation in these scenes has generated a particularly spirited array of T-shirts, bumper stickers, and buttons including "BITE my pillows, BUST my headboard, and BRUISE my body any day," "Bite me Edward," "I have OED — obsessive Edward disorder," "Who needs heaven when you have Edward?" and "The Forbidden Fruit Tastes the Sweetest." These extremely popular proclamations reveal that while the series is purportedly promoting an abstinence message, this is not necessarily the message seducing fans. Rather, as sites such as *RavisHim* (or ravish him) and *Robsessed* reveal, Edward (and Robert Pattinson) have become modern-day incarnations of the romantic rake — a literary type that "steals innocence" from the likes of Tess of the d'Urburvilles yet is portrayed as irresistible.

Jacob, the romantic foil, also exhibits his passion in violent format (as will be discussed in more detail later in the chapter). However, when he does so, many fans reject his character. This reaction is unsurprising given that Jacob's actions are clearly sexual assault. Though Edward is described as similarly rough, strong, and forceful in their sexual encounters, the key difference is that Bella desires Edward and their physical relationship is consensual. Thus, fan rejections of Jacob play into a key cultural meme — that of "No means no" and only mutually consensual sexual acts are acceptable. Further, while Edward and Bella discuss their relationship, making mutual decisions about their actions, Jacob instead forces Bella against her will. As he holds her face and forces her to look at him, she tries to yank free, relating that he is "holding too tight, till it hurt" and that she tries to object, only getting out the "N" sound. The text in *Eclipse* thus suggests Bella was about to say "No" (*E* 330).

As this scene reveals, saying no is often not enough to deter unwanted sexual advances. In fact, as many studies have shown, the best tactic is to fight back vigorously rather than to acquiesce. Yet, the myth that nonresistance is the best bet still permeates cultural narratives. This is exactly the tactic Bella opts for in the saga. As she relates, "I pretended I was a statue and waited. Finally, he let go of my face and leaned away" (*E* 331). In real cases of assault, such passive nonresistance often leads to an escalation of the violence. Hence, the message the text sends here — that becoming a statue is your best option — is off the mark. Yet, we can see why this message would be alluring to a female audience inculcated with ideas that girls are weaker, that "girls don't hit," and that playing the role of damsel in distress will protect them. Intriguingly, becoming statue-like is exactly what Edward instructs Bella to do to prevent his own passions from escalating. Thus, he has inadvertently instructed her to be a passive target.

This underlying rape script and focus on sexual violence that permeates the saga is far from unique — indeed, sexual violence is a common part of most romance fiction. While some have claimed this is due to a female penchant for "rape fantasies," many scholars argue, to the contrary, that male violence is so often depicted in fiction not because women fantasize about it, but rather because it is a fact of their lives. Male brutality is so common in texts because it is increasingly common, normal even, in real life. Or, as Katz puts it, "Americans like to boast we're 'the freest country on earth,' yet half the population doesn't even feel free enough to go for a walk at night" (*Macho Paradox* 1).

As Radway describes, "It seems likely that the romance's preoccupation with male brutality is an attempt to understand the meaning of an event that has become almost unavoidable in the real world. The romance may express misogynistic attitudes not because women share them but because they increasingly need to know how to deal with them" (72). While the readers Radway interviewed found "explicit preoccupation with male violence nauseating," she found that when the violence was romanticized it became acceptable, desirable even (76). To be acceptable, Radway contends, the violence must be "clearly traceable to the passion or jealousy of the hero" (76). Indeed, if male violence is portrayed "correctly" (or in a way that readers like rather than reject), it can make the reading experience more pleasurable by providing the comforting message that such violence is spurred by love/lust, or as Radway puts it, readers' "willingness to see male force interpreted as passion" (76). It seems these representations of sexualized violence in a romantic context are also likely bred from readerly desire to justify and come to terms with the rape culture in which they reside.

This idea is not new — in fact, Molly Haskell in a 1976 *Ms. Magazine* article claimed that violent fantasies are not indicative of masochism but rather allow women to come to grips with their anxiety and fear surrounding the prevalence of sexualized violence. In short, romanticizing such violence partly nullifies the ubiquity of rape and assault in the real-world, permitting female readers a "happy ending" in spite of widespread textual (and real world) male violence. As Radway contends, "The process enables a woman to achieve a kind of mastery over her fear of rape because the fantasy evokes her fear and subsequently convinces her that rape is either an illusion or something that she can control" (214). However, this fictionalized presentation of male violence has very real consequences. As Radway notes, it provides a female reader with "a false sense of security by showing her how to rationalize violent male behavior and thus reconcile her to a set of events and relations that she would be better off changing" (216). It further suggests that if females control their sexuality, if they are "good girls," they will lesson the likelihood of being raped. In *Twilight*, the underlying rape script, the whole idea that Edward, Jacob and other males can't control themselves, is redolent of this kind of rape apologist line: If you (females) don't tempt us, you will be fine. But, if you "ask for it" (by walking down dark alleys like Bella or being "too pretty" like Rosalie), then you have only yourselves to blame. In other words, when you are not "good" and don't abide by abstinence, violence happens.

Violence Against Women: Not Just a Twilight *Issue*

While various characters' storylines frame females as targets for male violence, *Twilight* does not present a hard and fast line regarding the issue of violence against women. Some parts of the narrative suggest that women are to blame for the violence done to them, others suggest that the way we construct masculinity inevitability leads to violence. Though the series offers a fairly realistic depiction of the types of violence women face in daily life, it ultimately delivers a message strikingly similar to *Beauty and the Beast*—that the "beauty" can turn the beast into a "prince" if only she loves him enough. But, perhaps the most worrying representations are the abusive relationships Bella has with both Edward and Jacob, and the fact that these relationships are presented in a positive, desirable light that promotes female readers to identify with Bella and yearn for these same types of relationships. In fact, Bella exhibits many of the characteristics common to abused women. She questions what defines normal behavior. She justifies the actions of the males in her life and has difficulty maintaining focus and drive (as when she goes into a catatonic depressive state when Edward leaves). She is negative and full of self-doubt, feels unworthy of love, and justifies or ignores the negative aspects of her romantic relationships. She is loyal to a fault, even though her loyalty in many cases is unfounded.[8] Though Bella certainly seems to be a modern-day Belle, hoping to transform her "beasts" into princes, other female characters offer less rosy pictures of interpersonal violence.

Esme's back-story, provided mainly through Meyer's correspondence with *Twilight Lexicon*, reveals a woman controlled first by her father then by a violent husband. Her aspirations to be a teacher out West were quashed by her dad, who didn't think this plan was "respectable for a lady."[9] Her father pressured her to marry Charles Evenson, but Esme soon discovered that "Charles's public face was very different from his private face; he abused her. Her parents counseled her to be a good wife and keep quiet." When Esme became pregnant, she ran away, living with relatives and working as a teacher. When her son died a few day after birth, "she had nothing left" and jumped off a cliff. Enter Carlisle, who "saved her" by turning her vampire. This story, though it hints at Esme's ability to be independent, ultimately capitulates to the notion that women are all "damsels in distress" needing the likes of Carlisle to save them. Without good males to protect/love them, the story suggests, women will be abused either by controlling fathers or by violent lovers. Their best recourse is to marry a prince and have his babies—as Esme's undying "maternal ache" testifies to.

Rosalie's story shares a controlling father and a violent fiancé, Royce King II, a very wealthy, socially prominent man. A week before their wedding, Rosalie comes across Royce and a group of his friends as she is walking home alone from a friend's house. They beat and rape her, leaving her for dead. Carlisle finds her, and, "not wanting to waste such a young, beautiful life, and thinking she could be a companion for Edward, Carlisle changed her." While the story of her rape is more in keeping with the reality of rape for women than Bella's Port Angeles scene (i.e., most rapes are committed by males known to the female rather than by strangers), Rosalie's story is problematic in that she is framed as largely unsympathetic and shallow. Her gang rape occurs because she is walking alone at night — a common act women are held responsible for in the real world where blaming the victim is ubiquitous. Rather than arguing that Rosalie should be able to walk alone without being attacked, Meyer inserts Carlisle as savior (again). And though Carlisle turns her, without her permission (as is his style), in order to be a mate for his vampire son, Edward (in a heinous form of vampire matchmaking), this is framed as heroic. At least Rosalie is given the ability to seek vengeance on her male attackers — which, as Anne Torkelson argues, "is unique in *Twilight*'s world of submissive, powerless women."[10] Torkelson further reads Rosalie's vengeance as empowering, noting that "though violence against men by women is hardly the solution to rape culture, Rosalie's agency makes a welcome change to Bella's damsel in distress and suicidal antics."

Rosalie is also unique in that she resists Carlisle's matchmaking and chooses Emmett as her mate. Later in the saga, she again rebels against the patriarchal power base of the Cullens, standing against Carlisle and Edward to protect the pregnant Bella. As Torkelson proposes, Rosalie's story "seems to suggest a positive and much needed message that women victims of violence and abuse can survive and reclaim power for themselves." However, as Torkelson concedes, this message is problematized given that "Rosalie only exhibits agency after she has gained superpowers" (n.p.). As a human, like the other women of the saga, she is powerless and under the control of men — she must be made a vampire (by a male!) in order to have any agency. Thus, rather than giving women power in their own right, the saga only affords females power when they become vampires — a change that is most often brought about by the benign patriarch, Carlisle. The solution for sexualized violence is thus not changing the actions of males or the construction of masculinity, but changing females into vampires, who, as will be discussed in what follows, follow the dictates of married monogamy — the true safety net for females according to the *Twilight* saga.

No Pre-Vampire Sex, Or, How to Marry a Vampire

In order to be eligible for this safety net, females need to remain abstinent and repress their sexual desire. While the series vacillates on many of its messages, one area it does not waver in is its representation that marriage before sex is inadmissible. Edward makes this particularly clear despite Bella's continual administrations. And, the fact Bella ends up pregnant on their honeymoon during their first sexual encounter serves as a reminder that if she had her way, she very well might have become pregnant out of wedlock. Further, the dangerous way sex is coded — as causing bruises and broken furniture — suggests that it must be undertaken very cautiously and with the "right" partner. Even then, as Bella's black-and-blue body reveals, sex is a dangerous undertaking. Alas, this does not deter the lusty Bella. She continues to be hot for her icy lover while he wallows in a dejected pool of vampire angst.

Given her desire to hide her bruises, we might read this encounter as leaving the tell-tale signs of domestic violence — signs that women in the real world also often need to hide. As Bella looks in the mirror, noting she is "decorated with patches of blue and purple," she concentrates "on the bruises that would be the hardest to hide" (*BD* 95). Since they are on their honeymoon on a private island, one wonders why she needs to hide these bruises, and, further, why she rather lovingly describes them as "decorations" that "blossom across the pale skin of my arm" (*BD* 89). The answer, of course, is that she needs to hide them from Edward, her controlling lover, so that she can get him to "decorate" her some more. Here again, the saga frames female sexuality as aberrant and damaged, as "asking for it," while Edward, the ultimate male, is "completely, maddeningly in control of himself" (*BD* 103).

It is not until Bella is a vampire that she is allowed to be an equal sex partner — it is then that she and Edward can have sex with "no caution, no restraint. No fear — especially not that. We could love together — both active participants now" (*BD* 482). As this quote reveals, pre-vampire sex (which is coded as premarital sex) is fear-based — the only way to make sex "safe" is to partake in it as a vampire (i.e., as an equal) within the confines of marriage (which of course still confers unequal "protected" status on females — even female vampires). To give Meyer the benefit of the doubt, we might read these depictions as revealing that women are in a lose/lose situation within patriarchy — either they are human sluts (who "deserve to be raped"), or they are angelic vampires (who can only enjoy their sexuality once married).

Watch Out for the Wolf Boy, Or, Why to Choose the White Male Hero

In addition to suggesting that abstinence is the best policy and married monogamy is the happy ending, *Twilight* also problematically frames Native American men as savage beasts — a framing that has historical precedent and links to the sexualization of men of color. As Peter van Lent documents, violent sexuality pervaded captivity narratives with native men framed as dangerous yet desirable noble savages (211). Analyzing the popularity of "Indian Romances," van Lent suggests that turning the native male into a romantic hero both renders his supposed violence sexy and ameliorates the history of colonization. "Loving him," van Lent writes, "a minority and a victim of much we regret — makes American dominant culture feel less guilty" (226). This is why, according to van Lent, native men are often hypersexualized and regularly presented (as is Jacob) with a "heavily muscled torso" (215–16). However, the love such romances portray is decidedly unequal, with the "Native hero who feels unwavering amorous devotion to the white heroine, who, in turn, struggles with the problem of commitment" (221). This description fits *Twilight*, where Jacob is devoted to Bella, yet she struggles with her attraction to him, ultimately choosing to marry her (white) vampire suitor.

Such racial triangles are a recurring staple, and, as with *Twilight*, the white woman (Bella) is presented as the "ultimate prize" for the good white lover (Edward) who the bad darker lover (Jacob) threatens to defile. Dyer reads this framing of the white woman as not only bolstering cultural conceptions of acceptable romantic pairings, but also perpetuating normative ideas about sexuality, race, and gender:

> The white woman is not only the most prized possession of white patriarchy, she is also part of the symbolism of sexuality itself. Christianity associates sin with darkness and sexuality, virtue with light and chastity. With the denial of female sexuality in the late nineteenth and early twentieth century ... sexuality also became associated with masculinity. Men are than seen as split between their baser, sexual, "black" side and their good, spiritual side which is specifically redeemed in Victorian imagery by the chastity of the woman. Thus the extreme figures in this conflation of race and gender stereotypes are the black stud/rapist and the white maiden [*White* 44].

Superimposing Dyer's claims onto *Twilight*, we can read Bella as the prized possession of white patriarchy. Her sexuality is denied and refuted by Edward, who is framed as the rightful sexual decision maker. Edward is able to control his "baser" sexual side via his love for the chaste Bella. Simultaneously, Edward's "black" sexual side is projected onto Jacob, who acts as the "black/stud rapist" who forces himself on Bella, sexually assaulting the "white maiden." Despite her anger, her initial resistance, and her obvious objection and attempts to say no, Jacob *smiles* when all is said and done! Here, Jacob is framed along the lines of the black male rapist, who, according to Winnubst, permeates the U.S. unconscious as nightmare (1).

The image of a "black male raping a white girl," Winnubst argues, has a mythic status that shapes notions of race, class, gender, and sexuality in the United States (2). Examining the trope of the vampire in relation to whiteness, Winnubst explores the history of racism, sexism, homophobia, and anti–Semitism in vampire narratives (7). Of particular interest to our present discussion is how "rapists are designated as 'raced' and how this benefits current constructions of gender and sexuality" (2). According to Winnubst, "It is the white straight male who benefits from demonizing black males and thereby further controlling white women by posing as their protectors (preferably while wearing crucifixes)" — as with *Twilight*, where Edward benefits by demonizing Jacob and framing himself as Bella's protector; and, while he may not wear a crucifix, he is certainly coded as a Christian/Mormon (as the next chapter will assert) (10). Conversely, Jacob is coded as a rapist — a representation with deep-seated historical resonance. As Katz maintains, "The images of the dark-skinned man as a threat to white women — and a threat to social order more generally — has been used for centuries by whites to justify all manner of racist social controls" (*Macho Paradox* 134).

If we believe Winnubst's claim that "sex and violence become the sites at which gender and race are negotiated," we might read *Twilight* as perpetuating various norms about all of these notions, namely, sex is dangerous (especially for females), violence is a result of failing to police one's sexuality or deter desiring beasts (i.e., wolves), gender needs to be policed so that proper relationships between strong men and passive women ensue, and race is something that — like gender — needs to be strictly regulated — especially considering the lustful tendencies of "dark" men. In regards to racialized sexuality, it is important to note that while Edward's sexuality is described as even more violent than Jacob's, his violence is depicted as sexy while Jacob's is framed as abhorrent. Though the consensual aspect is key here, so is the history of what types of men are allowed to be violent and what types of male violence are traditionally considered sexy — in short, white men's violence is often framed as heroic (think Rambo), while raced violence is savage and dangerous (think Western films, the nightmare of the black rapist, etc.).

In keeping with these precedents, *Twilight* frames Jacob as guilty. Though he promises, "I would never, never hurt you, Bella," indeed he does, and readers are encouraged to condemn Jacob (as many fans do). Instead of examining the wider cultural contexts that make such acts of sexual assault common, readers are able to place all blame comfortably at Jacob's doorstep. This also has the advantage of elevating Edward in their eyes, reaffirming the good guy/bad guy binary.[11] Such a clear-cut depiction is certainly alluring to readers, as it suggests that they, in their real lives, will be able to tell the difference between potential Edwards and Jacobs. Unfortunately, as noted above, the depiction is also laden with racial connotations, suggesting that white guys are the better choice (as will be further explored in chapter 7).

Additionally, *Twilight* falls into the trap of idealizing white females as "poster virgins" who are "young, good-looking, straight, and white" (Valenti 44). Simultaneously, the saga depicts women of color as *naturally* a part of a sexually violent culture where indigenous wolf-men are liable to scratch one's face off (via the narrative of Sam and Emily). While it is true that indigenous women are disproportionately victims of interpersonal violence, the saga serves to reinforce what Valenti names "a disturbing cultural narrative ... that 'innocent' white girls are being lured into an over sexualized culture, while young black women are already part of it" (47). Rather than examining the legacy of colonization and how this leads to inflated levels of violence in communities of color (and how white men are the perpetrators of much of this violence),

Meyer's saga shows Bella as at risk when with Jacob (the wolf of color) but safe with Edward, who ironically has far more potential to harm Bella and who is far more regularly domineering toward her.

First Comes Love, Then Comes Marriage

While the saga's undercurrent of sexual desire and frequent spicy scenes can certainly make for exciting reading for the young adult audience at which the books are aimed, it does not necessarily do much for all those young girls who are given abstinence-only education by day and bombarded with hyper-sexualized imagery via popular culture at night. Rather, it wraps up the same contradictory messages in a new vampire package — be like the virginal human Bella but think about sex all the time. Given that the United States has the highest rate of teen pregnancy and abortion in the industrialized world, as well as the highest rate of teen STDs and inordinately high numbers of violence in teen relationships, *Twilight*'s failure to even once mention contraception/protection in it's pages let alone explore the underlying causes of sexualized violence is disappointing. Granted, it's fiction, and we cannot expect (nor should we necessarily desire) that fiction be instructive. However, we must remember that such fiction certainly shapes how we behave in the real world and, especially for females, frames the type of romance/sex we desire — as the work of Radway and Modleski makes clear.

As Radway determines, readers don't react well to the suggestion that "sexual passion is not always earth-shattering or even necessary to a strong and stable relationship"; they don't want books that suggest "the romantic dream is an illusion" or that "women ought to lower their expectations and rest content with lesser men" (177–78). Rather, females' reading of romance promotes what they are told by the wider culture, that "their very worth as individuals is closely tied to their sexual allure and physical beauty" and, as they are taught by their families, churches, and via abstinence-only sex education, "their sexual being may be activated only by and for one other individual" (177). This narrow definition of female sexuality, as Levin and Kilbourne testify, and "encourages girls to focus heavily on appearance and sex appeal" while simultaneously making gender roles "increasingly polarized and rigid" (5). This increasing polarization takes place in a society still governed by a compulsory heterosexuality that "accepts as a given the institutions of heterosexuality and monogamous marriage" (Radway 213). Yet, as Radway sees it, the need for this ritual retelling of the heterosexual romance is in itself "a symptom of the ongoing instability of the heterosexual solution to the oedipal dilemma, that is, as a ritual effort to convince its readers that heterosexuality is both inevitable and natural and that it is necessarily satisfying as well" (14). Narratives in which "heterosexuality can create a fully coherent, fully satisfied, female subjectivity" are thus at the service of traditional patriarchy and eroticize the message that married monogamy allows for the true (and safe) awakening of female sexuality (Radway 14).

Indeed, the goal of romance, as Radway aptly defines it, is for the heroine to achieve "oceanic merging with a nurturant, heterosexual lover"—a merging that *Breaking Dawn* certainly presents (153). The trickle-down effect of the saga further frames heterosexual romance as the only possibility, as evidenced, for example, in Gresh's *The Twilight Companion*. At the outset of the "romance quiz," she addresses her readers as follows: "I assume that you are a female" (or, in other words, *the* audience for such a quiz) (184). "If not," Gresh writes, "just pretend for the purposes of this test that you are a girl"—yes, because we wouldn't want to suggest that males may be interested in *Twilight* and certainly *not* that anyone is harboring same-sex desires (184).[12] Gresh's heteronormative bolstering of the saga can be summed-up via lines such as "given that I've already mentioned that Bella and Edward have a baby in *Breaking Dawn*, it's obvious that the two also get married in the book"—yes, because obviously marriage is the *only* option and babies *only* arrive *after* marriage (236). Thus, not much has changed since Snitow's 1983 summation of the romance: "The heroine is not involved in any overt adventure beyond trying to respond appropriately to male energy without losing her virginity. Virginity is a given here; sex means marriage and marriage, promised at the end, means, finally, there can be sex" (135). *Twilight* differs slightly in that Bella sexually pursues Edward, yet, as his rules win out, it is true that there is no sex in the series until the two are married. Thus, although the series importantly gives Bella sexual agency, Edward sets the rules for the relationship. Moreover, Jacob, the wolf of color, is problematically framed as a sexual beastie.

Chapter 6

The Soul of the Vampire

Sparkly Mormons, Female Eves, and Unconverted Wolves

John Krakauer, in his bestselling expose on Mormonism, *Under the Banner of Heaven*, argues that "there is a dark side to religious devotion that is too often ignored or denied. As a means of motivating people to be cruel or inhumane — as a means of inciting evil, to borrow the vocabulary of the devout — there may be no more potent force than religion" (xxi). Bertrand Russell similarly asserts that "every single bit of progress in humane feeling" and "every moral progress, has been consistently opposed by the organized churches of world"; he names religion "a disease born of fear and as a source of untold misery to the human race" (24). While *Twilight* certainly doesn't aim to promote inhumanity or incite evil, it nevertheless has a shadow side underlying its more glittery representations of first love — an underlying religious script that is undoubtedly colored by much of the anti-woman, pro-patriarchy, sexual Puritanism that shapes the religion of its author. Though religious readers no doubt see this as a plus, the hidden nature of this potent force that informs the narrative begs examining.

If religion is such a good thing, and if Mormonism is as wonderful as the author's devotion to it suggests, why must the fervent religious foundation of the saga be not only silenced in the text, but also only tepidly endorsed (and sometimes vehemently denied) by the author and many fans? Further, given a general turn in the direction of the religious right witnessed in U.S. culture in the era of *Twilight*'s release dates, as well as its championing of one currently popular strand of religious tenet — the championing of abstinence — it is somewhat unexpected that the saga and the fandom go to such lengths to pretend the lure of the story is not rooted in a deep religiosity. However, as the United States has had a historically contradictory relationship with belief — pretending on the one hand to be a profoundly secular society while radically departing from its claims of separation of church and state on the other, *Twilight*'s contradictory attitude toward religion is perhaps best viewed as a reflection of America's own vacillating stance toward belief.

While most polls show that 90 percent of Americans believe in God, the United States still has a reputation as a secular nation (Krakauer 68). This is conceivably related to America's view of itself as a society championing intellect and reason. Faith, as Krakauer asserts, "is the very antithesis of reason," and, as such, it does not gel with so much Americans hold dear — logic, pragmatism, common sense (xxiii). And though our recent federal and state budgets belie the claim that we are a country that cares about education, we certainly have a long and deep-seated devotion to valuing intellect. Yet, as Krakauer reminds us, "faith, by its very definition, tends to be impervious to intellectual argument or academic criticism" (68). Religion thus does not sit well with our societal championing of individual self-reliance nor with America's cultural deference for edification. Even so, the United States is a nation steeped in religiosity.

Mormonism as an American Faith

Perhaps no religion is more American than Mormonism. Just as America presents itself as the only true democracy, so, too, does Mormonism claim to be the world's only true religion (Krakauer 4). This is not to say that most faiths don't claim such veracity, but rather to suggest that Mormonism justifies its status as true and good in much the same way America has historically justified its own tenets and actions— with recourse to reason, to historical "truth," to manifest destiny. Fawn M. Brodie, whose book, *No Man Knows My History: The Life of Joseph Smith*, is considered paradigmatic, describes Mormonism as a "potpourri of American religious thinking spiced with the fundamental ideal of inevitable progress" (380). And this "progress," as she notes, is very much about economic progress, or "the goal of perpetual prosperity" (ix). Saturated with what Brodie names "the Yankee enthusiasm for earthly blessings," Mormonism energetically identifies God "with material prosperity," so much so that Brodie names this as "the most vigorous tradition transmitted by Joseph Smith" (ix, 402). Noting that Mormonism considers wealth and power a basic blessing of both earth and heaven, her biography of Smith reveals him to be your classic Horatio Alger (188). He came from a very poor family — indeed his penning of the Book of Mormon was in part aimed at preventing foreclosure of the family farm (Brodie 18, 55). A tremendous salesman with a shady history working as a money digger and diviner, Krakauer indicates that "he could sell a muzzle to a dog" (55–56). From humble, dubious beginnings, Smith tenaciously climbed economic and status ladders to become a revered prophet and founder of one of the world's wealthiest religions. Supposedly revering the U.S. Constitution "as a divinely ordained document," Smith ran for president in 1844 (Krakauer 107). Though he never held public office, his standing as a living prophet and renowned leader places him alongside other American icons that used their wits to achieve the so-called American dream.

At the time of Mormonism's founding, the United States was gripped by an era of extreme religious experimentation, known as the Second Great Awakening, a time that Krakauer describes as a "super-heated, anything-goes religious climate" (55). Mormonism, Brodie further explains, "is drawn directly from the American frontier, from the impassioned revivalist sermons, the popular fallacies of Indian origin, and the current political crusades" (69). Springing from the milieu of frontier America, "Mormonism's strictures and soothing assurances— its veneration of *order* — beckoned as a refuge from the complexity and manifold uncertainties of nineteenth-century America" (113). Indeed, we might surmise that the current surge in Mormonism (it's one of the world's fastest-growing religions) and the concomitant popularity of a fictional saga so steeped in the tenets of the faith, speaks to the complexity and manifold uncertainties of *twenty-first-century* America in similar ways. While some have described the twentieth century as "unprecedentedly secular," the twenty-first is thus far steeped in religiosity (Gordon and Hollinger 3). From the long war in Iraq and Afghanistan, to our increasingly knotty ties with Israel, from our federal government support of abstinence-only education and the Global Gag Rule to our battles over same-sex marriage (as with California's controversial 2009 Proposition 8), the United States is currently embroiled in all sorts of actions and legislations that have religious convictions at their core. Though this turn to a more overtly religious society can be traced to the late twentieth century and the double term of the profoundly religious president George W. Bush, the ramifications of his religiosity are still playing themselves out in the Obama era.

In terms of *Twilight*, we must remember that Meyer penned the saga during Bush's reign, at a time when federally funded religious belief was at an all-time high, when the nation fetishized virginity as it had not since the Victorian age, and when legislation trying to mandate homophobia into law was proposed in numerous states. We must also be cognizant of the fact that the author is a devout Mormon and admits that "unconsciously, I put a lot of my basic beliefs into the story."[1] Whether "unconscious" or not, many of the "basic beliefs" of her Mormon faith saturate the saga. In addition to incorporating tenets to do with sexuality, such as Mormonism's insistence that premarital sex is not only sinful but also an act that can lead to eternal exclusion from the "celestial kingdom" of heaven, the saga also includes general Mormon notions such as the championing of obedience to authority and a respect for industriousness and ongoing edification.[2] Yet, Mormon scholar Margaret Toscano argues that Meyer subverts Mormon dogma in two distinct ways—first, she puts love before obedience, and second, she rejects the notion of moral purity maintained by exclusion (21). Detailing five Mormon themes that recur in the saga (the importance of free will, eternal marriage and family, the Mormon concept of heaven and hell, the literalness of the supernatural, and the divine destiny of humans), Toscano's essay asserts that Meyer also "re-interprets Mormon doctrine" and does not, contrary to some claims, "simply and uncritically [import] Mormon ideas wholesale into her work" (21–22).

Though Bella's virginity is framed as a life-or-death matter, and equated to the potential loss of Edward's soul, Meyer privileges love over obedience to authority — a departure from Mormon tenets. While Bella is chastised for disobeying male authority in the text, especially that of Charlie and Edward, her rebelliousness leads to a happy ending. Bella's life (and morality) are put at risk, yet her character, a modern Eve, reveals that "evil must be experienced in order to become truly good" (Tosacano 34). Further, Mormonism's much different conception of the Fall, which sees it as fortunate, is played out in Bella as an Eve who must "fall" in order to experience her happy ending. Mormons also believe God was once human and suggest God, Jesus, and Adam were permutations of the same being (we can see this through Edward as a character who takes on the role of all three). In keeping with this fine line between male and god, a male is believed to have the possibility of becoming a full-fledged god in the afterlife who can be "the ruler of his very own world" (Krakauer 83). In the texts, we might see Carlisle as this male/god, ruling over own his own immortal kingdom on earth. Here, in her exultation of divine, heroic males, Meyer is in line with, rather than resistant to, her Mormon belief. However, her depiction of Bella as an equal (or even as superior) to Edward and Carlisle in *Breaking Dawn* suggests females also deserve to be full-fledged (vampire) gods. Yet, while the saga subverts Mormon tenets in certain regards, in others it stays true to the faith.

Not only are males conceived as supreme, though; so is the white race. Though Mormons no longer hold to the "divinely ordained supremacy of the white race," the echoes of this belief still infiltrate the Church and certainly can account for the divinely white Cullens, who are the saga's heroes (Krakauer 83). Likewise, the clearly delineated demarcations between good and evil link to the Mormon tenet that "there are two churches only; one is the church of the Lamb of God, and the other is the church of the devil" (Krakauer 69). Bella, through her alignment with Edward, is able to become a "lamb of God" (or, in other words, a Mormon), while the Volturi and renegade vampires are clearly aligned with the "church of the devil." And, just as there "was an appealing simplicity to the book's central message, which framed existence as an unambiguous struggle between good and evil," so, too, does *Twilight*'s unambiguous framing of the Cullens as good and the Volturi as evil appeal to an audience eager to immerse themselves in a story devoid of the ambiguity of modern life. Finally, the Mormon's disdain for abortion and homosexuality is evident in Bella's insistence that terminating her pregnancy is *not* an option and the saga's general erasure (and disdain) for anything but married, heterosexual, reproductive monogamy. Just as Mormon couples have a sacred duty to have children, so does Carlisle "give birth" to a Mormon family; Bella, the newest family member, carries on this tradition, giving birth to a daughter able to heal the divide between saints and gentiles.

While Mormonism is sometimes viewed as an extreme religion, or even a fanatical one, many of its beliefs and practices are very in keeping not only with mainstream Christianity but also with mainstream America: work hard, value education, honor your parents, get married, have kids, do good works. Indeed, we might place *Twilight*'s popularity as similar in scope to the popularity of the Mormon religion itself—a religion that, as Brodie and Krakauer argue, speaks to the popular tenets of Americanism. When Krakauer argues that Mormonism is "so thoroughly American" that "God lets it be known that the Garden of Eden had been located in America," he might just as well be speaking of *Twilight*—which is so thoroughly American as to replant the story of Genesis on the Olympic coastline, apple and all (Krakauer 70).

Given Meyer's devout Mormonism, the religious traces of the saga are not surprising. What is surprising, though, is her use of a vampire/wolf/human triad to explore religious mythos. Noting she is regularly asked, "What's a nice Mormon girl like you doing writing about vampires?" Meyer reveals she is aware of this seeming contradiction. Though vampires are very steeped in religious mythology, Mormonism as a religion tends to steer clear of these more monstrous notions—it is, if you well, a PG version of Christian mythos, devoid of succubi and other female beasties. Focusing instead on what Dijkstra names the "holy trinity of womanhood—mother, wife, and daughter," Mormonism, like *Twilight*, focuses on the angel side of the angel/whore dichotomy (64). More prosaically, as the faithful are not allowed to watch R movies, use profanity, or partake in "aberrant" sexual practices such as oral sex or masturbation (more on this later), it is unexpected for a Mormon author to take up vampires—historically sexual and R-rated creatures—as her focus of choice.

Vampires as Religious Outsiders

Alas, the supposedly soul-less vampire is given a new twist in the *Twilight* series. Founding vampire mythos claims a demon mated with a human and produced a vampire. *Twilight* vampires, in contrast, have no such sordid sexual past. Rather, the Cullens are born as a result of religious persecution. In the saga, their bloodlust and social ostracization can be read as a metaphor for the prejudice religious outsiders, such as Mormons, face. Rather than the more traditional representation of the vampire as evil, the saga enacts what can be read as a vampiric quest for salvation. While in Stoker, Dracula seduces other men's women and, by extension, threatens the foundations of patriarchy generally and Christianity in particular, in *Twilight*, the Cullen vampires are the saviors who seemingly have the potential to rid humanity of its evil ways. Taking on the role of the evil count are both the Volturi and the wolves—it is these two heretical groups that threaten the missionary work of the Cullen vampires with Edward functioning as a virtual Christ, saving Bella from her human sins.

Carlisle is the son of a Anglican pastor who, in 17th-century London, led vampire hunts. Not only can his father's intent to persecute vampires be linked to the saga's conflation of vampires *as* Mormon (more on this later), but also it is significant that Carlisle, ultimate patriarch of the Cullen clan, was born during a time of extreme religious persecution. At first cooperating with his father's vampire jihad, Carlisle is attacked by a blood-sucker one fateful evening in the London sewers.[3] Given the likelihood that his own father would kill him, Carlisle goes into hiding for several days. Once he emerges, he still lives in virtual exile, first with the Volturi then as a doctor in New England. This meme of having to hide one's true self is of course resonant in relation to Mormon history — Mormons had to hide their polygamous practices specifically and their more "extreme" religious practices generally. As Brodie notes in her biography of Smith, "Few episodes in American religion history parallel the barbarism of the anti–Mormon persecutions" (130). These persecutions forced Mormon migration westward — much like the Cullens' forced exile to the western corner of United States. Historically, Mormons were variously attacked by mobs, by the media and by the government. Eventually, their founder was murdered. As Brodie emphasizes, "Wherever the Mormons went, the citizens resented their self-righteousness, their unwillingness to mingle with the world, their intense consciousness of superior destiny" (380). Here, the resentment toward Mormons seems to echo that directed toward the Cullens in Meyer's saga. As evidenced in the Forks high school cafeteria scenes, other students resent the Cullens' aloofness. The Cullens are viewed suspiciously by the town's human inhabitants; they are "outsiders, clearly not accepted," according to Bella (*T* 22).

Besides the general disdain humans have toward the Cullens, they are also persecuted by other vampires— or, symbolically, by other people of faith. If we read the Volturi as representing Roman Catholics (as religious scholar John Granger does), we might surmise that the Volturi are so intent on policing the Cullens because they represent a threat not only to vampire existence but also to the power of older, established religions. Their new "vampire Mormonism," if you will, threatens the Volturi's power, much like modern Mormonism threatens to topple the stronghold on belief of other major religious players, Catholicism being one of them. This equation between vampirism and religious persecution is rendered overt in *New Moon*, as when Alice informs Bella of the legend of the Christian missionary who drove vampires from Volterra (438). The people of Volterra commemorate their safe, vampire-free city in the very celebration Edward plans to expose himself during— suggesting on the one hand that vampires are not the trouble-makers they are made out to be and, on the other, that vampires (as stand-in Mormons) are *still* persecuted, as Edward is by the Volturi.

The Cullens, and Edward in particular, also nurture a sense of persecution to their benefit — a practice in keeping with Mormon identity. They are able to excuse their wealthy, exclusive existence using the justification that they are disbarred from human society. As such, they become martyrs rather than gluttons, saints rather than sinners. We might read Edward, who insists on viewing himself as a monster even though his "vegetarian" ways frame him as saintly, as a vampiric Joseph Smith — a man who Brodie argues "learned to use persecution as a means of identifying himself with the great martyrs" (88). Edward's decision to leave Forks for Bella's sake in *New Moon* is in keeping with this persecution meme — he martyrs himself for Bella, much like Smith ultimately gave up his life for his followers (and that Smith did so to hide the damning polygamous practices of his brethren might be linked to Edward's attempts to hide his love for Bella *and* to protect his family's vampire identity).

Brodie contends that Smith knew "persecution was inevitable as the sunrise, and to it the only answer was power" (258). Carlisle and Edward seem to know this as well. They amass power via wealth and degrees as well as by expanding their coven in number. Might we also read Meyer, though, as seeking a similar sort of power via the mainstreaming of her fictional saga? Through it, she has been able not only to amass personal wealth, but also to bring a new level of awareness to (and mainstreaming of) Mormonism. Just as Smith "saw to it that the sufferings of his people received national publicity," is Meyer seeing to it that her growing cadre of fans will see the condemnation of her faith as unjustified (Brodie 259)? Though Mormonism is coded in the text rather than overt, and though I am not suggesting Meyer consciously set out to write a Mormon reclamation, I think the textual explorations of the persecuted Cullens clearly resonate with the historical persecution of her faith.

Further, the saga's interest in salvation more generally points to a narrative that is profoundly concerned with matters of the soul. From the Genesis narrative that frames *Twilight* to the ultimate battle that closes *Breaking Dawn* (and is redolent of the epic battles in The Book of Mormon as well as in the Christian Bible), the saga is infused with religious underpinnings throughout. Though Bella claims to be "fairly devoid of belief" in *New Moon,* her faith in Edward, and her insistence he has a soul, belies this claim. Edward and Carlisle both believe in God, heaven, and hell — but only Carlisle believes "there is an afterlife for our kind" (*NM* 37). Though Edward insists that evolution is a rather preposterous explanation for existence, thus revealing his belief that vampires were created by God, he thinks vampires have lost their souls. This is his motivation for not wanting to turn Bella. However, Bella later calls him on this, insisting he doesn't truly believe in eternal damnation.

Whether or not Edward will admit he believes vampires have souls, he is certainly intent on saving Bella's *human* soul. Much of his insistence they remain abstinent is framed in this pursuit specifically, while his desire to rid the world of its evil ways more generally frames him as a Christ-like savior. In *Twilight*, he rescues Bella from Tyler's errant van, offers Volvo-driven salvation of her purity in Port Angeles, and sucks James' venom from her bloodstream to save her life. In *New Moon,* his voice protects her from her destructive inclinations with motorbikes, and then his spirit offers comfort as she nearly drowns after her infamous cliff-jump. In *Eclipse,* he protects her from Victoria, beheading the virtual Medusa in a move more Perseus- than Christ-like. Finally, in *Breaking Dawn,* Edward injects venom into her heart in a final act of "salvation"—turning her into a vampire as she is about to die. Granger argues this transition represents the conversion from gentile to LDS, noting Mormons "believe that when a non–Mormon is baptized into the Church, the convert's Gentile blood is cleansed from their body and they are given a new internal makeup" (159). Smith and Brigham Young both spoke of this as purging of blood, explaining that conversion cleansed Gentile blood from the system and replaced it with Mormon blood. In Bella's case, human (i.e., non–Mormon) blood is replaced with vampire venom. As the goal for Mormons is to gain divinization, we might read the conversion to vampire as offering eternal life or, in Mormon terms, eternal salvation.

Though Granger argues that the saga functions in the main as a Mormon religious screed, his work also contends that the saga is so popular as it offers a more general ode to faith. Arguing that *Twilight* is as popular as it is "because it smuggles the core religious message of the Western tradition, the Fall of man and his return to union with God through His Word," Granger acts as a sort of *Twilight* prophet in his own right, vociferously insisting the saga is about "our life with God," which he names as "the central drama and relationship of human existence" (146–47, 76). Though I disagree with Granger that "we seem to have been designed for the pursuit of myth and self-transcendent experience more than we are for either rational thinking or watching television," I do admit that the saga itself, whether consciously or not, functions as a fictional quest for transcendence (218). Granger bases his writing on Mercea Eliade's claim that in secular culture, literature serves a religious and mythic function (xi). While literature *can* serve this function, I differ with Granger on his insistence that all fiction inherently serves faith as well as with his claim that readers *want* it to do so (141). I don't know about you, but I am not in pursuit of "God's love for man" when I pick up a book like *Twilight* (86). But if, as Granger contends, books "foster our spiritual growth and transformation," for those so inclined, what kind of "fostering" does *Twilight* offer (20)?

A Morality Lesson for Females: Advancing Patriarchy via Mormon Vampires and Evangelical "Morality"

Just as the Mormon church is "piloted by over one hundred middle-aged, elderly men who are its spiritual leaders," so, too, are the vampires (and werewolves) of the saga piloted by men (Laake 13). While American culture is generally patriarchal, Mormon culture is more specifically so—the right of male rule is thoroughly coded in both its scripture and its practice. A Mormon lesson manual for boys explains it this way: "The patriarchal order is of divine origin and will continue throughout time and eternity. There is, then, a reason why men, women and children should understand this order and this authority in the households of the people of God.... It is not merely a question of who is perhaps best qualified. Neither is it wholly a question of who is living the most worthy life. It is a question largely of law and order" (Laake 40). There you have it — it doesn't matter how admirable or capable you are, it merely matters that you are male. This never-ending "divine" order is echoed in *Twilight* not only in the vampire and wolf society, but also in the human world. Schools, hospitals, law enforcement — all are represented as having men at the helm. The patriarchal underpinning of Mormonism is of course not unique — it is in fact rooted in much scripture, including the Old and New Testament. This patriarchal foundation, according to Laake and others, results in a male-led church where "dissent isn't tolerated" (Krakauer 31). In this institution women learn that men are "the heir to the patriarchal order and would be the head of our house" (Laake 167). This leadership of home and family extends well beyond the everyday though. Indeed, men learn they will become gods in the next life "capable of creating and ruling their own worlds" (Laake 40). This afterworld belief, enforced every Sunday, has a place for female goddesses, too— they will be allowed to bear their husbands' spirit children for all eternity (Laake 40). As in life, men will rule, and women will mother.

This structure is echoed in Meyer's saga with all primary leadership roles held by men. Carlisle, Aro, Sam, and Charlie are each patriarchs ruling their own little kingdoms. In contrast, women are "the wives," who are like the females of the Volturi world that "never leave the tower" (or figuratively don't get to leave the panopticon of patriarchal power).[4] Sure, Bella may be a "queen" by the series' end, but she is still firmly ensconced in a world ruled by men. Further, her power is dependent on her role as Edward's wife and Renesmee's mother. Bella's power derives from these roles— as does women's power generally within the Mormon church. As Granger puts it, "The moral of Bella's story is that of the faithful Mormon wife. By adhering to the law of chastity until marriage, by fidelity to her man, and by giving birth to children," she is able to become "a super-powered near immortal" (205).

Back in the real world, males hold the Mormon priesthood from the age of twelve, which brings with it the literal power to act for God, but women are excluded from the priesthood.[5] Wives are expected to be fully obedient and can only get to heaven through a man. And, as late as 1987, Mormon leader Ezra Taft Benson declared that "contrary to conventional wisdom, a woman's calling is in the home, not the marketplace" (Laake 235). Though *Twilight* allows Alice stock-market savvy and gives Rosalie mechanic skills, for the most part it suggests a woman's calling is still in the home (as discussed in chapter 4). In fact, we might surmise that women are given a modicum of skill and independence due to the cultural context from which Meyer is writing — a society that claims to be "post-feminist," or that likes to pay lip service to the fact that the battle for women's liberation has been won.[6]

Yet, even within the Mormon church, a decidedly nonfeminist institution, there has been much rumbling in recent decades regarding male privilege and female subservience. Laake's book documents these rumblings, noting that as the civil rights era dawned, church leaders scrambled to justify male rule and to frame feminism as a blight upon the church and all it stood for. Noting that her father often told her that "the women's movement was Satan's way of trying to weaken the family," Laake recounts reading church magazines such as *The Improvement Era* and *The Ensign* only to find very anti-woman pieces. In 1964, Mormon leader David McKay urged, "No other success can compensate for failure in the home" (72). Yet, as Laake documents, the messages became more alarming by 1972, when "the rhetoric had heightened, at least partially in response to feminism" (129–130). For example, Thomas Monson's "Women's Movement: Liberation or Deception?" claimed, "So long as Mormon women cling to the simple ideal of home and joyous family life, so long as they feel the measure of their creation is homemaker ... so long is the church and nation safe" (130). Monson labeled women who pursued careers and independence as "the Pied Pipers of sin who have led women away from the divine role of womanhood down the pathway of error" and encouraged women to accept three challenges for the 1970s: "Sustain your husband.... Strengthen your home.... Serve your God" (Laake 130).[7] As Krakauer contends, "Over the years the Mormon leadership has made numerous pronouncements about the 'dangers' of the feminist movement and has excommunicated several outspoken feminists" (24). Perhaps Mormonism's most lasting legacy in relation to feminism in the current era is its defeat of the Equal Rights Amendment. As is widely documented, the church very effectively motivated Mormons to vote as a block against ratification of the ERA, a move that many agree prevented the amendment from what had previously looked to be easy ratification. Much like their recent forays into passing Proposition 8 in California in 2009, the bill that would have legalized same-sex marriage in the state, LDS involvement in politics tends to favor the patriarchal, heteronormative status quo — a status quo that leaves females as the handmaidens of the church (and society).

In *Twilight*, we can see the echoes of the earlier antifeminist pronouncements as well as the more recent political actions enshrining marriage as that between a man (as fully functioning human/potential god) and wife (as subservient helpmeet). For example, Renee is framed as a relative failure due to her divorce, while those like Esme, who "cling to the simple ideal of home and joyous family life," are rewarded. In addition to falling in line with Mormonism's views of the female role, *Twilight*'s messages regarding gender are also in keeping with another powerful religious block in the United States—the Evangelical Christians. As K. J. Swanson explores in her work, Evangelicals have largely embraced *Twilight*, seeing it as offering particularly good messages for adolescent females. As Swanson remarks, "The majority of Evangelical response to *Twilight* has been one of praise for its morality" (n.p.). In fact, there are already a smattering of full-length Evangelical Christian reads of the saga including *Touched by a Vampire, Escaping the Vampire,* and *The Twilight Phenomenon.* Different from John Granger's religious treatise on the saga, these texts do not so much set out to explore all the religious themes and messages of Meyer's work, but rather to survey what the saga has to offer in terms of morality lessons for females. Swanson identifies four categories of praise common amongst such books in which the authors (1) appreciate the saga's messages about resisting sexual temptation and remaining chaste, (2) emphasize the nobility of the male protector while championing female passivity, silence, subservience, and beauty, (3) present love as sacrifice, framing females as the ones who need to make the sacrifices, and (4) celebrate the victory over sinful nature, framing sex as sinful and female sexuality as not to be trusted. While Swanson admits that such concerns are not new for the Evangelical book market — indeed she notes that evangelicals have been trying to answer the question of what it means to be female for years— she illustrates that *Twilight*'s popularity has provided a new and booming market of "instructional guides to help readers personify authentic femininity."

In what Swanson terms a *theology of sexuality*, such books display basic distrust of female sexuality and enforce power differentials in male/female relationships that normalize male sexual aggression. Thus, while Mormons and Evangelicals surely do not agree on everything, they do seem to concur regarding the dangers of the feminine. And *Twilight*, for the most part, seems to gel with their shared notion that a female's place is next to (or beneath) a man. As both belief systems ascribe to divinely ordained patriarchy, it is hardly surprising that their worldviews are far from woman friendly.

However, even the most male-privileging of beliefs still have feminists in their ranks— and Mormonism is no exception. Indeed, as self-defined Mormon feminist Maxine Hanks argues, "It makes sense that Mormon women would be feminists: within male centered religion and discourse, feminism and feminist theology are necessary" (xi). Hanks, along with Jana Riess and Holly Welker, are feminist Mormon scholars who have responded to the series, with Hanks being the most complimentary and Reiss and Welker being more critical. While Reiss argues we need to be "concerned about the regressive gender stereotypes" (9), Welker notes the series is a product of "really gross Mormon ideas about gender" (6). Hanks, on the other hand, contends that *Twilight* speaks to a Mormon feminist sensibility and asserts that Meyer promotes and enacts feminist theology via her authorship.

While I agree with Riess and Walker that the series is certainly problematic in regards to its bolstering of gender norms, I also concur with Hanks that Meyer is no antifeminist — or, as Toscano puts it, Meyer "is no assertive feminist, but she is also not simply a 'Mormon housewife' who unthinkingly accepts and regurgitates LDS Church Dogma" (21). Via its focus on female characters and the suggestion that they share power with the male (vampire) leaders, the saga echoes the long battles within the church for women to share the priesthood as well as to resist male leadership and pro-polygamy arguments. For example, Emma Smith, Joseph's first wife, was widely reported to be very headstrong and rather vociferously opposed polygamy (more on this later). Others note that the feminine deity basic to Mormon theology presents the possibility of a more woman-friendly religion. However, as the "mother in heaven" is a shadowy and elusive figure in Mormon theology, a feminist-friendly religious practice has not come to pass (Wilcox 3). Rather, Mormons grow up singing "Oh my Father," and contemporary leaders do not encourage worship of the heavenly mother (Wilcox 12). Rather, the idea of a female god seems mainly to have resulted in a trickle-down from "mother in heaven" to motherhood as an exalted role on earth. Thus, while John Granger contends that Mormon women have it better than other females of faith due to their conception of God the Mother, this elusive deity has not brought about much real-world power for women. Similarly, the Mormon conception of Adam and Eve's expulsion from heaven as a fortunate fall has done little to empower modern-day Eves.

Bella's Fortunate Fall: The Vampire Eve

Unlike most branches of Christianity, Mormons view the fall as a necessary progression that allowed for the experience of life in a physical body, the right to choose between good and evil, the opportunity to gain eternal life, and the ability to experience joy. Eve's role thus presents the possibility of being conceived less as the cause of man's fall from grace and more as a conduit through which humanity was allowed joyful corporeal existence. However, given Mormonism's strong patriarchal ideology and insistence that women's primary roles are that of wife and mother, as a religion, Mormonism has not (at least not in formal doctrine or within mainstream Mormonism practices) become strongly Eve — or woman — positive. We might, though, read Bella as a modern Eve who does (by saga's end) wield a great deal of power, becoming a superheroine vampire of sorts. Indeed, Meyer's texts encourage a reading of Bella *as* Eve. For example, the first time Bella encounters Edward in biology class, she wonders why Edward seems so tense around her, noting, "He didn't know me from Eve" (*T* 24). In addition to the Genesis quote that opens the first book of the series, an unbitten apple famously bedecks the cover, Alice throws away an "unbitten apple" the first time Bella sees her, and Bella toys with but does not bite an apple while eating with Edward in the cafeteria (*T* 19). This first text in the saga thus sets Bella up as an *obedient* Eve. Yet, as the saga continues, we might read Bella's decision to enter the world of vampires and werewolves as representing her "fall" from human innocence. After she kisses Edward in a decidedly Eden-like meadow, she experiences all that Mormons associate with the fortunate fall—physicality, joy, free agency, and, by the close of the saga, eternal life. The super–Eve status she attains in *Breaking Dawn* is not achieved before her due penance in childbirth, though. Just as in the Bible where God tells Eve, "I will greatly increase your pains in childbearing," so does *Twilight* give us a Bella/Eve who suffers great pains not only during birthing, but also throughout her pregnancy (Genesis 3:16). Thus, the series presents us with a newfangled Eve that is less willful/sinful than the biblical Eve, but one who still endures hardship/pain so that she might experience eternal life—she is a martyr Eve in a sense, one who never bites the apple, but who willingly suffers the consequences nevertheless.

Averill reads Eve in relation to the saga in her work, exploring Eve as a "biblical feminist" and Bella as her decidedly nonfeminist descendent. Averill argues, "The tradition of patriarchy presents the Adam and Eve myth as a cautionary tale, meant to alert Judeo-Christian men to the wayward and tantalizing wiles of female sexuality." Yet, as evidenced above, this claim is not in keeping with Mormon conceptions of "the Fall." Averill, reading Eve's acts in Genesis as offering "key moments of mythic female agency," asserts that biting the apple defies "the male-god rules." However, in *Twilight*, Bella does *not* bite the apple." "Leaving the apple un-bitten," Averill explains, "turns back the mythic clock, giving Meyer the opportunity to tell a tale in which woman/Eve opts not to act, or rather chooses to submit." Though Averill does not frame her reading with reference to Mormon theology, it seems the Mormon take on the fall is crucial here—the fortunate-fall view that Mormonism upholds means that Bella, in *not* biting the apple, risks *not* experiencing corporeality, free choice, eternal life, and joy. Yet, though Bella doesn't bite the apple in the Genesis-inflected scenes of *Twilight*, she does indeed leave the figurative Garden of Eden, progressively tasting more knowledge about vampires and werewolves (and her own sexuality) as the saga continues. She falls, in a sense, into a supernatural world and experiences all the things Mormons see the biblical fall as making possible. She, like a "biblical feminist" Eve, does not submit to God/Edward's dictate that she stay human (Averill n.p.). Rather, she puts her mortality to a vote and succeeds, by saga's end, in her quest to become a vampire.

In addition to her stated desires for an egalitarian relationship in the series, Bella continually expresses her sexual desires. According to the Mormon reading of the fall, sex is a necessary and good thing, a "spiritual exercise" (Granger 180). Indeed, as Granger notes, "Sex within marriage is ... the only means to personal salvation and immortal life" (181). Yet, as Granger details, *only* sex within marriage is acceptable: "Sex outside marriage is the quick road to hell"

(181). This is why we have the somewhat paradoxical representation of sex as pleasureful and life-sustaining on the one hand, and as dangerous and soul-destroying on the other. Bella thus also seems to function as a descendent of Lilith, Adam's first wife in some versions of Christian legend who was known for her unabated lust. As the story goes, Lilith was created at the same time as Adam and refused to become subservient to him. Thus, she left Eden, opening the way for Eve — a more docile biblical "first" female. Bella, in her role as Lilith, repeatedly attempts to seduce Edward. Like the succubus Lilith is sometime read as, Bella repeatedly tries to persuade Edward to have sexual relations with her, effectively trying to drain him of his soul or "virtue." Yet, Edward's stalwart refusal allows the Mormon "Law of Chastity" to be upheld. Offering what Granger argues is a "spiritual message for the hook-up and 'friends with benefits' generation," the saga does not refute the pleasures of sexuality but does, quite unequivocally, contend that such pleasure should only happen within the confines of marriage (54). In multiple ways, the texts indicate that Bella would be putting her life at risk by having premarital sex with Edward. However, in keeping with the stricter codes of sexuality directed at women, there is not an ancillary danger for Edward. As vampire, he would not be risking his own life, only his virtue. This is in keeping with the higher importance the LDS church places on female chastity and concurs also with views toward "celestial marriage" in which men may have many wives but women can only ever have one husband. In Mormonism, chastity and virtue for women is described as "that which was most dear and precious above all things" (Moroni 9:9), and the Lord "delight[s] in the chastity of women" (Jacob 2:28, 31–35). Edward, as a figurative devout Mormon in the text, subscribes to this Law of Chastity, encouraging Bella to do the same.

Marriage as Bella's (Bruising) Crown of Glory

By the saga's end, Bella's narrative is in keeping with the Mormon conception of marriage as a means to female salvation and childbirth as "a woman's crown of glory" (Granger 182). Laake, noting her desperation to marry, confirms this view, sharing,

> I knew that my success in this life and the next was dependent on it. The importance of such a marriage was the primary lesson of my Mormon girlhood, when it had been repeatedly impressed upon me that if I failed to marry a faithful Mormon man in a ceremony performed in a Mormon temple, I would be denied access to the highest level of Mormon heaven [17].

Though Bella is not desperate to marry in this way, her capitulation to Edward's marriage demands is ultimately presented as the right choice that leads to the saga's happy ending. And, just as marriage is the means for eternal life for women in Mormonism, so, too, does marriage result in Bella's transformation into immortal vampire. Further, she quickly also fulfills "a woman's highest purpose" within Mormonism-she becomes a mother (Laake 158).

However, the saga also at least tangentially touches on the darker side of relationships and marriage — domestic abuse. Laake argues that this issue "is glossed over at best" by the church, and, "at worst, the church is blatantly supportive of abusers" (202). Noting that "as recently as April 1992, one of the highest leaders of the church, Elder Richard Scott, counseled all victims of abuse ... to rely upon God's help for healing," Laake's work reveals that women who are abused are often counseled to stay married (202). Sharing that a friend confided in her, "I can't tell you how it feels that this man who is supposed to take me to heaven might beat me up," Laake's disclosure that suffering abuse is preferable to divorce according to the LDS Church can be read in relation to the saga's suggestion that relationships are not always fairy tale perfect (128). While on the one hand, Bella's black and blue body (the result of her wedding night with Edward) might be read as an embrace of violent sex as sexy, on the other, it might also hint that if abuse is to happen, it *need* be coded as sexy so that the higher purpose of marriage can continue unabated.

Further, the representation of Bella as covered in not only bruises but also feathers brings to mind the history of tar and feathering that Mormons were subject to. As documented by Krakauer, Brodie, Laake, and others, Joseph Smith was tarred and feathered various times in the early days of the religion, as were a number of the Mormon faithful.[8] That this practice was associated with the desire to castrate Smith is also evident in Krakauer's documentation of the mob that attacked Smith in 1832, a mob that brought with them a doctor prepared to "emasculate" Smith (118). As a literal punishment associated with shame and powerlessness, the practice can also be read as figurative emasculation — as an attempt to take away the potency of Smith's power.

In *Breaking Dawn*, Bella, not Edward, is symbolically tarred and feathered and not emasculated but subject to male abuse. Given Mormonism's supposed celebration of sex within marriage, why is Bella "punished" for sex? Is this just an extreme initiation into the "spiritual exercise" of married sexuality, or might it indicate that sex for women within Mormonism is not always as wonderful as promised (Granger 181)? Though Meyer may not intentionally have used this imagery to hint at the history of tarring and feathering meted out against Mormons as punishment, as a devout Mormon and an avid reader she is surely aware of this facet of Mormon persecution. She probably is also familiar with Smith's claim that he ripped open beds and pillows in search of the first draft of his book, which was lost or stolen — a chapter of Mormon history that offered a setback for Smith's claims of prophecy (55). Thus, perhaps this scene, which raised so many hackles for its representation of a bruised and battered (yet post-coitally euphoric) Bella, can be read as a figurative re-envisioning of Mormon persecution — one that renders such punishment erotic rather than disgraceful.

As per other representations of domestic abuse and sexual assault in the book, they are far less glowing than the tar-and-feather honeymoon scene. For example, Jacob is presented as an unthinking cad for forcing Bella to kiss him, while Sam is framed as unable to control his temper, resulting in Emily's scarred face. Is it coincidental that these other, more condemned incidents are carried out by the Quileute rather than the Cullens, or might we read the Mormon view of indigenous peoples as coming into play?

White and Delightsome Vampires versus Cursed, Russet-Skinned Wolves

Brodie, arguing that Smith's intentions for the Book of Mormon started as "a mere money-making history of the Indians," documents the cultural contexts that likely spurred Smith to name Native Americans as a cursed race (83). Detailing how the "Indian mounds" that dotted Smith's New York location resulted in various legends that attempted to explain their purpose, Brodie contends that Smith capitalized on the desire to explain indigenous peoples and history to the benefit of his new religion (34–35).[9] Written at a time when the subject of race was a particularly heated moral and political debate, Smith's scripture solved the origin of Native Americans and blacks, presenting each as uniquely "cursed" and separate from whites (Brodie 172). Referring to this factor as leading to "the discrimination that is the ugliest thesis in existing Mormon theology," Brodie notes that Smith's religion promised a sort of equality but one that was grounded in "white and delightsome" skin where once those "cursed" accept Mormonism they will "rejoice" and "many generations shall not pass away among them, save they shall be a white and delightsome people" (174, 93). Smith was thus offering Native Americans, as Brodie details, "not restoration, but assimilation, not the return of his [sic] continent, but the loss of his identity" (94). This, she argues, "did not seem a genetic absurdity to a people who were being told in sober history books that the pigment of the red man in New England who had adopted the white man's way of life had actually become lighter than that of his savage brothers" (94).[10]

The Book of Mormon contains the history of two warring races, not vampire and werewolf as in *Twilight*, but white and nonwhite: one a "fair and delightsome people," the other a "wild and ferocious, and a bloodthirsty people; full of idolatry and filthiness ... wandering about in the wilderness, with a short skin girded about their loins, and their heads shaven" (*Book of Mormon*, Jarom 20). These two races Smith named the Nephites, who were "peace-loving and domestic," and the Lamanites, who were "bloodthirsty and idolatrous" (Brodie 43–44). These two races supposedly fought for 1,000 years, with the evil, dark-skinned Lamanites eventually killing off the white Nephite race. In this genocide, the darker-skinned Lamanites were said to have slaughtered the Nephites, leaving only Moroni, son of the heroic Nephite leader Mormon, who would eventually lead Smith to the gold plates that contained the Book of Mormon.

Smith's scripture abounds with references to white-skinned people as good and pure (much like *Twilight*) and to dark-skinned people as "loathsome," "filthy," and as "full of idleness and all manner of abominations" (Nephi 12:23). While those with white skin are "exceedingly fair and delightsome," those cursed with dark skin are "not ... enticing unto my people"; indeed this is why God "did cause a skin of blackness to come upon them" (Nephi 5:21). Yet, if these cursed people accept God (and more specifically Mormonism), "their scales of darkness shall begin to fall from their eyes; and many generations shall not pass away among them, save they shall be a pure white and a delightsome people" (Book of Mormon, Nephi 30:6).

Believing in a scripture in which God darkens the skin of unbelievers and sinners, and lightens the skin of those that please him, resulted historically in a religion with an ugly history of racial discrimination. Brigham Young, the prophet who took the mantle of leadership after Smith's murder, expanded the racist doctrine of the church and is widely reported to have been far more overtly racist in his teaching than Smith. Under his leadership, blacks were named as the rightful "servants of servants" and formally disbarred from priesthood, a policy the church refused to relinquish until 1979.[11] Even after overturning the ban on black priesthood, the church continued to practice "official racism" according to many (Krakauer 93). As reported by a 2007 article in *The Salt Lake Tribune*, for example, "The blacks-as-cursed belief continues to be circulated at the grass-roots level and supported in quasi-official publications such as *Mormon Doctrine* and the *Mortal Messiah....* All attempts to get the church to repudiate these notions have been rebuffed."[12] Such beliefs also resulted historically in Mormons' thoroughly documented history of "framing Indians for crimes" committed by Latter Day Saints (Krakauer 245). In addition to disguising themselves as Natives and committing murder and theft, Mormon leaders also encouraged Natives to attack gentiles with promises they would share their plunder (Krakauer 213). Thus, not only does Mormon scripture codify racism as ordained by God, but also Mormon practice reveals that cultural exploitation was an acceptable practice. What, however, does all this have to do with *Twilight*?

For starters, we might read the Quileute wolves as "cursed" with their ancestral history of shape-shifting. Edward's emo-brooding aside, the Cullen vampire life is presented as blessed and opulent. In contrast, the "russet-skinned" Quileute are cursed with the burden of shape-shifting — a fate Jacob particularly rails against. While the Cullens are presented as exceedingly "white and delightsome," as blessed and god-like (as the next chapter will more thoroughly examine), Quileutes such as Jacob are forced into a life of wolf servitude, one brought about, significantly, by the arrival of the (Mormon) vampires.

The legend of the Cold Woman shared in *Eclipse*, whose white skin and golden hair made her face "magical in its beauty," details how the "spirit wolves" guarded the tribe from vampires in the time before the Cullens' arrival (256). The bloodthirsty way of the "cold ones," who brought death to generations of Quileute, might be interpreted in relation to the legacy of colonization and westward expansion — a legacy that Mormons did not initiate but nevertheless benefitted from. Due to the invasion of their land by "cold ones," the Quileute must "carry the burden and share the sacrifice their fathers endured before them" (259). This aspect of the saga can be argued to function as a sort of (reparation), framing the white cold ones as evil invaders and the Quileute as an innocent people merely protecting their land and lives. When Carlisle and his coven arrive (who might be read as the good, migrating Mormons rather than the evil white colonists who preceded them), he and Jacob's great-grandfather make a truce: if they promise to stay off La Push land and continued their "vegetarian" diet, the Quileute would not, as Jacob puts it, "expose them to the pale-faces" (*E* 125).

This treaty between the Cullens and the Quileutes can be read in relation to the historical precedent of Mormon and Native American attempts to work together to defend themselves against what each saw as the dangers of westward expansion by White America, or, in Jacob's terminology, "the pale faces." For Mormons, this expansion threatened their newfound peace in Utah (and resulted eventually in the Utah War); for Native Americans, more tragically, this expansion resulted in displacement and genocide. And, if we read the Cullens as persecuted Mormons, forced to migrate further and further west before finding their virtual Zion in Forks, we might read the Quileute as the descendents of the dark-skinned Lamanites who, if only they will accept Mormon/vampire ways, will be able to become themselves a "white and delightsome" people.

As Brodie asserts, as Mormonism moved west, Smith hoped the displaced Native Americans "would soon swell the ranks of his church," and Mormons "never ceased to proselyte eagerly among American Indians, despite the fact that with miscegenenation Indian converts do not become, as Joseph Smith promised in an implicitly hostile phrase, 'a white and delightsome people'" (121, 425). And, just as Smith wrote the Book of Mormon in hopes of drawing both white and nonwhite converts, so does the saga seem to have an eye toward conversion (Brodie 93). Though the Cullens are hardly full of missionary zeal and do not proselytize to the wolves, the same cannot be said of Bella. As a new convert herself, she is akin to a zealous young missionary trying to convince Jacob and the others that the Cullen way of life is admirable. By book's end, Jacob has indeed been converted to this line of thought — though not through the sermonizing of Bella but rather through another religious laden aspect of the saga — imprinting.

Premortal Romance: Or, How to Become "White and Delightsome" by Imprinting on a Human-Vampire Baby

As Maxine Hanks asserts in "Mormon Vampires? Religion and *Twilight*," one of the distinctly Mormon aspects of the series is its emphasis on soul mates and the "imprinting" that occurs in pre-existence (n.p.). Latter-day Saints believe that all souls live a premortal life as "spirit children," and, as Mormon writer Eric Jepson explains in his piece "Saturday's Werewolves: *Twilight*, Monsters, and Mormons," this belief is often associated with what he names "a classic Mormon literary pattern: the Premortal Romance." [13] In this pattern, so-called spirit children "come to Earth, and when they meet, bond immediately" (Jepson). As another Mormon scholar, Tyler Chadwick, concurs, "This narrative trope is based in the LDS doctrine that we existed as spirits in the presence of God prior to mortal birth, an official teaching that gave rise to the folk doctrine of premortal coupling (i.e., that male and female spirits promised to find one another on Earth and to marry for eternity)".[14] Chadwick cites this trope as a much more likely inspiration for imprinting than the one claimed by Granger — that imprinting is Meyer's apologist response to John Krakauer's condemnation of polygamy in *Under the Banner of Heaven*.[15] I am inclined to agree with the Mormon scholars on this point, especially given that Granger bases so much of his argument on the assumption that Meyer read and was thoroughly familiar with Krakauer's text — an assumption that is not bolstered by any proof other than that Krakauer's book was published shortly before Meyer's writing of *Twilight*.

While imprinting does offer a fairy-tale version of love, it doesn't really speak to polygamy. In fact, in the text, the claim is the wolves imprint on *one* female (there is no suggestion a female can imprint on a male nor that there could ever be same-sex imprinting). However, polygamy does exist in the Quileute past — Bella learns in *Eclipse* that the ancestor Utlapa takes "a young second wife and then a third" (248). Admittedly, this is framed as a negative excess that garners disdain from the tribe, but, so, too, was the polygamy practiced by the LDS faithful pre–1862. Thus, while imprinting is portrayed as inevitable (as well as quite innocent) in the saga, polygamy is painted with a more critical brush. Here, Meyer falls in line with the historical precedent of Mormon women being less than jubilant about the practice of plural marriage; notably, Emma Smith, Joseph's first wife, opposed the practice, even threatening to take a second husband of her own.[16] Meyer continues this tradition it seems, exalting the one woman/one man model via the various Cullen couples. Yet, via the imprinting meme projected onto the Quileute wolves, Meyer is also able to render taking child brides, a mainstay of polygamy, less abhorrent.[17] While the real-life Smith commanded girls at least as young as fourteen to marry him or face eternal damnation, in *Twilight*, imprinting frames December–May pairings as innocent. Indeed, Meyer goes to great lengths to show Quil, who has imprinted on the toddler Claire, as a sort of male nanny rather than a love interest. The texts also emphasize that until the female imprinted upon is an adult, the relationship is not romantic or physical, but nurturing. Via this narrative packaging, Meyer is able to sugarcoat Mormon's polygamous past as well as to offer a contemporary version of premortal romance, a model that is in keeping with the Mormon championing of eternal marriage and family.

As Jepson observes, "Werewolves really latch on to the whole eternal marriage thing." Yet, Meyer complicates the rosy version of premortal romance that has shaped Mormon literary history by exploring the loss of agency that such romance entails. Seeing as Meyer calls "free will ... a huge gift from God," her fictional portrayal of premortal romance complicates Mormons' beliefs about agency, as Jepson suggests.[18] What Jepson does not consider, though, is the gendered and racial implications of Meyer's portrayal. Bella, a white female, is able to choose who to love — Edward *or* Jacob. Jacob, a Quileute minority, like his wolf brethren, has no such choice. Indeed, this is one aspect of the saga that angers Anita Wheeler, a Quileute storyteller that names Jacob's imprinting on baby Renesmee as sickening and abhorrent, as well as counter to Native culture.[19] As Wheeler's indignation suggests, Meyer's imprinting not only offers a fairy-tale version of polygamy and premortal romance, but also projects the uglier side of these practices and beliefs—child brides and forced marriage — onto Native others— a move that both appropriates and misrepresents indigenous culture. Being as the saga champions the love of Edward and Bella as ideal, it ironically projects the one true love narrative onto the figurative white Mormons of the text and plural marriage/premortal romance onto the indigenous Quileute — a projection that handily reverses the real-life polygamous practices of some Mormons.

This presentation of the Quileute as Mormon, at least given their history of polygamy and their imprinting as newfangled premortal romance, might be read as fictionally enacting what Joseph Smith had hoped for—conversion of the "cursed" Lamanites to "white and delightsome" people. Believing that conversion could "purge out the old blood" and make Native Americans the "seed of Abraham," the Book of Mormon, much like *Twilight*, suggests that conversion is the means to a better life on earth and to salvation beyond (Brodie 175). In Jacob's case, by the close of *Breaking Dawn*, not only has he lost his hatred and mistrust for vampires, but he has also in effect become one of the faithful. Imprinting on Renesmee, he has joined the Cullen fold (Edward even calls him "son") and will, we can presume, produce Mormon-hybrid babies that, given Renesmee's ultra-white skin, are likely to be more "white and delightsome" than his own "russet" color. Thus, just as Christianity has historically been presented as a civilizing force for indigenous peoples, so, too, does *Twilight* present its fictional Mormonism as able to "save" the rather hotheaded and wayward Jacob.[20] This depiction seems all the more problematic when put in the context of *real* Quileute history, where, in 1881, Christianity descended forcefully upon the Quileute when A. W. Smith established a school and renamed the Quileute with biblical monikers such as Esau, Levi, and Sarah (Powell and Jensen 41). Then, in 1895, Shakerism was introduced. Predictably, Quileute beliefs "were replaced by the explanations of missionaries and school teachers after contact" (Powell and Jay 47). We can presume the same may happen for the fictional Quileute in *Twilight*, who will likely lose their "legends" of the Third Wife and Taha Aki and instead rely on a Cullen-ized view of history.

Making Mormonism Sparkle: Twilight as Mormon Apology

As documented in the film *American Mormon*, LDS is likely one of the most misunderstood religions in America. And, if this documentary and *Twilight* commentary on the Web are to be believed, it is a religion that still garners much derision. The wearing of "magic" garments, the secret temple ceremonies, the cult-like handshakes, the fairy tale-looking temples, the tithing — the list goes on. These aspects of the belief, not to mention the formal stance against homosexuality, the strict gender codes that give males the majority of power, and the racial history that besmirches the faith, make Mormonism a suspect religion in the eyes of many. This is perhaps why Meyer has not gone to great lengths to promote herself as a Mormon author. In fact, when talking to fans or the general public about this book, one of the most common reactions I heard was "She is Mormon? Really?" While *Twilight*ers know this, many lay readers and less-fixated fans do not. As such, it's not surprising that not all that much discussion is dedicated to the Mormon underpinnings of the book — in fact, it's far more common to read the book in relation to Christianity generally, as the many Evangelical responses already published attest. Due to the paucity of such analysis, there has not (as of yet) been much discussion of how Meyer (intentionally or not) pens what can be read as various critiques of her faith. John Granger and Maxine Hanks both touch on this aspect of her work, both leaning toward the argument that while there are certain strands of the saga that seem critical of the faith, for the most part, Meyer has created a devout Mormon series.

Granger reads the series as "a sympathetic presentation of core LDS beliefs and a defense of controversial ideas that divide Mormons and their gentile neighbors," arguing that the saga "glosses and gilds problematic LDS history" (ix, x). Suggesting that Meyer offers a "wish-fulfillment apology for the faith" complete with "implicit criticism of its failings," Granger's reading fails to consider that religion, not Mormonism itself, might be the bigger ideology that Meyer (and readers who respond to the text) delves into (150). As a practicing member of the Greek Orthodox church who claims literature is helping our supposedly sadly secular culture find its way back to God, Granger is hardly an outsider to faith. Rather, he is a proud religious cheerleader, suggesting that those of us who do not subscribe to Christianity are "zombies" with empty lives (76). This does not render his analysis useless by any means, but his failure to clearly announce his own religious leanings seem disingenuous. In effect, his book comes off as a "believe this, not that" type of screed that paints Mormonism as a sort of wacky faith that requires its members to become apologists (as he argues Meyer does).

But Granger does consider the gender dynamics that come into play in Meyer's veiled responses to her religion, asserting, "Meyer takes a roundhouse shot at the Prophet in Rosalie's origin story" (212). Suggesting that Rosalie's fiancé, Royce King, is a representation of Joseph Smith as misogynist, Granger indicates that Meyer rails against Mormonism's history of mistreating women. Given that Rosalie shares the last name "Hale" with Smith's first wife, she might possibly be read as a fictional version of Emma, but then wouldn't we also have to consider Emmett, and his lusty corporeality, as another possible incarnation of Smith? Granger doesn't suggest this. Instead, he reads Edward as "obviously" representing "the Mormon Prophet, Joseph Smith" (166). Indeed, it seems many characters represent Smith according to Granger — Royce, Carlisle, Edward. While this interpretation is conceivable, Granger fails to analyze how Smith (and his supposed fictional representations) are problematic amalgams of god, man, and monster. To be sure, there is a great deal of damning historical documentation about Smith — he is characterized as an egotistical womanizer, charlatan, and child-rapist. As such, Granger's suggestion that Meyer grapples with her adoration for the prophet Smith and contempt for the man Joseph begs much more nuanced examination.

Granger is more convincing in his exploration of Leah as "Meyer's picture of the intelligent woman born into LDS faith." Such women, Granger argues, are put "into competitive and close contact with misogynist Mormon machomen," where they have no freedom within "the group think of Mormonism and institutional discrimination against women" (214–15). Though reading Leah as allowing for the exploration of what Granger calls "the dark side of Mormon life" is an intriguing concept, such a read also seems to call for an examination of why her character is so negatively portrayed (214). If indeed Leah represents an independent and intelligent LDS woman that has little choice but to leave the religion in order "to be fully human, a woman, and to use her talents freely," isn't Granger suggesting that no "talented" women would remain in such a faith (215)? This not only seems derogatory, but also goes against his unabashed championing of Meyer, who, though certainly talented, has remained devout. It also fails to address the fact that not all Mormon males are "misogynist macho-men." Here, the racial connotations of his read are interesting as well. He never mentions that Leah is an indigenous woman who would, as such, be read as a "cursed" descendent of the Lamanites nor that the "macho-men" she rallies against in the text are similarly cursed. As such, shouldn't we read her "tragedy" (as Granger calls it) in relation to this aspect of Mormonism (215)? On the one hand, we might see Meyer as condemning the racist underpinnings of her belief by portraying Leah and the wolves sympathetically; on the other, we might read their beastliness and inability to think for themselves as promoting the idea that they are indeed descendents of the "lesser" Lamanites.

Finally, if Granger wants to substantiate his claim that Meyer is penning a revisionist, more female-friendly account of Mormonism, failing to consider Renesmee as a female savior figure seems a glaring omission. Referring to her as a "God-man androgen" and even suggesting Bella is a "little Christ" (145, 127), Granger consistently neglects to grapple with the gendered implications of this read. Why is Edward Christ and Bella only "little Christ"? Why is the history of Mormon feminists and the strong-resisting role of Emma Hale never brought into consideration? These omissions seem particularly odd, especially given Granger's assertions that Mormon males are "misogynist macho-men" and his simultaneous derision of feminists.

Hanks, as noted above, offers a more feminist reading of the saga, asserting, "I think she [Meyer] is doing feminist theology."[21] Emphasizing that it is safer to do such work in the present day, Hanks notes that Meyer still received an "implied slap on the hand" from the Deseret bookstore, the preeminent Mormon book purveyor in Salt Lake City. Hanks argues that Meyer brings the patriarchal and feminist forms of theology into dialogue in order to teach spiritual lessons. Claiming that Meyer is "both orthodox and heretical" in her writing, Hanks concludes that she both promotes and resists Mormon views of marriage, family, eternal progression, and polygamy. On marriage, Hanks points out that Meyer holds to the view that it should be monogamous and binding, but she also presents marriage as an institution that is not perfect. She links this to Meyer's representation of spiritual imprinting, which is in keeping with Mormon belief in premortal existence, but emphasizes that Bella has two soul mates— Edward and Jacob —which is, she says, "a heretical reading."[22] She argues that this as well as her focus on the third wife "reverses polygamy with polyandry," elevating the female role as constitutive and also suggesting that not only men can love more than one mate in their lifetime. Claiming that Meyer's work offers "a daring divergence" from Orthodox Mormon teachings, Hanks sees Meyer as carrying out "shamanic work." While I hesitate to name her oeuvre as prophetic or healing, I agree with Hanks that there is definitely a deep religious vein running throughout Meyer's texts, and that this gridding is not wholly supportive of Mormon theology specifically or Christian teachings more generally. There is, as Hanks suggests, a strange admixture of championing religion (albeit subtextually) and simultaneously critiquing or attempting to justify her theology's more pernicious aspects— especially in relation to the role of women and the Mormon history of polygamy/racial doctrine. Of course, Meyer cannot go too far in her critique even if she wants to do so, or she, too, would, like Hanks, be excommunicated. We might, in fact, read her as similar to Edward—convinced she may be damned if she goes too far outside the parameters of (Mormon) virtue and trying ever so hard to resist the sweet smell of forbidden fruit. Writing, it seems, has allowed her to explore some forbidden territory — love of more than one man, sexual activity outside of marriage, the notion that motherhood may not be enough (or pleasant) for all women, the suggestion that modern-day Eves might be better served if they are allowed to equally hold power, to be, as Bella puts it, more Superman than Lois Lane.

Chapter 7

Got Vampire Privilege?
*Or, Why You Should Marry
an Undead White, Wealthy,
Heterosexual Mormon*

While the cultural phenomenon surrounding *Twilight* now boasts several million devoted fans, the series' unexamined representation of privilege is rarely a topic of discussion. However, when read in relation to systems of power, the saga upholds many dominant ideas about race, class, gender and sexuality in ways that idealize rather than question or subvert existing inequalities. Though the series does have some components that might be read as questioning hierarchical and prejudicial thought systems, overall, it supports various normative ideologies and most pervasively, as I will argue, romanticizes white privilege and the continuing rule of whites over "the Other"—which, in *Twilight's* case, is the Quileute. Yet, in *Breaking Dawn,* when the werewolves and vampires put aside their distrust of one another to protect Bella, the series examines how prejudice can be overcome. Via explorations of certain "races" so to speak, of humans, vampires, and werewolves, and how these groups can coexist and even care for one another, the series suggests that legacies of racism can be undone. However, given that the saga frames white vampires as the saviors and effectively colonizes the Quileute wolves, the solution Meyer's work enacts is in keeping with a colonial viewpoint. Further, the failure to question male privilege, wealth inequality, or heteronormativity in the saga results in narratives that—though certainly entertaining—are rather dubious from a progressive political perspective.

Structurally, the series relies on a divide between humans, vampires, and werewolves. Indeed, it is the relationships and tensions between these groups that ground the narrative. Read as a racial allegory, a white, working-class human chooses between an ultra-white, ultra-privileged vampire and a far less privileged wolf of color. The saga thus echoes older tales of conquest and imperialism, though instead of the white cowboys and Native Americans who populated Western films, we now have vampires and werewolves vying over borders as well as women. The love triangle at the series' core is also imbued with racial connotations, with a white vampire in competition with a Native American shape-shifter. Their characters are contrasted using various binaries that equate Edward with whiteness and Jacob with the indigenous. Edward is associated with wealth, civility, intellect, godliness, beauty, and married monogamous heterosexuality — all categories that confer privilege in the contemporary United States. In contrast, Jacob is a working-class, relatively uneducated "noble savage" associated with animality, primitivism, and dangerous sexuality. Like Bella, readers are encouraged to choose between these two different suitors — one who is extremely privileged (Edward) and the other who is a cultural outsider or Other (Jacob).

As such, the saga circulates extensively around issues of privilege. However, this focus remains relatively unspoken and underanalyzed, just as systems of privilege do in the real world. By housing her narrative in a supernatural frame, Meyer (and readers) are able to use the "it's just a fantasy" excuse — a response that aims to curtail serious consideration of how this fiction reflects and promotes certain views of race, class, gender, and sexuality in the real world. This invisibility of privilege, as noted by scholars, "strengthens the power it creates and maintains. The invisible cannot be combated, and as a result, privilege is allowed to perpetuate, regenerate, and re-create itself.... Privilege is invisible only until looked for, but silence in the face of privilege sustains its invisibility" (Wildman and Davis 615). Given that privilege is normalized in American culture, holders of privilege often fail to see their own social advantages. In the case of white privilege, as Wildman and Davis argue, privilege functions to render whiteness invisible: "Whites do no look at the world through a filter of racial awareness, even though whites are, of course, members of a race. The power to ignore race, when white is the race, is a privilege, a societal advantage. The term 'racism/white supremacy' emphasizes the link between discriminatory racism and the privilege held by whites to ignore their own race" (620).

Yet, despite the pervasive undercurrents that render *Twilight* a modern colonial text, most existing scholarship either ignores issues of privilege altogether (gender analysis being an exception) or mentions such topics only tangentially. In "The Tao of Jacob," for example, Rebecca Housel makes no mention of race — an especially odd omission given the essay's focus on Jacob as a character "aware of social isolation connected with social difference" (237). Though Housel nods to Jacob's Quileute heritage she never explicitly examines race. Other books, like Gresh's *Unofficial Guide* and Jones' *Touched by a Vampire*, also fail to cover issues of privilege and race. One of the first published essays to examine such issues is — to my knowledge — my own "Civilized Vampires Versus Savage Werewolves: Race and Ethnicity in the *Twilight* Series," published in *Bitten by Twilight* in 2010. And, if my own surveys, discussions with fans and students, and participation in *Twilight* conventions is any indication, it seems most celebrate Meyer's inclusion of Native Americans. Indeed, the first time I spoke publically on the topic at *Summer School in Forks,* an audience member came up to me aghast that I would suggest there might be a problematic side to Meyer's use of the Quileute in her narratives. This "any representation is better than no representation" seems a common response, one that some Quileute tribal members themselves accept. Detractors are wary to be critical of Meyer and the interest and boon her work has brought to this tiny tribe — so wary that those I interviewed declined to be named.

However, if we examine *Twilight* in the context of racism in the United States more generally, in relation to the horrid history of the decimation indigenous people have suffered, and with an awareness of how Christianity generally and Mormonism more specifically are related to larger colonial and missionary projects, it is no stretch to see that to ignore race in the saga is a glaring omission. To speak to the cultural context in which the *Twilight* phenomenon occurs, I would concur with Dyer that race is never *not* a factor — even in our supposedly post-racial milieu. As Dyer puts it, racism is a "non-consciousness that we all inhabit" (White 7).

Twilight *Constructions of "The Indian"*

In regards to the Native Americans' experiences post-contact, I propose that this history cannot be ignored if one is to offer a full analysis of *Twilight* and the cultural work it is doing. As scholars such as Howard Zinn and Ward Churchill remind us, indigenous peoples have been systematically annihilated, acculturated, and/or exploited since the colonial project began on what is now U.S. soil.[1] Not even considered citizens until 1924 and not given universal suffrage until 1957, indigenous peoples are arguably the most ill-treated and underrepresented minority globally. Literature historically played a huge role in the framing of Native Americans as uncivilized and savage, and Meyer's texts, I argue, carry on this project.

As Paula Gunn Allen argues,

> No Indian can grow to any age without being informed that her people were "savages" who interfered with the march of progress pursued by respectable, loving, civilized white people. We are the villains of the scenario when we are mentioned at all. We are absent from much of white history except when we are calmly, rationally, succinctly, and systematically dehumanized [49].

The saga's failure to rework such negative stereotypes of Native Americans thus places it within a long line of white-penned narratives that variously appropriate and/or misrepresent indigenous culture and legend. As noted in the introduction to *Fantasies of the Master Race,* "Literature crafted by a dominating culture can be an insidious political force, disinforming people who might otherwise develop a clearer understanding of the struggles for survival faced by an indigenous population" (Jaimes 1). Meyer's text indeed "disinforms" people about the Quileute, leading them to believe on the one hand that their legends include werewolves and, on the other, rendering the indigenous struggle for survival invisible. Most myths regarding indigenous culture have been similarly penned by whites, and thus, as Elizabeth Bird argues, "these stories, at a mythic level, explain to Whites their right to be here and help deal with lingering guilt about the displacement of Native inhabitants" (*Dressing in Feathers* 2). In fact, in *Twilight* it is the white vampires who are displaced and the wolves who attempt to commit metaphorical white vampire genocide.

Contributing to what Bird names "the fabrication of the Indian by White culture," *Twilight* produces a modern myth that equates whiteness with goodness and frames indigenous people as less-evolved savage beasts (3). It thus allies with Churchill's claim that "literature in America is and always has been part and parcel of the colonial process" (39). This colonial process has tended to either romanticize indigenous culture or construct it as lesser, abnormal, and pathological.[2] While some have argued that Meyer's inclusion of indigenous characters is positive, her co-opting of Quileute legend smacks of a privileged colonial view that historically saw Native Americans as savages that had to be either destroyed or acculturated.

Further, due to historically sedimented privilege, whites are still the classifiers, and Native Americas are the classified. As Vine Deloria asserts, "For most of the five centuries [since contact], whites have had unrestricted power to describe Indians in any way they chose. Indians were simply not connected to the organs of propaganda so that they could respond to the manner in which whites described them" (66). While Native Americans have a particularly rich history of literature and while the number of indigenous-produced, -directed, and/or -written films is growing, they still do not have a mainline to the "organs" of the media, so to speak. Instead, as Dyer posits, "White people create the dominant images of the world and don't quite see that they thus construct the world in their own image" ("Matter of Whiteness" 12). In Meyer's case, her image of the world is colored by both her white privilege and her Mormon belief system, and, just like Bella, who does not see her white privilege, neither does Meyer seem aware of the very important messages about race that her fiction contains. As the late Zinn recognized, representation of Native Americans involves very important ideological choices, especially since indigenous people have been misrepresented and largely silenced within mainstream texts for centuries (9).

Though Meyer's text is a fantasy, we cannot pretend that such fiction does not shape real-world views about race and class— gunshot Westerns were largely fantasy, too, and think of the lasting legacy they have left us with in terms of Native Americans being seen as savage warriors who scalp too often and drink too much. And, as the media is, as Stuart Hall names it, a "powerful source of ideas about race" where notions of racial otherness "are articulated, worked on, transformed, and elaborated," it is imperative to be cognizant of the racial messages that texts contain (20). According to Hall, "Primitivism, savagery, guile and unreliability" still underpin media representations of indigenous people and show them most often as "cunningly plotting the overthrow of 'civilisation'" (22). In *Twilight*, we see this first in Billy Black's attempts to keep Bella away from Edward, then more extensively in the Quileutes' plan to attack the Cullen vampires and/or kill Bella in order to prevent the birth of her half-vampire child. Since the Cullens are depicted as refined and enlightened, the animosity the wolves hold toward them is framed as misguided.

While the texts themselves largely ally with the white construction of "the Indian," the casting choice of Taylor Lautner also falls in line with a long history of non–Native actors being cast to play indigenous parts.[3] Though Lautner claims to be part Native, his assertions seemed disingenuous coming as they did after the media brouhaha over the casting of a non–Native actor to play the part of Jacob Black. Lautner seemed instead to be "Going Indian," as Robert Baird names it, or falsely claiming indigenous heritage, a phenomenon with strong historical precedent (131) . Tinsel Korey, cast to play Emily, enacted the same sort of ruse, claiming to be Native/First Nation when in fact she is East Indian.[4] Despite the historical outrage associated with the casting of non–Native actors to play Native roles, Korey's deception seemed to fall mostly under the radar. However, after the ruckus over Lautner's casting, Native actors were cast to play Sam, Embry, Quil, Jared, and Paul for the second film, though none of them are Quileute. Alex Meraz, who plays Paul, was mindful of the weightiness of his casting, sharing,

> During the process of casting, when I was waiting to hear word if I got a role or not ... I prayed every night. I was asking for permission even to represent the Quileute tribe. I was putting out a lot of good thoughts. In essence, even though we're taking some of their mythology, their creation story and it's mixed in a fantasy, still we're taking from the culture. Being Native, we needed to be conscious of that and ask permission to the people of the past, present and of the future for it. It's a very conscious thing. Native Americans, they have a right to be protective of their stories [Topel n.p.].

Putting a rather positive spin on the saga's depiction of the Quileute, Meraz further explains:

> I think also, as representatives for Native Americans in this franchise, we have a responsibility not to be a bad image.... We're portraying Natives and that's what they're going to see. I think it's time for us to kind of rewrite what Hollywood's take on Native Americans was, which was long hair blowing, noble kind of people, leather and feather period pieces. So now you see something in a contemporary setting, and you see us to be humans. It's great [Topel n.p.].

While it's true the saga avoids the usual tendency to depict Natives as only living in (or stuck in) the past, Meraz's claim that the saga shows them as humans glosses over the fact that the texts (and the film adaptations) focus on the *wolf* identity of the Quileute — on their animality more than their humanity. But the texts and films *do* show an indigenous people in a modern setting, allow them to be key, heroic characters, and avoid some of the more negative stereotypes (i.e., the drunken Indian).

Vampire Imperialism

The fact that the saga speaks so extensively, albeit indirectly, to issues of privilege — and to race especially — places it within a long history of vampire fiction. As Gelder's *Reading the Vampire* relates, vampire lore is intricately related to imperialism, capitalism, and issues of race. Arguing that much British fiction functions as "imperial Gothic" that "reflects Britain's interests in, fantasies about and suspicions of the East," Gelder reads *Dracula* as promoting an anti–Semitic mythology (11). More generally, he argues that *Dracula* speaks to the master/slave dialectic and "can help us to understand why we are compelled to create the 'other' as the object of our hatred and our hunger" (134). Auerbach makes similar claims, contending that "xenophobic fear" inspires *Dracula* and that the novel explores the nightmare "of a racially alien foreigner ruling and transforming England" (148). While the Count is framed as an abhorrent racial other, 20th-century vampires have become increasingly sympathetic cultural outsiders (as explored in chapter 1). However, despite their Otherized status, vampires often wield a great deal of privilege. Anne Rice's vampires, for example, are akin to vampire aristocracy and are, as Auerbach puts it, "beautifully devoid of social consciousness" (154). The Buffy series also traded in quite a bit of unexamined representation of privilege, with white middle-class Americans as its heroes and nary any humans or vampires of color in sight.[5] Some writers have lamented this trend in vampire fiction, though, and have attempted to redress it in their work. Charlaine Harris, for instance, is critical of the tendency to equate being American with being white and middle class.[6] Her Sookie Stackhouse texts circulate around issues of race, sexuality, and class in ways that question prejudice and existing systems of power. Jewelle Gomez's *Gilda Stories* also critiques societal norms, focusing in particular on historically entrenched racism. *Twilight*, in contrast, is more in keeping with *Dracula* in its execution of racialized vampire mythology — especially in its adoption of a colonial gaze.

Twilight frames America as the new frontier for vampires (with Forks being the Western resting place of these good pioneers), constructing Europe (and Italy in particular) as the old world, and La Push (and nonwhite society) as "outside," Other, and poverty-stricken. We might read the Cullens as the "good Americans," the Volturi as old-world power, and the Quileute as noble savages *in need* of colonization. In fact, Edward describes the Volturi as "a very old, very powerful family of our kind," noting, "They are the closest thing our world has to a royal family, I suppose" (*NM* 19). Edward frames their rule as a necessary evil, telling Bella in *Breaking Dawn* that "the Volturi aren't supposed to be the villains, the way they seem to you. They are the foundation of our peace and civilization. Each member of the guard chooses to serve them. It's quite prestigious; they all are proud to be there, not forced to be there.... They're only alleged to be heinous and evil by the criminals, Bella" (580).

Here, calling the Volturi the "foundation of ... peace and civilization," Edward characterizes their power as maintaining order. In so doing, Edward depicts them very much in keeping with white colonizers of the past who justified their conquest of the globe as obligatory and framed their control over other cultures as a "civilizing" force. Just as America ultimately broke with its European roots in order to found a "new" country (which of course depended on the displacement and genocide of the existing population), so does Carlisle, a vampire Columbus of sorts, create his own virtual vampire empire on the western edge of the new world — an empire that of course requires the local natives to be subdued — as indeed they are by the saga's close.

Twilight *as Colonial Text*

Twilight furthers the representation of Native Peoples as savage (a representation *necessary* to the colonial project) by presenting them as wolves. Robert F. Berkhofer, in *The White Man's Indian: Images of the American Indian from Columbus to the Present*, argues that over four centuries of imagery have sedimented the notion of the "good Indian" as someone who "was hospitable to invaders and whites, was thought to be strong, noble, calm, and brave, and assumed to live a life of liberty, simplicity, and innocence" (28). The "bad Indian," on the other hand, was associated with nakedness, lechery, polygamy, promiscuity, and was thought to be cruel to captives, take part in constant warfare, and mistreat women. Meyer draws on both of these traditions, presenting the Quileute as a brave and simple people, and championing those who are kind to whites (such as Jacob, Seth, Billy). Yet her saga is infused with the stereotypical legacy of the bad Indian as well — the wolf boys are perpetually half-naked, their people are given a history of polygamy via the story of the third wife, they are shown to be unnecessarily prejudiced against the good Cullens and eager to wage war against them, and, via the storyline of Emily and Leah especially, they are shown to mistreat women.

While Meyer explains her inclusion of the Quileute as coming about due to her visit to Forks and discovery of their legends, noting that she didn't plan for the wolf strand of the narrative at the outset, it cannot be denied that representing a real indigenous people as wolves is in accordance with a colonialist viewpoint. I am not suggesting that this viewpoint was intentional on Meyer's part. However, as the famous essay by literary theorist Roland Barthes, "The Death of the Author," makes clear, authorial intent is largely a moot point. Meyer readily admits that she had concerns about her depiction of the Quileute. When asked by a fan if she had "any negative recourse for the fictional portrayal of their tribal members as werewolves," Meyer answered:

> I was pretty worried about this myself. However, to this point I've had nothing but positive feedback from Native Americans, both Quileute and otherwise. I actually got a letter on MySpace from a girl who is the daughter of one of the council members (she titled her message Quileute Royalty), and she loved the werewolf thing. The common theme in the positive feedback that I've gotten is that the Native Americans I've heard from like that my Quileute characters are fully formed characters whose ethnicity is just one aspect of who they are, rather than their main feature.[7]

Here, Meyer's comments reveal that she had some sense she was taking liberty with another culture's legends and history. However, by telling the story of one fan, who she significantly names as "Quileute Royalty," Meyer deflects criticism. Then, by obliquely referring to positive feedback about her lack of focus on ethnicity, she further averts the question of portraying tribal members *as* werewolves. In effect, she skirts the question, avoiding the implications not only that is she appropriating another culture's legends, but also that her adaptation of said legend turns Quileutes into werewolves—a shift that is decidedly *not* in keeping with traditional Quileute legend. In another question-and-answer session, when asked why she chose certain settings, she shared, "I was nervous about what the real life citizens of Forks would think, and more especially what the real life people of La Push would think — I'd taken some rather big liberties with their fictional history, and I wasn't sure if they would find it amusing or irritating."[8] Again, she reveals an awareness that her "liberties" might be taken as an affront. What she does not seem aware of, though, is how said liberties build upon a history of appropriation in the name of white, colonial interests. Further, as pointed out by Willis-Chun, Meyer fails to recognize her profit as cultural theft. As Cynthia Willis-Chun argues, "Meyer's decontextualization and revision of the Quilteutes' legend did them violence because they were no longer products of the tribe, but of the author" (273). Meyer's framing of their legends as "fictional history" is troubling in its suggestion that their history and legends are "mere fairytales" where "she denies the sacred context of these stories, altering them for her (own) commercial purposes" (Willis-Chun 273).

Meyer's well-known stories about dreams inspiring the *Twilight* series are especially interesting here — just as dreams are filled with our subconscious longings, beliefs, and desires, so too is our writing — thus, while she might not have *meant* to appropriate Quileute history nor include a racialized, colonialist view, she nevertheless does. Moreover, by rendering the oppression that colonialism relied on and the white privileges it fostered invisible, the series works to maintain the status quo. By presenting "vampire privilege" as incredibly desirable in her texts, Meyer, by extension, presents such socially constructed privileges as acceptable. Though I doubt Meyer is intentionally writing from such a colonial view, her sociohistorical positioning cannot help but shape her knowledge as well as her depiction of Native culture. Or, as Sherman Alexie argues, "When non–Indians write about us, it's colonial literature. And unless it's seen that way, there's a problem."[9] Yet, Meyer does not seem aware of this colonial view; rather, she frames herself as an innocent fan of Quileute mythology. As she shares:

> The Quileute (*Quill*-yoot) legends Jacob tells Bella in chapter six of *Twilight* are all genuine Quileute stories that I learned when I was researching the tribe (which is a real tribe with a truly fascinating and mystical history). All are actual Quileute legends, except for the vampire myth about the "cold ones." I latched onto the wolf story (the actual Quileute legend claims that the tribe descended from wolves transformed by a sorcerer).[10]

Though Meyer "latched on" to these stories, as far as I can tell, she did not correspond with any Quileute peoples nor seek out the Tribal Council to enquire whether it was okay to depict their legends in the series, let alone to determine whether her Google research was correct. Rather, she read about the Quileute on the internet, just as Bella does in the series. Meyer freely admits this when discussing how she decided on the Forks setting and the inclusion of the Quileute, noting, "I turned to Google, as I do for all my research needs."[11]

A modern James Fenimore Cooper, who, "like so many authors of his time ... knew little or nothing of Native Americans directly," Meyer carries on a long tradition of white authors who know little to nothing of indigenous peoples nevertheless establishing them "as a significant literary type in world literature" (Berkhofer 93, 11). While Cooper gave us Natty Bumpos, Meyer has given us the Native American as modern werewolf. She follows the convention of not allowing Native characters to marry the heroine, which, as Berkhofer points out, disallows Native characters to ever function as a hero (94). She also carries on the tradition of using indigenous characters as "backdrop" and thus, as is the norm with such fiction, raises "no real criticism of American values" (98).

As Rob Schmidt, of the blog *Newspaper Rock*, argues, such non–Native co-optation of indigenous history tends to distort Native legends and culture and results in the perpetuation of negative stereotypes. As Schmidt writes,

> Non-Natives have a long history of borrowing Native legends, stories, concepts, beliefs, and practices. And then simplifying them, changing them, sometimes bastardizing them beyond recognition. The result is a mishmash of mistakes and stereotypes amid nuggets of actual information.

In Meyer's case, one of the founding legends of the Quileute as being descended from wolves is "bastardized" into depicting Quileute people as werewolves. One of the few printed accounts of this legend reads as follows:

> Then kwati, the Transformer, went on and reached the Quileute land. He saw two wolves. There were no people here. So kwati transformed the wolves into

people. And he told these people, "For this reason you Quileute shall be brave, because you come from wolves. In every manner you shall be strong," said kwati [Andrade 85].

Notice that the legend emphasizes the strength and bravery of the Quileute. Meyer, though, also emphasizes their violence and animality. The traditional colonial stance that her work conforms to translates into the white characters in the series, be they vampire or human, being presented as more civilized — the nonwhite Quileute, in contrast, are exoticized, animalized, and turned into either "noble savages" or howling beasts. Just like the government agent sent to La Push in 1883 who gave Quileute children names from the Bible and American history (effectively erasing their own culture and history), so does Meyer stamp a new name on their cultural legends— werewolf. This designation has been so effective that fans repeatedly ask about werewolves in Quileute legend, an action that understandably dismays tribal storytellers.[12]

As for characters in the series, Edward also adopts a colonial view, telling Bella that "werewolves are unstable. Sometimes, the people near them get hurt. Sometimes, they get killed" (*E* 30). Here, Edward is akin to a white man talking about the dangerous men of color that violate and endanger white women. This is an interesting switch given that historically Native peoples were far more peaceful than their colonizing counterparts (*and* in the *Twilight* universe, vampires are actually far more dangerous to humans than the Quileute wolves). But, in keeping with the white view of history, the white Cullen vampires represent a colonizing force whose worldview and actions ultimately benefit the lives of the Quileute by story's end. Further, the representation of the wolves as less civilized, as closer to nature, and as running in packs all accords with the historical justifications that argued that colonization was necessary to tame savage peoples. Further, when Edward shares with Bella that Carlisle is responsible for the truce between the Cullen vampires and the Quileutes, he presents his family as a noble clan of benevolent rulers who act as a civilizing force. Bella *naturally* adopts this view in *New Moon*, assuming the wolves are savage killers. In the final book of the series, *Breaking Dawn*, the idea that the colonization of the wolf is necessary is further promoted when the Cullens introduce "culture" to Jacob, inviting him into their home. Sleeping and eating outside at first, in various states of undress, he is gradually "civilized" and moves inside the house, or into the white world. Esme feeds and clothes the wayward wolf-boy, offering him shelter and sustenance.

In regards to the wolves' past history with the Cullen's, Edward shares with Bella that "we outnumbered them, but that wouldn't have stopped it from turning into a fight if not for Carlisle. He managed to convince Ephraim Black that coexisting was possible, and eventually we made the truce" (*E* 30–31). Here, the Cullen vampires are again represented as the civilizing force in contrast to the wolves. This is interesting given that historically Native peoples were far more peaceful than their colonizing counterparts; the vast majority of Native peoples were not warriors, but lived in communal societies valuing what Disney dumbed down into "the circle of life" in *The Lion King*. As Paula Gunn Allen in *The Sacred Hoop* notes, according to the native view, "life is a circle, and everything has its place in it" (1). Colonialism, she argues, is what tore this web apart. Alas, this aspect of Native American history is lost in the *Twilight* universe, and Meyer depicts the Quileute as dualistic, hierarchical, and patriarchal.

This historical representation is particularly ironic given that patriarchy was *introduced* to the Quileute *by whites*. As detailed in George A Pettitt's study, *The Quileute of La Push*, "There is no evidence" of "allegiance to any one chief until the naming of a chief and sub chiefs by white men about 1855" (4). Yet, even though Pettitt admits that the Quileute were not a hierarchical, patriarchal culture prior to colonization, he nevertheless continues to focus on men and male customs of the Quileute in his study. As he hails from a patriarchal culture, and is writing in the 1950s, his own cultural conditioning superimposes patriarchy onto Quileute culture. Meyer, over 50 years later, enacts a similar "patriarchal-ization" of the Quileute. As Gunn Allen documents, traditional indigenous culture was usually gynocratic and was never, she claims, patriarchal before "contact" (2). Rather, the "colonizer's patriarchal perspective," which "is based on the white man's belief in universal male dominance," led to the "patriarchalization" of indigenous culture (32–33). Over the years, what she names "colonialist propaganda" led to the false belief that Native Americans were male-dominated (32).

Though Meyer claims that the Quileute legends Jacob tells Bella in chapter 6 of *Twilight* are genuine, various depictions of Quileute culture in the series are decidedly *not* genuine. For example, according to the "Legends" chapter in *Eclipse*, Quileute society does not allow women to be warriors, treats wives as property, seems to care only about the fathering of sons, and honors women only for their mothering role and their willingness to sacrifice their lives for their children. More specifically, in *Eclipse*, the story of the third wife, who sacrifices her own life to allow the defeat of the cold woman, is entirely fictional. Bella, after hearing this story, relates. "I was trying to imagine the face of the unnamed woman who had saved the entire tribe, the third wife. Just a human woman, with no special gifts or powers. Physically weaker and slower than any of the monsters in the story. But she had been the key, the solution. She'd saved her husband, her young sons, her tribe. I wish they'd remembered her name" (*E* 260). While it is certainly in keeping with Native belief to value the strength and sacrifice of strong women, it is *not* in keeping with such lore to forget such a pivotal figure's name — rather, this reveals the colonial standpoint of Meyer — a woman who comes from a religion and culture that devalues the importance of females and nonwhite people. To say nothing of her fictional depictions while claiming "genuine" knowledge is a gross injustice.

As Andrea Smith argues, "Indian nations were for the most part not patriarchal and afforded women great esteem, Indian women represented a threat to colonial patriarchy as they belied the notion that patriarchy is somehow inevitable" (285). In regards to Quileute culture specifically, Pettitt reports that many Quileute "bear their mother's name and quietly state that they can't remember who their father [wise]" (74). Further, the fact that premarital sex and/or out-of-wedlock pregnancy was not condemned by the Quileute indicates they did not accord to the misogynistic views engendered in patriarchy where women become property of men, taking their names and being "given" to them in marriage. Pettitt also notes that the Quileute don't place a high importance on rank or hierarchy, yet, when he pressured them to name "important people," three of the five names they gave to him were female. Considering he conducted his research in the 1940s, an era far more zealous in its patriarchy than current times, the Quileute beliefs and practices regarding women are refreshingly egalitarian. Yet, in her texts, Meyer depicts the Quileute as *more patriarchal* than either the Cullens or the people of Forks. This depiction, though likely subconscious, is undoubtedly informed by Meyer's Mormon beliefs.

Championing Whiteness as Next to Godliness, Or, Bella Makes the White Choice

Taking such proclamations from the Book of Mormon into account puts a different spin on the ways in which the Quileute are represented in the series. As a reminder, according to Mormon belief, Native Americans, referred to as Lamanites, are descendants of Hebrews who "strayed" and became "cursed" with dark skin.[13] The promise of the Lord to the Lamanite descendents according to Mormonism is that they shall yet receive the gospel and become a white and delightsome people (as explored in the previous chapter). In *Twilight*, these teachings materialize in Meyer's depiction of the delightfully pale vampires and the animalistic Quileute — whose key character, Jacob, is tellingly given the surname "Black." In contrast, the good Cullen vampires are presented as ultra-white.

Of course, the championing of whiteness that the texts enact can also be read in relation to Christianity generally. As Dyer notes, whiteness has been historically associated with godliness. Referring to the "whitening of the image of Christ," Dyer argues that constructing god as white has perpetuated notions of white superiority, framing whites as more spiritual and godly than raced people (17). Dyer, who grounds his approach to whiteness via an analysis of religion, race, and imperialism, insists that Christianity has "been thought and felt in distinctly white ways for most of its history" with reference to "the gentilising and whitening of the image of Christ and the Virgin in painting; the ready appeal to the God of Christianity in the prosecution of doctrines or racial superiority and imperialism" (17). This argument relates particularly to Edward and Bella. Bella repeatedly refers to Edward as God-like and angelic, emphasizing his whiteness. In *Twilight* alone, she claims Edward has "the face of an angel," "the voice of an archangel," and relates that "I couldn't imagine how an angel could be any more glorious" (19, 311, 241). She also refers to him as "my perpetual savior," as a "godlike creature," and notes he "looked like a god" (166, 292, 65).

For her part, Bella accords to "the image of the glowingly pure white woman," an image that Dyer reads as related to the Virgin Mary and Eve (17, 29). As Dyer asserts, "In Western tradition, white is beautiful because it is the colour of virtue. This remarkable equation relates to a particular definition of goodness ... purity, spirituality, transcendence, cleanliness, virtue, simplicity, chastity" (72). Arguing that all concepts of race are also concepts of bodies, Dyer asserts that "black people can be reduced (in white culture) to their bodies and thus to race, but white people (are not) reducible to the corporeal" (14). Contending that white people are associated with transcendence and spirituality and nonwhite people are allied to immanence and corporeality in the Western imagination, Dyer's work offers a fruitful approach to examine the white/dark and spiritual/bodily binaries the *Twilight* saga circulates around.

While the white hero and heroine of the saga are consistently associated with transcendent, eternal love (and link specifically to Mormon notions of eternal progression and eternal families), the raced characters are connected to mortality, immanence, and the body. They are focused on for their darkness. For example, when Bella first sees Jacob and his friends at La Push, she notices the "straight black hair and copper skin of the newcomers" (*T* 117). She describes them as "all tall and russet-skinned, black hair cropped short" with "strikingly similar hostility in every pair of eyes" (*E* 263, 323). As the series continues, the Quileutes' dark faces are emphasized repeatedly in a fashion reminiscent of the notion that all raced people look the same. While Edward's eyes and hair are gold, Jacob's are dark. His last name is Black, and he, like other Quileute characters, is associated with a lack of light — his house has "narrow windows," and he has "long, glossy black hair" that hangs "like black satin curtains on either side of his broad face" (*NM* 130, 131). These descriptions suggest that his vision is shrouded, that he does not see things clearly — he is not like the all-knowing Edward whose mind-reading skills are shown as a benevolent power used to protect Bella.

While Edward's whiteness is portrayed as next to godliness, Jacob and other Quileute characters' russet-colored skin and black hair are associated with animality — an association with religious as well as colonial roots. In addition to its depictions of the Quileute characters as literally and figuratively darker, the series also features a number of other characters whose villainy is either associated with nonwhite skin and/or black hair and clothing. One of Bella's would-be killers in *New Moon*, Laurent, for example, is described as having olive skin and glossy black hair in the book and is played by an African

American actor in the films. The evil Volturi, their name redolent of black vultures, are repeatedly associated with their long black capes and "dark ruby eyes" (*BD* 118). Felix and Demetri, two of the Volturi guard, have an "olive complexion," and Aro has jet black hair (*BD* 463). In the film adaptation of *New Moon*, these evil characters are visually associated with darkness and savagery: Laurent tries to eat Bella in the meadow, and the Volturi make lunch of a group of unsuspecting human tourists.

Even the raced vampire allies are portrayed as more savage than their white counterparts. In *Breaking Dawn*, the animal-skin-wearing Amazonian vampires are depicted as "feline" (*BD* 612) with "long black braids" (612). Bella observes, "It wasn't just their eccentric clothes that made them seem wild but everything about them" (612). Noting their "restless" eyes (612), "darting movements," and "fierce appearance," she relates, "I'd never met any vampires less civilized" (613). The Brazilian workers featured earlier in the book on Isle Esme during Edward and Bella's honeymoon are similarly associated with darkness. The "tiny coffee-skinned woman" with "dark eyes" is "superstitious" and speaks in what Bella describes as an "alien tongue" (114, 136). Meyer's settings are also imbued with light/dark symbolism. Forks, the small-town, predominantly white, good old-fashioned American locale, is associated with its white inhabitants, while La Push, as a contrasting outside, is populated by the "russet-colored" Quileute. Here, the texts structurally enact a culture/nature and civilized/savage split. While Forks drips with nostalgia for (white) days gone by—from the nice small-town sheriff (Charlie) to the quaint old cars (Bella's truck), La Push is associated with untamed and uncontrollable nature. It is during her first visit to La Push that Bella learns about the cold ones. It is both a place where she is put in danger (via storms, motorcycle riding, and cliff diving) and a place where she learns dangerous things (about cold ones and werewolves). Forks, in contrast, is a place where she is repeatedly saved by Edward and where she is able to retreat to the safe havens of her father's house and the white — literally and figuratively — Cullen mansion. Most of her injuries are sustained outside of Forks— in Arizona, in the forest, in the mountains, or at La Push. Structurally, Forks is the safe zone. As the town's name indicates, Bella is at a fork in the road and must choose between the white vampire knight (Edward) and the dark-skinned wolf (Jacob).

Yet, the metaphorical connotations of the town's name are never expanded upon to include any consideration of the racial realities of the Forks setting. In the texts, there is no explicit indication that Forks includes nonwhite inhabitants within its boundaries nor any consideration of the racialized dividing line between Forks and La Push. As blogger Debbie Reese notes, this erases the real-life racial tensions that permeate the area:

> Tension between vampires and Quileutes, but no tension between the white people in Forks and the Quileutes. Because it is fantasy, we've got to suspend disbelief and accept the vampire/Quileute tension. And, because it is fiction, we're encouraged to

believe that the people of Forks and the Quileutes get along. But, relations between whites and Quileutes have been complicated [n.p.].

These complicated relations involve a history of less-than-friendly relations between whites and Quileutes, from whites resisting Quileute children attending school in Forks to disputes over fishing and timber rights. Meyer thus not only misrepresents Quileute culture and legend but also fails to represent the realities of racism and poverty that shape this area of the world in particular and the United States in general. And, as Brianna Burke argues in her essay "The Great American Love Affair: Indians in the *Twilight* Saga," Meyer's texts serve the dominant ideology that undermines native sovereignty and cultural survival.[14] Given that Native Americans are the poorest group in the United States with the lowest incomes, poorest housing, lowest education rates, and highest rates of unemployment and domestic abuse, the failure to seriously address any of these issues in the texts, the fandom, or the wider cultural phenomenon is remiss. Similarly ancillary texts such as Gresh's devote a half-page sidebar to the Quileute, and cite only a website as source (41). While Meyer's failure to address problems with poverty amongst the Native American community or the racism that Native Americans regularly endure *could* be brushed off via the claim this is meant to be a fantasy, not realistic historical fiction, it is even more problematic when texts devoted to analyzing the saga fail to consider issues of race and privilege.

Got Vampire Privilege?

In the series, while being a Quileute dooms one to life in "on the res" and/or existence as a perpetually violent/naked wolf, being a vampire accords one all sorts of privileges that echo real-world white privilege, or the social capital afforded to those with white skin. For example, the Cullens' beauty, wealth, and intellect are linked to their whiteness. When Bella first sees them, she is unable to stop staring, noting, "Every one of them was chalky pale.... Paler than me, the albino" (*T* 18). She goes on to relate that they were all "devastatingly, inhumanly beautiful" (*T* 19), describing their faces as ones "you never expected to see except perhaps on the airbrushed pages of a fashion magazine, or painted by an old master as the face of an angel" (*T* 19). Although Bella never uses the word "white" in this description, the references to models, classic art, and angels link the Cullens to images that are associated with whiteness in U.S. culture. As the series progresses, Cullen beauty continues to be linked to whiteness, from their pale skin to the clothes they wear to the white mansion they reside in. Edward, in particular, is associated with white perfection. He has a "perfect" body that is "white, cool, and polished as marble" (*BD* 25).

Yet, the whiteness of the Cullens is never explicitly linked to their privilege in the texts. This accords with white privilege in the real world, which functions as an unmarked, naturalized category conferring superiority on those with white skin. Much like in the real world, such privilege is not recognized but serves as an unexamined and desirable norm. In one of the most influential essays examining such privilege, "Unpacking the Invisible Knapsack," Peggy McIntosh argues that whiteness works as a hidden system of advantage in our world. Yet, as McIntosh notes, the majority of whites do not recognize the unearned privilege their whiteness confers upon them. She explains: "I have come to see white privilege as an invisible package of unearned assets that I can count on cashing in each day, but about which I was 'meant' to remain oblivious.... Whites are taught to think of their lives as morally neutral, normative, and average, and also ideal" (78). Dyer similarly notes that whites do not acknowledge their whiteness and that this in itself is a function of power. Asserting that in Western culture whites play predominant roles, Dyer maintains that "at the level of representation ... whites are not of a certain race, they're just the human race," emphasizing that "this assumption that white people are just people, which is not far off from saying that whites are people whereas other colours are something else, is endemic to white culture" (10–11).

In *Twilight*, Bella never names Edward as racially white, nor does she consider the mixed-race connotations of her friendship and possible romance with Jacob. She does not, in effect, *see* race, including her own. This failure is in itself a trapping of white privilege, and her failure to recognize her own racially based privileges results in a text that renders white privilege invisible. In kind, young readers of the series are not encouraged to examine the racial power dynamics that shape their own lives; rather, they are given the facile message that race does not really matter, that we should all just focus on getting along (or on nabbing ourselves a super-cute vampire boyfriend). Indeed, as Meyer and her ultra-white vampires do not seem aware of their white privilege, it is not surprising that the (predominantly white) fans do not recognize or address the underexamined view the texts foster. This erasure of race is, I argue, linked to the way the series offers an unexamined representation of white privilege delivered in a "colonial viewpoint" style.

Characters in the series and readers of the series alike are encouraged to accept whiteness as the *norm*, and to desire, without question, the privileges whiteness brings. Simultaneously, characters in the texts learn that "brown men" are dangerous beasts. Readers are repeatedly offered stereotypical and inaccurate portraits of the Quileute, who, in Meyer's world, have been morphed into wolf-people. Representations of Jacob and his werewolf tribe offer particularly delimiting depictions of race, ethnicity, and cultural mythology, representing Native Americans as savage animals, as has so often been the case in colonial texts. Native Americans, we learn, are the wild, uncivilized werewolves who (unlike their vampire counterparts) cannot control their violence or their desires. Their brown skin (constantly focused on in the books) is contrasted to the marble-white skin of the vampires. Further, the werewolves are associated in various ways with the "uncivilized" and "savage"—they are more violent, they do not actively choose who to love but experience "imprinting," they run in packs, they are prone to group-think and unexamined hierarchical power structures, and they smell, howl, eschew clothing, and so on. Compared to the "high-culture" of the Cullens and the Volturi, who appreciate music, art, and the "finer things," and who fittingly look like classically beautiful statues, the werewolves are smelly, wild, and all too natural. Yet, these stereotypical representations of race and culture in the texts have often been celebrated, as if Meyer is being inclusive and culturally sensitive. However, when one looks at the saga via a privilege lens, it becomes apparent that various binaries are upheld that perpetuate rather than question dominant ideologies—dichotomies such as white/black, light/dark, transcendent/immanent, and mind/body. It is to this last binary that I will know turn.

Edward as Mind, Jacob as Body

Edward is undoubtedly positioned as a mega-mind in the series. Not only can his laser brain read the thoughts of others, but he also has various graduate degrees, is well-spoken and well-read, and is distanced from his ice-cold body. Jacob, in contrast, is grounded in corporeality — his bodily size, color, and temperature are constantly focused on in the books. Further, as a werewolf, Jacob and other Quileute characters are associated in various ways with the unruly body. The wolves' bodies run hot, and their physical anger cannot be contained. For example, in *New Moon*, Paul, a wolf pack member, cannot control his anger and erupts into wolf form to fight Jacob. And Sam, the wolf pack leader, reportedly lost control and attacked his fiancé Emily, permanently disfiguring her face and body. More generally, the werewolves' lack of clothing further emphasizes their status *as* bodies.

Edward, on the other hand, is depicted as a restrained, civilizing mind. His "impossibly selfless" (*E* 49) nature is proven when he does not try to prevent Bella's continuing friendship with Jacob as well as through his politeness and magnanimity when dealing with the wolves. He is represented as always thinking about Bella, as having her best interests at heart. He is a good influence who encourages her to pursue college. And, he denies his own bodily desires in various capacities. As a vegetarian vampire, he controls his bloodlust; as a 106-year-old virgin he controls his sexual desire. On the other hand, Jacob, a modern-day Tonto, is the trusty fun-loving sidekick —fixing Bella's motorbike, holding her hand, cheering her up — but never capturing her heart or conquering with his mind. Readers, like Bella, are encouraged to see Edward as the smart choice for the brainy heroine Bella.

Furthering the emphasis of the body/mind binary is the sexualization of the wolf body. Echoing traditional representations, of colonized peoples, the series overtly sexualizes the Quileute characters, representing Jacob (and the other wolves) as perpetually in a state of undress. This is in keeping with historical representations as scholars such as van Lent and Bird explore. Captivity narratives depicted Native men as dangerous yet desirable noble savages and warriors according to van Lent. Van Lent suggests that turning the Native male into a sexy, romantic hero both renders his supposed violence sexy and ameliorates the history of colonization. Noting that "the representation of Native Americans without clothes is a very old tradition. Even during the age of exploration the earliest narratives and accompanying sketches drew considerable attention to the Natives' scant clothing or total lack of it," van Lent's work can be read in relation to how *Twilight* functions not only in keeping with traditional Harlequin romance formulas (as argued in chapter 2) but also in keeping with the subgenre of "Indian Romance" (217). This genre relies on the "heavily muscled torso" of Native male, leading to both sexualizing Native men and emphasizing their "natural" propensity for violence (van Lent 215–56).

In terms of the sexualization of Native Americans, the focus on Jacob's nudity is in keeping with a history of white representations of Native men as more bodily, more brute, and more animalistic than white men. Although Bella obsesses over Edward's attractiveness, too, it is most often his eyes that she fixates on. The traditional notion of eyes as "windows to the soul" is key here. While Bella most often concentrates on Edward's head — his hair, eyes, and mouth, she appreciates Jacob's warm skin and muscled torso. Once again, Edward is rendered as mind, Jacob as body. In these various representations, Jacob is associated with bodily activities and desires. Through his mechanic work, his excessive need for sleep, his hot temperature, and his hot-headedness, he is grounded in his body — and, significantly, a body he cannot control. The sexualization of Jacob (and the other wolves) became even more pronounced with the film adaptations wherein an often-shirtless Taylor Lautner, the actor who plays Jacob Black, flexes his muscles for the camera. The texts offer a precedent for this representation though, focusing as they do on the wolves' lack of clothing. As van Lent notes, "The representation of Native Americans without clothes is a very old tradition" (217). This tradition began with early narratives and sketches and continued through to modern films where indigenous peoples seem to be in a permanent state of undress. In *Twilight*, this nakedness is justified via the transformation from wolf to human and is so ubiquitous that Bella asks Jacob, as noted earlier, "Is it really so impossible to wear clothes, Jacob?" (*E* 215).

The images surrounding the film adaptations play on this wolf nudity, portraying the "wolf pack" wearing shorts only. All of the actors had to "muscle-up" for their roles. Most notably, Taylor Lautner packed on 30 pounds of muscle in order to secure his role as Jacob for the second film adaptation. Burke names this as part of a larger cultural trend in which Native American males can never live up to the ways they are presented in the media. To be fair, some of the white male actors are also very muscular (most notably Kellan Lutz), but the books themselves and the film adaptations do not sexualize the white vampires in the same way nor to the same extent as the Quileute wolves. Overall, Edward is beautiful and god-like, while Jacob is "hot" and muscular. As Dyer notes, sexuality is often characterized as dark and bestial in the Western imagination, with nonwhite males portrayed as more overtly and uncontrollably sexual, while "the whiteness of white men resides in the tragic quality of their giving way to darkness and the heroism of their channeling or resisting it" (28).

In the texts, Edward is indeed able to resist his "dark" sexual side, while Jacob is not. This is interesting in relation to the historical tendency to depict the vampire in relation to dangerous sexuality. Burton Hatlen analyzes this in relation to the western belief that dark men are more (dangerously) sexual than white men. Like Winnubst, he reads the vampire as a symbol for the black rapist: "Dracula's skin is, of course, pale; but his black clothes and cape, his affinity with the night, and his penchant for entering bedrooms at midnight through windows combine to make him an archetype of the dreaded black rapist" (129). Yet, *Twilight* takes away these dark symbols, dressing its vampires in white and giving them the ability to abide daylight. In turn, it projects dark vampire sexuality onto the Quileute wolves, framing them as sexual predators. In fact, Jacob sexually assaults Bella — sedimenting the age-old claim that brown men are dangerous beasts who will besmirch pale women. Winnubst names this as a nightmare pervading the Western unconscious in which "the white girl is designated as the most highly cathected target of 'raced' male violence; and rapists are designated as 'raced'" (2). In *Twilight,* Bella is the target of such violence via Jacob's sexual assault. Though the text frames this as "just a kiss," the fact that Jacob is her beloved best friend makes this act all the more abhorrent. Indeed, the text indicates that raced men are prone to violating those they love as in the cases of Jacob/Bella and Sam/Emily. Edward, in contrast, is represented as a savior and, significantly, a defender of Bella's chastity. He warns Bella that "werewolves are unstable. Sometimes, the people near them get hurt. Sometimes, they get killed" (*E* 30). This warning prompts her to ponder Emily's scars: "I saw in my head the once beautiful face of Emily Young, now marred by a trio of dark scars that dragged down the corner of her right eye and left her mouth warped forever into a lopsided scowl" (*E* 30). This, the most overt case of domestic abuse in the series, along with Jacob's sexual assault and psychological manipulation of Bella, pits Quileute wolf-men as violent savages in contrast to Edward the manly, always-in-control protector, Carlisle the do-gooder, the Volturi police force, not to mention the real police chief in the book — Charlie Swan who is, surprise, surprise, a white male. Jacob, in contrast, is a wild wolf-boy who, in reference to Emily's facial scars, jocularly admits "hanging out around werewolves has its risks" (*NM* 330). The text substantiates Jacob's claim with its representation of violence as a genetic trait for the Quileute.

Further, through the narrative choice to have wolves experience "imprint-ing," the saga takes away their free choice in regards to whom they will love. Especially in a book that values true love above all else, removing choice in aspects of love renders the wolves' imprinting as an inferior form of love. More-over, the fact that two wolves in the story imprint on pre-toddlers constructs them as rather creepy pedophile types. And, though Jacob argues that "all this mandatory love-at-first-sight was completely sickening!" and refers to "all that imprinting werewolf garbage," by the series' end, he has happily imprinted on Renesmee. Symbolically, he both gives in to his "animal nature" and assimilates into white vampire culture.[15]

Whiteness and Wealth and Heterosexual Monogamy as Ideal

Related to what I would argue is a colonial depiction of Native Americans in the series is an unexamined championing not only of white privilege but also of class privilege. As the Mormon Church is exceedingly wealthy, with current assets of, at a low estimate, $30 billion, and as the church itself is not critical of wealth but rather actively works to amass it, it is not surprising that wealth is held up as virtuous and good in the *Twilight* series by Meyer, the devout Mor-mon author. The Cullen family is a model of both industry (amassing a mini-empire) and education (with a slew of degrees between them). This strand of the narrative is in keeping with what Krakauer names the "optimistic cosmol-ogy" where the "virtue" of Mormons allows for the amassing of wealth with no worries of greed. "Making money was a righteous pursuit," he notes. "The Lord smiled on the rich, as well as those who aspired to become rich" (112). Further, the text's championing of wealth is analogous to its championing of whiteness — and on the other side of this positive depiction of *white* wealth is *dark* poverty. In the saga, the ultra-white Cullens have access to endless wealth while work-ing-class Bella has to "marry up" in order to gain access to their knapsack of privileges.[16] Significantly, her marriage literally results in her becoming *more white*; her turn to vampire means she will now be as pale as her beloved Edward.

And, the Cullens are presented as living the good life, and their activities and tastes are associated with high culture: they like classical music, appreciate art, value education, like to travel, and have sophisticated fashion and home décor know-how. Their home is depicted as opulent, decked-out in white and gold with an accompanying garage populated with luxury cars. Isle Esme (an island off the coast of Rio de Janeiro owned by Edward's vampire mother, Esme Cullen) carries on the white opulent theme with a master bedroom that Bella dubs "the white room" (*BD* 100). Edward is similarly associated with wealth, as when he gives Bella a five-carat diamond and casually remarks, "I inherited quite a few bobbles like this" (*E* 43). His gold eyes and hair, as well as the gold bed in his room and his shiny Volvo, associate him with riches. In contrast, Jacob's house resembles "a tiny barn," and his garage consists of "a couple of preformed sheds that had been bolted together with their walls knocked out" (*NM* 131, 133). Rather than luxury cars and designer duds, he has an '86 Rabbit and wears sweats or "ragged, grease smeared jeans" (*E* 77). Edward has multiple college degrees and composes symphonic lullabies, whereas Jacob fixes cars and has to be reminded by Bella to do his homework. Here, the differing class levels, as well as the way whiteness is associated with wealth and intelligence and non-whiteness with physicality and manual labor, contributes to the racial divide.

Bella, though she has white skin privilege, is economically more in line with Jacob. Referring to the "scarcity of my funds," she details her "decrepit computer" and refers to her dad's small two bedroom house with its "shabby" chairs and lack of a dishwasher. Bella reveals she lived in a "lower-income neigh-borhood" back in Arizona and is relieved when she sees that most of the cars in the Forks high school parking lot "were older like mine" (*T* 5, 43, 14). Later in the series, Jacob suggests Bella is attracted to Edward's wealth, but she denies this. Although she is represented as not initially liking being the recipient of the Cullens' gifts, by the series' end she has enjoyed parties, a designer wedding dress, a luxury vacation to Isle Esme, and boasts a fancy cottage complete with a new closet full of clothing. When Bella chooses Edward at the series' close, she also chooses wealth and all the privileges it brings — she also chooses, as noted above, to become *more white*.

Alas, as with the saga's failure to depict the realities of poverty and lack of sovereignty of indigenous peoples, it also fails to address the realities of socioe-conomic disparity in the United States. Though I am not suggesting that fiction be required to address such realities, the series' unexamined advocation of wealth begs consideration — especially given the rough economic reality that contemporary readers live in. But, like the romance genre it echoes, the saga offers a facile presentation of riches, suggesting that any young heroine might "marry up" into a Cullen-like family. Departing from the Austen and Bronte texts it pays homage to, *Twilight* does not critique socioeconomic inequalities and the imperative placed on females to better their position through marriage. Rather, it romanticizes wealth via celebrating "the bloated accounts that existed all over the world with the Cullens' various names on them"; revealing the Cul-lens have "enough cash stashed all over the house to keep a small country afloat for a decade," the texts never condemn their wealth, let alone frame it as exces-sive or greedy (*BD* 647). Depicting Bella's rise from an antique truck-driving girl who could fit all her clothes in one suitcase to a woman whose closets are filled with designer duds and who drives luxury cars as a dream come true, the saga enacts a typical rags-to-riches romance fantasy. Unlike the Sookie Stack-house series, whose working-class protagonist mistrusts wealth, Bella never questions the Cullens' riches.

The story of the poor, downtrodden beauty falling in love with the rich and powerful guy is nothing new in the world of fiction, and this series is, of course, meant to be fantasy. However, the problem arises when we consider that readers are encouraged to uncritically view the wealth and power of the Cullens as desirable. The unfair advantages the Cullens have in terms of their ability to accumulate wealth are never analyzed, let alone put in any sort of negative light — rather, the Cullens are seen as demi-Gods who rescue Bella from her working-class life of run-down cars and old computers. Given that the United States has the most unequally distributed wealth and income in the world and that the gap between rich and poor here is bigger than in any other industrialized nation, the unquestioned idealization of wealth in the series is problematic. As critic bell hooks argues, we over-identify with the wealthy because media socializes us to believe they are better — *Twilight* certainly accords with this claim, prompting us to see the wealthy vampires as better, and encouraging readers to applaud Bella's rise from working-class nobody to Mercedes-driving vampire-ess.

In addition to uncritically celebrating whiteness, to appropriating Quileute legend, and to privileging wealth, the saga also supports married, heterosexual monogamy as ideal. Serving as a quasi-defense of traditional marriage, the saga closes with all of its main players paired off — even baby Renesmee has been paired with Jacob, and the long-time bachelor Charlie has found love with Sue Clearwater.[17] In *Twilight*, as in wider U.S. society, marriage is a highly regulated privilege exclusively granted to heterosexual couples. While these marriages can cross species and racial boundaries (vampire/human, wolf/vampire, white/non-white), there is no suggestion that marital relations between partners of the same sex could occur. Quite to the contrary, the inclusion of various homophobic sentiments from characters suggests that the *Twilight* universe is a decidedly heteronormative place. Given that Meyer is Mormon, a belief system that is notoriously heteronormative, this depiction is not surprising. Yet, some sentiments expressed in the text seem to go above and beyond Meyer's staying true to her Mormon roots into the territory of actually making fun of nonheterosexuals. For example, in *Breaking Dawn*, when Quil says to Jacob, "I don't notice girls anymore," Jacob jokes, "Put that together with the tiara and makeup, and maybe Claire will have a different kind of competition to worry about." Here, Jacob suggests that Quil being "made up" at a birthday party indicates that he might be gay; Quil responds by making kissing noises at him, asking: "You available this Friday, Jacob?" In a similar vein, Leah teases Jacob about his heartfelt goodbye to Quil, snickering, "*Thought you were going to make out with him*" (*BD*, emphasis in original, 265). Here, the fact that the Quileute characters are the only ones to voice homophobia is ironic given the fact that Native culture is historically more accepting of diverse expressions of gender and sexuality. Such sentiments would be far more realistic out of the mouths of Meyer's demi-god Mormon vampires. Alas, the Cullen crew do not *voice* their homophobia, but their actions certainly suggest that married monogamy is the only viable model.

As Mormonism names homosexuality as an unspeakable sin, the Cullen's silence around the issue is to be expected. Indeed, the saga for the most part completely silences homosexuality, concurring with the "love that must not speak its name" approach. However, scholarly responses to the saga have analyzed its heteronormativity. Kane, for example, argues, "The ascendency of the Cullens in contemporary popular culture raises questions about the implications of celebrating vampires that exalt in an ordered world where sexuality is drained of homoerotic elements, phallically driven, reproductively oriented, and kept within the constraints of the patriarchal family" (104). Kane further contends that the series is replete with "essentialist heterosexual imagery," especially in relation to Bella and Edward's physical relationship (114). Heterosexual sex, she argues, is naturalized. Exploring how this depiction not only allies to cultural contexts surrounding anti-gay marriage debates and legislation but also comes out of a context in which gay/straight alliances are now common in schools and diverse expressions of sexuality have become more tolerated, Kane reads the series as "part of a cultural backlash against queer figures" (116). On the other hand, scholars such as John Granger cheer the saga's celebration of "normal" marriage. During a talk at *Summer School in Forks*, he quipped, "Obviously for there to be a love relationship we have to have one of them be a man."[18] Here, his pronouncement that romantic love can only take place between a male and a female concurs with the saga's message that only heterosexuality *can and should* exist.

The Problem with Vampire Privilege

To conclude, the incredibly privileged view of life Meyer constructs in her *Twilight* universe is never examined or critiqued within the narrative; rather, the Cinderella-esque saga sends out-moded messages about being saved (in various ways) by a white hetero vampire-prince who can jet off to his family's own private island with no considerations for bank account balances let alone undergoing racial profiling during his travels. The message that such an under-examined representation of whiteness, wealth, and heterosexuality gives to readers is that these privileges are desirable. Further, by rendering the oppressions such privileges are dependent upon invisible, the series works to maintain the status quo and further sediments white, wealthy, male, heterosexual, Christian privileges. While claims that we live in a post-racial, post-feminist world have become increasingly common (especially following Obama's election), the United States is far from the diverse utopia many pundits claim. And, while the *Twilight* texts are indeed fictional, we cannot discount the power such fiction holds over our lives, over the socialization of young readers, and we need to, even as fans, be critical about some of the more delimiting messages the series offers about race, class, gender and sexuality.

Chapter 8

Consuming Desires
Can You Buy That Twilight Feeling?

Though an exact count of fans is hard to calculate, the number of *Twilight*-related blogs, forums, and fan sites confirms that the *Twilight* fandom is enormous. Echoing the popularity of *Buffy* and *Harry Potter*, the series has spawned an undeniable cultural zeitgeist. Fans spend huge amounts of time and money on the franchise, buying *Twilight* merchandise, traveling the country (indeed, the globe) to attend *Twilight*-themed events, making pilgrimages to Forks, devoting their time to reading/writing blogs and fan-fiction. Fans do not merely read and discuss the books or see the films, but become consumed by the *Twilight* world. In what follows, I explore the fandom and the resulting franchise, arguing the *Twilight* phenomenon speaks to the consuming desires of the contemporary moment. The phenomenon has resulted in the commodification of the saga and its settings, into an unprecedented movie franchise aimed predominantly at young females, and into a thriving *Twi*-net world brimming with websites, blogs, podcasts, fan-boards, videos, and fan fiction. Examining the addictive metaphors that permeate consumer culture in general and the *Twilight* fandom in particular, this chapter indicates the ways contemporary culture promotes addiction not only to products, but also to ideas, subcultures, and activities.

Reading *Twilight* as enacting a new form of "vampire capitalism" that places traditional representations of love, romance, and sexuality within a tantalizing world of newfangled vampires and consumer desires, the chapter explores the franchise's use of slick packaging and catchy slogans to ignite our desires to consume. Like the ads that allure us into buying things we don't need, *Twilight* and its surrounding commodification builds on the messages that dominate real-world advertisements, which flatten out the difference between love, desire, sex and consumerism. Moreover, the franchise's framing of females *as* consumers is in step with the construction of the female as commodified object on the one hand and as the ultimate consumer on the other. As such, it incorporates many of the capitalist messages girls and females are already accustomed to—namely, that they should be hard-working yet ever-ready to shop, devoted to family yet consumed by commodity desires, committed to not "over-eating" yet insatiable in their quest for body improvement. This chapter thus explores why the celebration of consumerism that *Twilight* both depicts and engenders is so seductive for contemporary fans and speaks especially to our advanced consumer capitalist moment.

Vampire Capitalism

Much scholarly work has focused on the vampire as a figure that both responds to and reflects capitalism. Karl Marx linked vampirism to capitalism, referring to capital as "dead labor," which is "vampire-like" and "lives only by sucking living labor" (qtd. in Gelder 20). As Gelder notes, "Marx drew on the metaphor of the vampire time and time again to describe its processes" and repeatedly "describes capital as a vampire nourishing itself upon labour" (20). Capitalism is defined by, according to Marx, its nature to consume in excess, which, in Marx's words "lives the more, the more labour it sucks" (257). The figure of the vampire as an insatiable capitalist able to "live more" only by sucking on the life-blood of others is an apt metaphor for the relationship between labor and consumption. Indeed, capitalism requires that its labor not only produce but also consume. Without the desire to "consume in excess," capitalism could not thrive. Yet, as Rob Latham documents in his article "Consuming Youth," "Marxists ... have been forced to admit that the desire animating capitalism is more complex than mindless gluttony, that the vampiric relationship between capital and labor involves libidinal investment, an erotic complicity" (130). Arguing that "the individual laborer has been irreversibly penetrated by and infected with consumerist desire, an unquenchable, acquisitive lust," Latham's work explores the consumer desire as both pleasurable and dangerous. Further, he reveals the way in which desires are commodified and labor is solicited via capitalizing on human pursuits of wealth, youth, status, etc. Reading the vampire as a capitalist boss-figure that turns her/his victims into exploited laborers, Latham contends that "the capitalism-vampire made willing accomplices of its laborer-victims by soliciting their desire with seductive promises—for example, perpetual youth — and profitably attaching it to an ever-expanding realm of commodities" (130). His assertion that "individual vampire texts illuminate specifically the historical phases of capitalism in which they are produced" proposes that vampire narratives provide a fictional lens through which to assess the realities of capitalism in the time periods of their production and reception (128). *Dracula* has been examined in this vein, with scholars such as Gelder, Auerbach, and Williamson interpreting the count as a figure that speaks to capitalism. Gelder, for example, links Dracula's wealth to mobility, suggesting that the vampire's ability to traverse national boundaries without national allegiance poses a threat to hierarchies of nation and class (14). Though Dracula is a cultural outsider and Other, who is coded as dark and foreign, his wealth gives him cultural capital. His character might thus be read as an incarnation of the West's fear regarding migration and reverse colonization. Gelder, arguing that Dracula "returns colonization to the colonizers," expands on these fears, reading the count in relation to the historical contexts of colonialism and cartography (12).

Reading the vampire as representing "an excessive form of capitalism" that "must be exorcised," Gelder contends that in framing Dracula as a bad capitalist monster "the novel enables (British) capitalism to rehabilitate itself, to cohere as an 'organic' process with a 'human face' which used money responsibly and sensibly" (19). While the capitalist as vampire was a common representation in the mid–19th century, this depiction has by no means died out. Rather, Anne Rice's textual vampires, as well as various vampires from film and television, represent the vampire as a consumer capitalist. In Rice, Louis, Lestat, and other vampires don't work yet are able to amass wealth (Gelder 119). Likewise, in *The Hunger*, Miriam Blaylock amasses not only lovers but also products. Her stylish dress and swanky New York condo speak to her wealth. Miriam is a modern-day vampire capitalist extraordinaire, stalking prey in night clubs and collecting vampire companions along with art and other upper-class markers. Those she turns lack her vital immortality, though, and thus might be read as of a lower class than she. Their ultimate fate, wherein they live forever but in a very aged, withered, but fully conscious state can be read as a metaphor for exploited labor — unlike Miriam, they are not successful capitalist bosses, but the laboring class who wither and (partially) die as a result of Miriam's entrepreneurial vampirism. In the film *The Lost Boys*, vampirism is again utilized to explore capitalism, but this time in relation to youth culture as "lost" in a maze of mindless, dangerous consumption.[1] Similarly, in *Near Dark*, the crazed vampire family members are presented as mindless consumer gluttons in contrast to the protagonist's wholesome family. *Buffy the Vampire Slayer* also nods to its cultural context of consumer capitalism, depicting high school culture as one concerned with fashion, products, and class status. And *Twilight*, as noted in the previous chapter, explores consumerism, ultimately championing wealth more so than criticizing socioeconomic hierarchies.

All of these various vampire texts explore "vampire capitalism," some of them celebrating economic formations that privilege the few (Rice, Meyer) and others critiquing amassing wealth as exploitive, dehumanizing, and resulting in dysfunctional family formations (*The Hunger, Lost Boys, Near Dark*). That the United States has spawned so many texts exploring vampires as either voracious or reluctant consumer capitalists is hardly surprising given its status as *the* consumer capitalist nation. Indeed, as Williamson argues, "The Western vampire is a creature of capitalism" that functions as a fitting figure for the "permanently transient culture of capitalism, adapting and evolving in order to keep pace with the cultural moment" (183). As such, Western vampires "advance" along with capitalism, responding to the vicissitudes of this profit-motivated ideology that, like the vampire, relies on consumption. Further, as Williamson explores, the vampire "expresses the pathos of the condition of the many in the West — the condition of alienation," a condition that Marx links to capitalist systems (183). This "borderline figure" is thus both producer and laborer, both consumer and consumed and, as an outsider, is alienated from humans, from her/his labor and the processes of production. Williamson takes this symbolism further, suggesting that the impossibility of achieving the capitalist dream makes us all outsiders, all metaphorical vampires. She writes, "When we do not achieve the success we are promised is open to all, we too are outsiders to the Anglo-American dream" (188). Capitalism ameliorates this outsiderdom, this alienation, with the lure of consumption. On this count, the media's role in supporting consumerism (or metaphorical vampirism where we "feed" off others' labor) cannot be overlooked. It is to these topics that I now turn.

Consumer Twi-*Citizens*

According to theorist Neal Postman, "We are a people on the verge of amusing ourselves to death" (4). Drawing on Orwell and Huxley, his work addresses our media-saturated culture as leading us into a "Brave New World" where media functions like an entertaining, thought-sapping "Big Brother." While studies show that individuals deny how much they are personally influenced by the media but admit *other people* are certainly influenced, there is no doubt that all of us, whether we like it or not, are influenced by our media (Durham 183). And, given that the media in the United States is a profit-driven industry owned and controlled by a handful of corporate conglomerates seeking to maximize their profits, it aims to construct U.S. citizens *as* consumers of products as well as consumers of the message that advanced capitalism is a fine and good thing. As Durham explores in *The Lolita Effect*, the media is a powerful mythmaker that promotes "ideas that are in the best interests of the most powerful groups in society" (188). These myths are "produced and disseminated by the people with the means to create and widely circulate them, and who will also benefit the most from them" (188). Geared toward a consumer, commodity culture, such myths promote certain ideas about gender, sexuality, race, class, citizenry, politics, belief systems, and so on. In effect, these media myths encourage us to *buy into* certain identities via the purchase of products, texts, and ideologies. Roland Barthes, one of the founding scholars of such myths, writes that "myth has the task of giving an historical intention a natural justification" (qtd. in Durham 183). In contemporary times, the historical intention to construct citizens as consumers has been rendered natural, as if the urge to shop were a biological imperative. And, just as vampires are addicted to blood, so are modern-day consumer-citizens addicted to products. Further, as Durham reveals, challenges to consumerism are made to seem foolish, while "the myth-

makers slyly suggest that conforming to the myths is edgy, hip, and rebellious"
(190). This plays out in myriad ways, most notably perhaps in the current
moment's obsession with edgy T-shirts proclaiming one's political, activist,
and/or ideological beliefs. We have been successfully misled, in effect, to believe
that purchasing T-shirts with catchy slogans is a political act. As Latham point-
edly asks, "Who is to drive the stake of critique through the vile undead heart
of consumerist desire?" (132). Not the media, which inculcates us with many
messages about consumerism and class, not only mirroring our (very American)
desires for economic achievement but also *producing* them.

As Diana Kendall explains, "In a mass-mediated society such as ours, the
media do not simply mirror society; rather, they help to shape it and to create
cultural perceptions" (139). Drawing on bell hooks, she further contends that
we over-identify with wealthy people (such as celebrities and politicians) because
our media socializes us to believe they are better (139). In fact, her claim that
"the blurring between what is real and what is not real encourages people to
emulate the upper classes and shut out the working class and the poor" could
well be directed at *Twilight*, a series that emulates its wealthy vampires and suggests that the working-class Bella's best option is to aspire to vampire status,
leaving the poor Jacob behind. Like the U.S. media generally, *Twilight* presents
white upper-middle-class lives as the norm and presents other lives as deviant.
Proving Day's claim that vampires are emininently commodifiable figures that
"are highly reactive to the market, providing a sensitive barometer of the social
reality in which they exist," *Twilight* vampires reflect contemporary American
desires for wealth and unfettered consumption (viii). Not only do they all have
designer wardrobes and designer cars, but they also live in a mansion, work the
stock market to their advantage, and own their own private island. The Gold-
man-Sachs of the vampire set, they do not feel any sense of guilt about their
wealth. This desire for riches and lack of concern regarding the consequences
of their consumption (including for how their gas-guzzling ways or indiscrimant
deer, lion, and bear consumption affects the ecosystem) reflects a culture that
wishes to consume without thought of bank balances or planetary consequences.

As Linn points out in *Consuming Kids*, ours is a culture saturated by consumerism, so much so that even war and environmental destruction are being
sold to us on a massive scale. While George W. Bush advanced the linkage
between being a good citizen and a good consumer in the sociopolitical realm,
the *Twilight* franchise is promoting links between being a good person, female,
fan, lover, etc., to the consumption of *Twilight* narratives and products. Giving
new meaning to the colloquial phrase "I shop, therefore I am," *Twilight* is creating a massive base of *Twi*-consumers whose slogan might be "I consume *Twilight* products, therefore I am." The power of this *Twi*-consumerism has helped
solidify the profit margins of the store Hot Topic during an economic downturn, has rescued the troubled film company Summit, and has launched the
careers not only of a number of actors, but also of a number of pseudo *Twi-*

celebrities who blog, emcee at *Twilight* events, and/or launch online and real-world businesses to cash in on the *Twilight* phenomenon.

Given that the author is affiliated with a religion far from shy about its own profit motives, this *Twi*-consumerism is a fitting trend. As Brodie documents, the communistic/socialist ideology that pervaded early Mormon days is now "vehemently disavowed" in favor of big business and financial wizardry (402). However, the profit motivation of one of the world's wealthiest religions is readily apparent. Contending that monetary skills are seen as equally important to spiritual excellence, Brodie documents how Mormonism enacts "an ingenious blend of supernaturalism and materialism" (295). Tithing is a core component of Mormonism that has resulted in "a vast pyramidal organization, in which the workers finance the church, advertise it, and do everything but govern it" (402). Framing believers of Mormonism as the labor that allows for its success, Brodie addresses the religion as an economic system that could not thrive without the labor/monetary power of its practitioners. This devoted "labor" has resulted in the Mormon Church's status as one of the most powerful economic institutions in the United States. Not only do Mormons control large sections of real estate, industry, and employment in their home state of Utah, but they also have vast interests in retail, insurance, the media, and real estate on a national level. With revenue of well over six billion a year, the church functions as a not-so-mini-empire with aims to colonize the globe not only with its belief system but also with its profit-maximizing ethos. *Twilight*, functioning as an admixture of a commodified transmedia text, a franchise, a fan-driven phenomenon, and a Mormon/capitalist friendly text, also has come to function as a not-so-mini-empire (hence the often-used term "fan-pire" to designate the *Twilight* fandom). However, in contrast to other recent texts' focus on well-to-do vampires (such as *The Hunger*'s Miriam Blaylock, Anne Rice's hedonistic, rock-star vampire Lestat, or *The Lost Boys'* consumer brat-pack vamps), *Twilight* charts the rise of working-class girl to vampire-queen, depicting Bella's transformation in keeping with the American Dream. Not only does she morph from ancient-truck-driving girl to Mercedes-owning super-vamp at the narrative level, but she also serves as a vehicle for real-life readers to play out their romantic fantasies and character/celebrity crushes. By buying into *Twilight*, so to speak, fans buy into the Mormon and capitalist-friendly message that wealth is desirable (and attainable), that someday their prince will come — and he will be a rich vampire able to rescue them from their woes, economic and otherwise.

The Feminization of Consumerism, Or, Why Girls Want to "Consume" Edward

A key aspect of being a fan for many *Twilight*ers is consumerism, or the buying of *Twilight* products. In addition to purchasing T-shirts, bumper-stickers, buttons, photographs, and just about anything else one can imagine, *Twilight*ers also purchase travel to partake in fan pilgrimages, buy tickets for various *Twilight* tours and events, attend concerts of *Twilight*-related bands, and procure books related to the saga or recommended by its author. They, quite literally, become *consumed* by their devotion to the franchise. Not only does the *Twilight* series make this type of consumption seem desirable, representing Bella and Edward's love as all-consuming in a positive way, but also the franchise beckons fans to consume as much *Twilight* as possible.

Summit Entertainment partnered with Creation Entertainment to launch the "Official *Twilight* Convention" with stops all over the country that sell out to crowds in the thousands, and each weekend represents the opportunity to immerse oneself in the *Twilight* world by seeing the celebrities that star in the films, watching "exclusive" footage, and attending *Twilight*-themed parties, balls, and musical performances. Such immersion, however, does not come cheap. With weekend packages usually starting well over $100 and sometimes topping out closer to $400 (which does not include travel or hotel), one must be a virtual wealth-privileged Cullen-type to attend such events. As autographs, balls, and concerts are an extra cost on top of the admission price, this Creation/Summit enterprise has been raking in the cash on a year-round basis. However, the *Twilight* franchise is far from unique in its consumerized goals, and it could not be so successful if it did not exist in a cultural context that already constructs its citizens *as* consumers. Building on the linkages between sex/romance and consumerism, consumption as a requirement of proper femininity, and the commodification of youth culture, *Twilight* taps into a number of cultural myths and shifts, commodifying itself in ways that benefit the author, the film-makers and actors, the companies associated with its dissemination (Summit, Creation, Little, Brown and Company), as well as the many pseudo *Twi*-celebrities who now make a living out of blogging about, reporting on, or working for the franchise.

The phenomenon also taps into the sexualization of consumerism, or the way that sex and sexuality are now regularly used to promote consumerism. This linkage is not aimed at arousing sexual or romantic desire, but rather to arouse desire for products; such images "are intended to sell us on shopping" (Levin and Kilbourne 15). As noted by Durham in *The Lolita Effect*, the impetus to be or feel sexy becomes "a reason to shop" (180). In relation to *Twilight*, the desire to become a vicarious Bella who is adored by Edward and Jacob becomes a reason to shop. The desire to feel like a part of the fandom becomes a reason to shop. The need to immerse oneself in the saga becomes a reason to shop, a justification to travel, and an impetus to attend various *Twilight* events. That the franchise sexualizes this consumption is evident in T-shirts with sayings that turn the (usually female) wearers into sexualized objects, such as those that read, "Bite Me Edward," or, "Property of Edward Cullen."

Concurrently, the male celebrities in the series are served up as sexualized fodder for the fans. The actors playing the Quileute wolves become the shirtless, muscled wolf pack, pictured on posters with smoldering gazes and seductive copy. The actors portraying the Cullen vampires are constructed as sexual icons as well — photographed shirtless, with come-hither stares, or even surrounded by naked women. The female celebrities, though the fandom is purportedly made up of heterosexual females, don't escape sexualization either. Their "hotness" is commodified on the covers of magazines, on day- and night-time talk shows, and in the endless interviews that speculate about their sexiness and/or sexual activity. Stories of a romance between Kristen Stewart and Robert Pattinson fuel this consumer/sex linkage, encouraging fans to buy magazines with stories about a real-world Bella/Edward love affair.

On the flipside of this sexualized and commodified production of *Twilight* is the way that the consumption of products, actors, and images is framed *as* feminine. While many female fans (and female-helmed websites) embrace this construction, this is partly why the backlash against *Twilight* is so strong. In fact, the ire directed at the fandom, the franchise, and even at female characters and actors seems a contemporary case of what Andreas Huyssen articulated as "the gendering of an inferior mass culture as feminine" in his 1986 article "Mass Culture as Woman" (5). While Huyssen places this gendering as emerging in the 19th century and then fading in the late 20th due to the inclusion of more women into "high culture and its institutions," the backlash against *Twilight* reveals that devaluing what is seen as feminized consumption is still *undead* (13). In fact, it still seems a truism that "mass culture is somehow associated with woman while real, authentic culture remains the prerogative of men" (3). In the same way that matters of importance, governing, leadership, power, and so on are associated with masculinity, the private sphere, emotion, and so on are still feminized. Similarly, men are primarily constructed as producers, makers, and doers, while women are associated with consumption, passivity, and the "I shop, therefore I am" mantra. Huyssen, noting Marx's "privileging of production over consumption," argues that "the lure of mass culture, after all, has traditionally been described as the threat of losing oneself in dreams and delusions and of merely consuming rather than producing" (8). This construction of woman as consumer has been consistently fortified over the years with the concomitant formation of woman *as* shopper. And, just as the *Twilight* texts frame women in such a way (Jessica shops for a prom dress, Alice is preeminent consumer, and Bella laments her feminine failure to be interested in shopping), so does the *Twilight* franchise court, construct, and perpetuate the notion of woman *as* consumer. In fact, by the close of the series Bella is presented as successfully adopting her feminine/consumer identity — not only of the blood that will now sustain her vampire existence, but also of fashion, home décor, and luxury cars. She also inculcates her daughter into this realm, raising what we can assume will be an ultimate little consumer. As she details in *Breaking Dawn,*

> Alice and Rosalie usually began our day with a fashion show. Renesmee never wore the same clothes twice, partly because she outgrew her clothes almost immediately and partly because Alice and Rosalie were trying to create a baby album that appeared to span years rather than weeks. They took thousands of pictures, documenting every phase of her accelerated childhood [528–29].

Renesmee is thus a consumer culture's dream female, needing new clothes constantly. And Bella, carefully detailing how she deliberately chooses "clothes that looked frilly and feminine" for her daughter, has morphed into the definitive consumer mom, buying into the notion that through purchasing power one exhibits motherly love (*BD* 675).

Yet, this construction of women as consumers that the texts and the fandom both reflect and perpetuate does not translate into more than power to buy. Rather, within the *Twilight* cultural zeitgeist, as well as within general culture, "women are wooed as consumers yet rejected as people," as Douglas puts it (*Where the Girls Are* 271). Similarly, females are wooed as consumers of *Twilight* but rejected by the culture at large as "silly girls" or "rabid fans."[2] Indeed, the persistently false claim that *Twilight* is an exclusively young girls' phenomenon speaks to this phenomenon — real people, real grownups, it is suggested, cannot like *Twilight*. If they do, there is something wrong with them. The dismissal of *Twilight* as trivial is thus at least partly motivated by the still-pervasive cultural dismissal of femininity and its associations with mass/low culture, with consumption, with frivolity.

Consumer Culture Gone Wild

At the same time as it constructs female characters and fans as consumers, so, too, does *Twilight* substantiate many of the messages that make consumer culture thrive. It validates the message that youth is desirable and can be obtained, that beauty is of tantamount importance, that one's appearance reflects what kind of person one is, that the car one drives, the house one owns, the products one buys demonstrate one's worth. As Latham argues, "Consumer culture offers a Faustian bargain, a vampiric promise of undying youth which transforms its initiates into voracious consumers" (140). *Twilight* offers a similarly Faustian bargain not only to its protagonist Bella, but also to its fans— buy this book, this Team Edward T-shirt, this convention ticket, and you, too, can experience youth, belonging, meaning.... And, just as youth culture "communicates through commodities," so do *Twilight* fans, exhibiting their Edward or Jacob affiliation, their love of Meyer, their desire to be "sparkly."

While, as Douglas notes, "one of the most important things any group can become in America" is a market, the *Twilight* market is largely rendered unimportant and trivial on many levels— by scholars, by religious establishments, by the literary world (*Where the Girls Are* 24). In effect, the only arenas that have embraced *Twilight* (and only to an extent) are the publishing marketplace, the popular press, and the movie machinery/award ceremonies—all of which of course are benefitting greatly from *Twilight*'s success. To speak first to the book market, *Twilight*, like the *American Girl* books, has become a "series to buy for"; like those bastions of girl fiction, which function as what Sharon Lamb and Lyn Mikel Brown call "cata-novels," or books that are filled with products so as to allow for the creation of endless tie-in products for readers to buy, *Twilight* is brimming with consumerist possibilities (167). Though Meyer undoubtedly did not have this in mind when penning her dream-inspired novel, which she claims she never envisioned the public reading, her placement within contemporary U.S. consumer culture (and her devotion to a religion that values capitalism) undoubtedly colored her saga — so much so that many *Twi*-products are direct adaptations of things presented in the books and/or films, such as Bella's green dress, wolf bracelet, and engagement ring, Edward's shiny Volvo, or any number of items displaying the Cullen family crest. Hot Topic and Nordstrom have capitalized on these product tie-ins in particular, launching clothing, jewelry, and cosmetic *Twilight*-themed lines.

In addition to supplying the market with a number of *Twi*-products, the saga was undoubtedly snapped up by a publisher due to its promising profit possibilities. As Marianne Martens documents, Little, Brown, the publisher of *Twilight*, is one of the major transnational conglomerates resulting from the 1980s mergers in the book world (244). This conglomeration resulted in books being seen/treated as "transmedia products" that can be profitable across multiple platforms and has led to the valuing of books that have this potential over and above "innovative and creative works of high literary merit" (Martens 244). In a market in which profit potential has taken primacy over literary value, it is not surprising that *Twilight* was swooped up with a lucrative contract. It is, as Martens argues, the perfect example of a transmedia product. Further, not only does it lend itself to film adaptations, merchandising, and cultural tourism, but it also promotes something publishers find particularly desirable — the repetitive consumption of primary and secondary *Twilight* books. As the popular badge "Hang out? Sorry, I've got to read *Twilight* again," reveals, fans do not read the books once — but twice, three times, twenty times. However, in order to profit from this consuming desire, the *Twi*-franchise must produce *new* items for fans to consume — new editions, product tie-ins, and so on.

As Radway's study revealed, books with romance at their core are particularly conducive to repetitive consumption, so much so that romance itself becomes a type of commodity that readers "buy" through reading certain books, seeing certain films, buying certain products, and traveling to certain places (117). Consumer culture tells us that consuming commodities is an effective way to deal with life's pain and disillusionments and results in a populace that believes it can buy happiness. For females especially, romance novels perform the same sort of function — by consuming them, we are able to, as Modleski argues, resolve conflicts that are not resolved in life (57). This, as Modleski notes, promotes a dependency on such literature, which functions as a narcotic. However, as with most dependencies, there are diminishing returns, and we thus need more and more of the "drug" (57). *Twilight* "pushers" are happy to supply us with more, offering up an endless array of books, products, and con-ventions—they even frame themselves as such by naming their websites things such as *Twi-Addicts* and *Cullen Boys Anonymous*. In conjunction with these other consumer opportunities is the construction of the author, the characters, the actors, and even the mega-fans *as* celebrities.

In the early part of the phenomenon, Meyer was definitely an active part of this *Twi*-celebrity, tirelessly giving readings, communicating with fans, and speaking at events. In turn, fans' idolized her as a celebrity in ways similar to earlier vampire fans adoration of Anne Rice. Described as "fan-friendly to a fault," Meyer made the list of *Forbes* top 100 celebrities at number 26. Though she has since pulled back from the *Twi*-celebrity gauntlet, she is still a "star" to her fans, many of whom fondly refer to her as "Steph," as if she was a personal friend. Here, fans are akin to Radway's Smithton women, who adore their favorite romance authors and endeavor to express their gratitude to such authors by attending autographing sessions (97). Thanks to the internet, though, *Twi-lighter*s need not travel to such events (though many still do). Instead, they are able to express their gratitude virtually or via buying star magazines.

As explored in the article "*Twilight* and the Production of the 21st Century Teen Idol," the franchise "is based upon a carefully constructed form of celebrity that encourages fans to blur the lines between the beloved characters from the *Twilight* books and the actors who portrayed them in the films" (Aubrey, Walus, and Click 227). This is particularly apparent with Robert Pattinson, who fans view as the real-life Edward. Even Pattinson concedes to this fact, joking, "Girls scream for Edward, not Robert. I still can't get a date" (qtd. in Aubrey, Walus, and Click 225). This positioning is indeed harkened in the books, where Edward is situated as a celebrity by his Forks classmates, his adoring family, and even by other vampires. Meyer furthered this Edward-equals-celebrity meme in inter-views and readings, noting she herself is a "fan" of Edward. This positioning, as the article noted above claims, appeals particularly to young heterosexual female fantasies where girls imagine their favorite stars falling in love with them. At conventions, the costly autograph signings capitalize on these fantasies, giving fans the opportunity to meet and speak to their idols. McRobbie argues that this type of "star crush" is particularly appealing to young female fans as it makes no physical demands and also allows them to gaze rather than be gazed at:

> The pictures which adorn bedroom walls invite these girls to look, and even stare at length, at male images.... These pin-ups offer one of the few opportunities to stare at body and get to know what they look like. While boys can quite legitimately look at a girl on the street and in school, it is not acceptable for girls to do the same back. Hence the attraction of the long uninterrupted gaze [13].

This female adoration for male *Twi*-celebrities in particular and for the saga generally also accords to Dyer's claim that "stars are made for profit" (*Heavenly Bodies* 5). They help to sell books, films, newspapers, magazines, fashion, and so on. These "heavenly bodies" are particularly resonant in our celebrity-steeped cultural moment, so much so that even people very tangential to the *Twilight* universe have become *Twilight* celebrities. In particular, the women who run two of the biggest commercial websites, *The Twilight Lexicon* and *Twilight Moms*, have become pseudo-celebrities in the *Twilight* world. As of December 2009, *Twilight Moms*, which started as a MySpace group, had over 33,000 registered users. The founder, Lisa Hansen, has become somewhat of a *Twi*-celebrity, testifying to this fact by wearing a pin at *TwiCon* announcing, "Yes, I am THE Lisa." The tendency of such people to wear pins and or T-shirts identifying themselves speaks to this phenomenon — "*Twilight* Moms" T-shirts both announce one's affiliation and proffer a certain "status" on the wearer. Fan studies scholars examine these fan hierarchies wherein "knowledge, access, and status determine one's standing" (Willus-Chun 269). In such hierarchies, some have *access* to Meyer or the film stars/makers, those bloggers or fan fiction writers who have lots of readers/fans themselves have *status,* and those who know the most about the *Twi*-world have *knowledge.* Such a stratification of fandom culture, as Williamson's study of Anne Rice fandom reveals, often results in a jockeying for position in which certain uber-fans attempt to police the fandom or claim to have specialized knowledge of the texts or access to the author (128).

In addition to the celebrity status of top *Twi*-bloggers, the Quileute tribal leader and their public relations representative have become celebrities of sorts, attending the *New Moon* premier in designer-loaned dresses. As reported in the *Peninsula Daily News*, tribal spokeswoman Jackie Jacobs "was vigilant in inviting every star they met to come and visit."[3] In Jacob's words, "We extended invitations to everyone....We want the world to come to La Push" (n.p.). While the accompanying commodification of settings in books is certainly not without precedent (Transylvania being a fitting example), this commercialization of the Quileute people and their La Push home is rife with contradictions. Before exploring this commercialization further, allow me to expand on the related ideas of cultural tourism and the commodification of culture.

Imperial Tourism and the Commodification of Culture

As documented by various scholars, the historical impetus to travel (and to write travel narratives) is allied to what Gelder names "imperial tourism," or travel carried out "in the service of Western interests" (9). Gelder reads *Dracula* as a prime example of this "imperial Gothic" fiction, which reflected in particular "Britain's interests in, fantasies about and suspicions of the East" (11). Stoker (much like Meyer) had never visited the setting of his novel, and relied heavily on travelogues (Gelder 3). Due to the great success of his work, Transylvania has, according to Gelder, been "more or less completely appropriated by vampire fiction and vampire films" (1). As Gelder continues, "One of the peculiarities of vampire fiction is that it has—with great success—turned a real place into a fantasy. It is impossible, now, to hear the name without thinking of vampires" (1). Fred Botting also explores the commercialization of Transylvania, noting the plans to open a "Dracula Terror Park" in Romania (203). While Botting and Gelder are writing about Transylvania, they could just as readily be writing about Forks, the real-world setting for Meyer's saga, which she fleshed out by relying not on travelogues but on Google.[4] And, much in the same way Transylvania has capitalized on its fictional representation in *Dracula*, so have Forks, Port Angeles, and La Push, to varying degrees, capitalized on themselves as the locales of the famous *Twilight* vampires, wolves, and clumsy heroine.

While the only place in Port Angeles that plays up its affiliation to *Twilight* is the Bella Italia restaurant, Forks has become a *Twilight* mecca. The struggling former logging town deliberately courted the saga and its fans with the Chamber of Commerce creating a *Twilight* brochure, constructing various photo opportunities throughout town, and naming July 20th "Meyer Day." Given that the Forks economy was devastated after much of the area was shut down for logging, the town's enthusiastic response to becoming the home of Bella and the Cullen vampires was understandably motivated by a crumbling local economy. Thanks to *Twilight*'s popularity and the town's efforts to capitalize on this, the income of Forks went up over 300 percent in the past several years (Shapiro 192). In addition to retailers entirely devoted to the saga, Forks motels, restaurants, coffee shops, and grocery stores use *Twilight* as a way to lure fans and up profits. One grocer has a hand-lettered sign out front that reads "Bella shops here," while *Twilight*-themed items have been added to many menus. This holy grail location, with a sign that reads "Welcome to the *Twilight* Zone," at the western edge of town, is the location that has most enthusiastically capitalized on *Twilight*'s success.

In contrast, Port Angeles has only one restaurant that courts fans, and even this location seems a bit curmudgeonly about its reputation as *the* restaurant where Bella ate those infamous mushroom ravioli. When I ate there in June 2009, I sat at the bar and thus could hear the conversations of the wait staff. Two of the waitresses lengthily bemoaned how they were going to "lose it" if one more couple tried to replicate Bella and Edward's meal. The bartender looked on in sympathy, nodding his support for *Twilight* fatigue. At the bookstore next door, a hiking-clad couple from Europe asked the man staffing the register what all this *Twilight* fuss was about. He tiredly gave them a short spiel. Though the bookstore displayed many *Twilight* books in its front window along with some cardboard cut-outs of characters, the worker obviously resented this, indicating as much when I spoke with him about *Twilight*. In fact, he was quite pleasant until I noted I was writing a book on the saga — this revelation brought about a marked shift in him, an "oh, you are one of *them*" type of stance.

Like Port Angeles, La Push has not become the *Twilight* mecca that Forks has. Though the Three Rivers Resort at the "treaty line" sells a Jacob Black Shake, the area is markedly uncommodified. This more fractious relationship to the series no doubt has historical roots, not only given the fact that the series offers a questionable portrayal of the Quileute people and appropriates their sacred legends, but also because Quileute culture (like many indigenous cultures generally) has belief systems and practices that do not gel well with consumer capitalism. On the one hand, *Twilight* is yet another colonial text wherein a white author uses Native American characters and mythology for profit/pros-elytizing purposes; on the other, the surrounding *Twilight* franchise goes against Quileute notions that land is sacred, that storytelling is an oral practice (not one to be printed and commodified), and that culture is not for sale. As the area has a long history of "hokwats" (the Quileute term for whites) traveling to the area in order to see a "real Indian," *Twilight* can be read as furthering colonial tourism. As noted in a 1976 study, "Thousands of outsiders pass through La Push each year in search of the 'noble savage.' They are usually disappointed. Not only are there no tepees and feathers, but the Indians don't seem particularly noble, or, for that matter, very savage. Where is the comfortable television stereotype of Indians?" (15). To update this observation to the present day, thousands of *Twilight*ers come to La Push in search of Jacob, but there are no shape-shifting wolves let alone marked links to *Twilight*— where is the comfortable stereotype of Natives as animalistic, half-naked, semi-savages that *Twilight* depicts? Just as "nineteenth-century tourists wanted to see traditional clothing and quiet nobility," so do 21st-century fans want to have a "real Indian" experience, but one that they now fuse onto Meyer's wolf-infused tail — they want to find Jacob and the wolf pack, to maybe taste Emily's blueberry muffins or see her facial scars (Powell and Jensen 4). Instead, what they find is a beautiful, uncommercialized beach framed by cliffs. The surrounding reservation, which is less than one square mile in area, is far from ostentatious, and, true to the books, the houses are rather small and unassuming.

Like the Western film genre, which often frames land as an empty, blank space for whites to inhabit and civilize, La Push is viewed by many as an area rife for *Twilight* take-over. This fact is evidenced by the many writers who question why La Push is not jumping on the franchising bandwagon, as if to do so would be the only option that makes sense. This view itself smacks of our colonialist history and capitalist present — many cannot view the world outside of this frame (or choose not to), failing to understand how power and profit is not a prime motivating force for everyone, including the historically noncapitalist Quileute. Admittedly, the Quileute nation and some of its people are profiting from the series, but this fact has the tenor of being tolerated, as seen as inevitable, rather than Forks' contrasting enthusiastic attempts to milk the phenomenon for all it's worth. As a result, most of the profit that capitalizes on *Twilight*'s Quileute connection goes not to the Quileute people themselves but to big corporations (such as Mattel, for its Jacob Black doll), and to the author and filmmakers. A side beneficiary is of course the Mormon Church (given Meyer's tithing). Ironically, a theology that frames Natives as cursed is amassing quite a bit of profit from Meyer's rather stereotypical portrayal of Native people — one that also upholds the idea they are not "white and delightsome."

As most Americans (and indeed most people the world over who are not indigenous) get their messages/ideas about Native people from Hollywood and/or in popular literature, the representation and ultimate commodification of Quileute culture that the saga enacts calls for a detailed analysis of the saga's cultural impact. Going along with the Hollywood tradition of turning Native peoples into "things to be consumed by popular culture," which has, for the most part, promoted a singular idea of "the Indian," *Twilight* has rendered the Quileute people a "thing" to be consumed (by, for example, buying a Jacob doll, "authentic" sand from First Beach, or a wolf bracelet) and has promoted the lonstanding notions of indigenous peoples as poor, animalistic, and violent (Cobb 207). As Cythia Willis-Chun points out in her work, Meyer's revisions appropriate Quileute legends, making them her property rather than theirs (273). Quileute legends, in effect, have become *Twilight* property. Meyer specifically and the franchise generally are greatly profiting from this cultural appropriation.

Scholar Laurie Ann Whitt names such appropriation "cultural imperialism," noting that the "the marketing of Native America" is "a particularly virulent form" of this practice (139). As Whitt and others document, the commodification of indigenous culture is deeply entrenched in Western Culture, and "whether or not it is conscious or intentional, it serves to extend the political power, secure the social control, and further the economic profit of the dominant culture" (140). Linking such commodification to a "conceptual assimilation" that "serves to extend ... the continued oppression of indigenous peoples," Whitt's observations can be put to productive use in the analysis of *Twilight*, a text that not only commodifies Quileute culture/legend, but also has resulted in massive degrees of "conceptual assimilation" wherein the Quileute have been incorporated into the prevailing *Twilight* culture not in keeping with *their* culture, but with Meyer's depiction of them (143). Meyer does a further injustice to the Quileute by suggesting their history is fictional rather than sacred or religious— as Willis-Chun writes, "She denies the sacred contexts of these stories, altering them for her own (commercial) purposes"(273). This is all the more ironic given that the Quileute don't believe you can "own" stories.

While the Quileute refuse to allow their music to be recorded for *Twilight* tours or to play ball generally with the franchise, many companies and individuals are doing all they can to generate as much profit from this zeitgeist as possible. From bumper stickers to posters, from key chains to T-shirts, from trading cards to lion and lamb pendants, both real-world and online stores devote themselves to the selling of *Twilight*-related products. There are Edward pillowcases and wall decals (so you can sleep *on* him, or he can watch you sleep!), a wine called "Sparkling *Twilight*," Jacob umbrellas, *Twilight*-themed make-up palettes, "*Twi*-lights" hair highlights, and you can even request that a *Twilight* image be emblazoned on your Chase credit card — imagine the possibilities: you can buy *Twilight* items with a *Twilight* credit card and, if you are really flush, even drive home your bounty in a shiny Edward-type Volvo!

From Fan Engagement to Consumer Fests: The Corporatization of Twilight Events

In addition to the endless array of *Twilight* products, fan events and conventions have become ubiquitous over the past several years. The first event I attended was *Summer School in Forks (SSIF)*, which took place June 25–29, 2009, at the Forks High School. The least corporate and smallest of all the events I have attended, *SSIF* attendees received a yearbook-like program entitled "Forks High School: Class of 2009" that included event information, a "Course Catalog" that detailed all the different panels, discussions, and "extracurricular activities" (which included a "field trip" to First Beach, a *Twilight* film screening, and a "Real Forks Prom"), and pictures/bios of the "Student Body" (or attendees and speakers). Organized by Ann-Laurel Nickel, who previously organized similar *Harry Potter* events, *SSIF* allowed scholars and fans to immerse themselves into the real-world setting of Forks as if they truly were Forks high school students, teachers, or inhabitants. To heighten the verisimilitude of this experience, panels (held in Forks high school classrooms) included frequent interruptions from the principal over the classroom intercom system. Details such as these suggested that the *Twilight* world was *real*, as did the labeling of lockers with Edward and Bella's names, the appearance of the Hillywood players (the well-known *Twilight* parody group who remained in character throughout the weekend), and one *Twilight* Dad who had died his hair Carlisle blonde after losing a bet with his daughter (he even wore gold contacts throughout the weekend).

Many in attendance seemed to relish this verisimilitude. For example, when I was checking in, I overheard two women enthusing about how when they landed in Seattle it was raining, as it had been when Bella landed. One joked she hoped to see Charlie driving up or spy a shiny Volvo on the drive out to Forks. Throughout the weekend, the atmosphere buzzed with excitement and camaraderie, with scholars, fans, and those who had come along to accompany family or friends engaging with each other over meals at the Forks High School cafeteria, on the bus ride to La Push, or in the handful of restaurant/retail establishments where we stood out as nonresident "*Twilight*ers." Though there were a handful of vendors on-site selling *Twilight* T-shirts and other paraphernalia, the consumer opportunities were markedly fewer than those at other events. *SSIF*, in contrast with *Twi-Con* and *The Official Twilight Saga Eclipse Convention*, was not hypercommercial — instead, the focus was on analyzing and discussing the texts and film (only *Twilight* had been released at this point), meeting others interested in the saga, and immersing oneself into the real-world setting. My next event — a podcast that took place during Comic-Con 2009 (arguably fandom's biggest U.S. event) — was markedly different.

To attend the July 24, 2009, Borders Bookstore *Twilight* podcast evening event, potential attendees had to wait in line outside the bookstore the morning of July 24 in order to get a wristband. When I arrived, about an hour before wristbands were scheduled to be handed out, there were about 120 people in line. Those waiting excitedly discussed their other *Twilight* experiences and all the Comic-Con *Twilight* happenings, sharing with each other about screaming upon seeing *Twilight* actors. The first 75 people in line had been promised they would be part of the "signing event," where as-yet unnamed stars would be in attendance, *if* they bought a *Twilight* product at Borders. Those around me in line discussed how they already had *everything Twilight*-related that Borders had to sell. Yet, once inside, they were more than willing to buy something in hopes of a signature — indeed, there was a virtual frenzy once we were inside the store, with people running around grabbing *Twilight* merchandise. In contrast to *SSIF*, where the books were front and center, not once while I was in line did I hear talk of the books themselves, only of the stars from the first movie adaptation. In fact, most in line seemed to know the names of all the cast members, even minor ones, and the majority of the talk was about celebrity spotting.

At the actual night-time podcast event, the panel of speakers (comprised of well-known *Twilight* bloggers from sites such as *The Twilight Lexicon, Twilight Moms, Cullen Boys Anonymous,* and *His Golden Eyes*) talked mostly about the pending *New Moon* Film. The podcast also included talk of *Twilight* events at Comic-Con, a comparative discussion of the 2009 Comic-Con *Twilight* events to those from 2008, a *Twilight* trivia quiz, and various personal anecdotes of the panelists' celebrity encounters. Though the talk was rather roundabout and repetitive, the enraptured audience listened intently, only becoming loud when expressing their excitement over the frequent "give-aways" that punctuated the discussion. While I did not attend any of the actual Comic-Con panels, I heard stories of people camping overnight to reserve a spot and was told that some people at the front of the line were selling their prime places in the ballpark of $300. This willingness to get close to *Twilight* celebrities at any cost is particularly apparent at the now-omnipresent *Twilight* conventions traveling the nation, where celebrity autographs start at $35 dollars each and can only be attained *after* buying admission to the conventions themselves, which range in cost from $20 for a one-day pass, to well over $300 for "VIP" full convention access.

Twi-Con, billed as the "premiere unofficial conference for Stephenie Meyer and the *Twilight* saga," was the largest to-date convention in the United States of its time and took place from July 30 to August 2, 2009 (*Twi-Con* Official Program). Over 2,800 people preregistered with 3,000-plus ultimately attending this event, which was "created for the fans, by the fans" and, according to the official program, fans came from "30 countries and four continents" to attend (*Twi-Con* Official Program). Summit's contract with Creation Entertainment and their "Official *Twilight* Conventions" have since supplanted *Twi-Con,* but at the time, this convention was a big deal to fans. Organized by four fans, it was far from smooth running. Registration was jammed and chaotic, with lines extending outside the Dallas Sheraton hotel location. In fact, registration moved so slow that the opening ceremony had to be pushed back. Despite these and other organization problems, *Twi-Con* was exemplary in its attempts to offer a participatory fan experience as well as in its attention to varied programming. Unlike the official conventions ran by Summit and Creation Entertainment that have since supplanted *Twi-Con,* the convention included break-out sessions (modeled after academic conference panels), video screenings, creative writing workshops, Hillywood Show dance instruction, and even "Cardio with the Cullens." With four days of scheduled programming, including concerts and an evening "Volturi Ball," the convention also included a large vendor hall and numerous photo/autograph opportunities with *Twi*-celebrities. For those in attendance, *Twilight* clothing seemed to be obligatory, with very few people not decked out in *Twi*-gear.

Though Summit and Creation entertainment were not formally involved with *Twi-Con,* they did send a representative to attend. One of the organizers saw this as "damage control" to appease fans who were disgruntled about the announcement that Bryce Dallas Howard would be replacing Rachel La Fevre to play the role of Victoria. At the debriefing session I attended as a panel organizer, we were warned to try and keep the Q&A and post-panel discussions positive and to diffuse fan disgruntlement or negativity. With a general "we don't want to anger Summit" tone, the convention organizers seemed to fear being critical of the corporate power behind the franchise, especially as they hoped "this is by no means the first and last *Twi*Con" (Official Program). Alas, although two *Twi-Cons* were planned for the summer of 2010, one in Las Vegas and one in Toronto, the Dallas convention would indeed be the first and last event of its kind. This fan-created event couldn't compete with the regular, national events ran by Summit and Creation. These conventions, unlike *Twi-Con,* do not include break-out sessions, any sort of "academic component," or opportunities for fan participation beyond taking pictures/getting autographs (each of which costs a pretty penny). Instead, they are, in the main, opportunities to "buy that *Twilight* feeling" (my phrasing). These official conventions represent the general corporatization of *Twilight*, where a participatory grassroots fandom has moved more and more toward a franchise model. Just as the second film was far more corporate than the first, so, too, have later conventions become more focused on promotion and profit than on participatory, shared involvement between fans. For example, at the *Official Eclipse Convention* held in Los Angeles in June 2010, one huge auditorium held back-to-back opportunities to see and hear *Twilight* celebrities. General admission seats were at the far side in the back, barely allowing visibility of the stage. Nearby, the vendor hall and various set pieces from the films (Volturi chairs, Bella and Jacob's motorbikes) offered minimal opportunities for participation via either shopping or taking photographs. Gone also were the interactive Q&A sessions of *SSIF* and *Twi-Con*. Instead, attendees could drop written questions into metal boxes labeled with the star/character names. Judging by the uniformity of the questions during celebrity appearances, these questions are carefully screened.

In addition to the more consumerized, more celebrity-focused conventions, *Twilight* bloggers, vloggers, parody groups, and reporters have simultaneously become more celebrified. For example, the creators of *The Twilight Lexicon* and *Twilight Moms* attend many of the conventions with "VIP status." Thus, while the *Twi*-net component of the fandom still has some of its participatory character (due in part to the nature of internet dialogue and its reliance on reader comments, discussion threads, etc.), it, too, has become more corporate, with the bigger sites now being commercial and the bloggers accordingly viewing their role as more "official" and "important." Having met the creators of *The Lexicon* at *SSIF*, I have watched how their status has morphed along with the conventions. While at *SSIF* they milled around and chatted with the fans, they now function as demi-celebrities, hiding behind curtains and insisting they are too busy to chat or for interviews. The creator of *Twilight Moms*, Lisa Hansen, exudes a similar aura of importance. Given that Hansen wore a button proclaiming, "Yes, I am THE Lisa," at *Twi-Con*, as discussed above, her opinion of herself as a *Twi*-star flourished rather early in the phenomenon. While the celebrity status of "uber-fans" is far from a new phenomenon, the *Twilight* franchise has courted this celebrification to unprecedented effect, courting bloggers and others at film sites and giving privileged access to select groups so that they might disseminate information about the filming, the *Twilight* stars, and other *Twilight*-related news. In effect, this group of "uber-fans" supplies all sorts of free advertising for the franchise, creating a constant buzz via "leaking" information to insatiable fans—a fan-block that, it is important to note, represents huge purchasing power.

Though Summit Entertainment was in a rather dire financial situation pre–*Twilight*, it has since grown into a profitable power player in the film industry—a feat all the more impressive given that Summit is an independent studio in a highly conglomerated film industry. But Summit is hardly the only one to profit from *Twilight*— the publishing industry, the retail market, and tourism have benefited in kind, making this phenomenon an extremely hot commodity in the current era of economic downturn. Mall tours, national conventions, concerts, autograph events and film screenings regularly draw huge crowds, while Hot Topic and Nordstrom have both capitalized on the *Twilight* clothing and accessory market to great effect. The desire to "buy that *Twilight* feeling" does not appear to be fading, with stories from the summer of 2010 of *Eclipse* premiere tickets going for $3,500 on Craigslist and the *Eclipse* "tent-city" testifying to this fact. As the popularity of the books and films continues to result in profits for Meyer and others associated with the phenomenon, the derisive commentary has accordingly become more scathing. Both media commentators and "anti-fans" continue to churn out criticism, much of it functioning as a gendered backlash against the predominantly female fan-base. It is to these concerns that I now turn.

Anti-Fandom and Gendered Backlash

Twilight has received mixed reviews from the outset, with the books being criticized and *Twilight*ers being derided as silly girls. Given that fans are often viewed with skepticism, especially when they are female fans, this is hardly surprising. As noted in "Biting Back: *Twilight* Anti-Fandom and the Rhetoric of Superiority," fans often come under public scrutiny with the common consensus being that fans are "geeks, nerds, and — possibly — a little crazy" (Sheffield 208). However, the emergence of fan studies within academia in the 1970s complicated this dismissal, suggesting that fans partake in active, often subversive activity. Founding scholars in the field, such as Fiske and Jenkins, championed fans as "crusaders with strategies, tactics, and political agendas" (Sheffield 208). However, later scholars questioned the largely celebratory depiction of fan culture that colored early studies, arguing that fan activity is not always subversive nor a democratic free-for-all — that, in fact, when fandom is framed *as resistance* consumer capitalism is bolstered (Williamson 113). While most of these noncelebratory studies have either taken the "fans as dupes" approach or focused on the economic components of fandom, or how fans function in the main as consumers, more recent studies have argued that fan activity is complex and varied, sometimes resisting the status quo, sometimes supporting, and sometimes acting as a populist form of academia in which fans function as incisive cultural critics.[5] Mark Jancovich, for example, suggests there is a link between academic studies of film and fandom, emphasizing that many fans, like many academics, are not cultural outsiders, but are middle-class, educated men. Many cultural studies scholars take this gendered analysis even further than Jancovich, examining the ways in which fans have largely been gendered male with fan activities described in masculinized terms. This emphasis on the gendered components of fandom is particularly relevant to *Twilight* fandom and the gendered backlash it has wrought. As theorists such as McRobbie and Modleski argue, cultural studies often position boys as resisting or subverting mainstream culture, while girls are either not considered at all or framed as dupes and/or uberconsumers.

This strand of contemporary culture studies has much historical precedent, though, as documented by Huyssen (discussed above). He documents how "high culture" has often positioned itself as masculine, repudiating women and femininity. Such a split has positioned women as a "reader of inferior-literature" who is "subjective, emotional, and passive," while man, on the other hand, is "positioned as producer, as creator of high/authentic art, as rational" (Huyssen 2). Modleski, in a similar vein, notes, "The practice of countless critics who persist in equating femininity, consumption, and reading, on the one hand, and masculinity, production, and writing on the other" ("Feminity as [Mas]Querade" 41). Or, as Gelder puts it, "The high cultural reader is imagined as contemplative; by contrast, the reader of popular fiction, the fan, is distracted" (119). In relation to *Twilight*, we can see how readers are framed as fans who fail to see these texts as "inferior-literature," while most critics (who are still predominantly male) position themselves as able to discern "authentic art."

Women, as Huyssen and Modleski document, have long been positioned as avid consumers of mass culture — indeed, they have been framed *as* mass culture (1–2). Indeed, in the 19th century, mass culture was "persistently described in terms of feminine threat," and mass or mob movements were framed as "raging" and "hysterical" — two highly feminized depictions (6). Arguing that "the fear of the masses ... is always also a fear of the woman," Huyssen's work further documents how the "universalizing ascription of femininity to mass culture always depended on the very real exclusion of women from high culture and its institutions" (6, 13). This exclusion still holds today and is certainly pertinent to *Twilight* and the related institutions of publishing, the film industry, and the media. As Huyssen puts it, "It has always been men rather than women who have had real control over the productions of mass culture" — this is still the case with the majority of filmmakers and film critics being male (13). This male control results both in "the persistent gendering as feminine of that which is devalued" and in rather angry reactions when female producers manage to crack through the male-dominated cultural production landscape (7). Indeed, women are often, as Modleski puts it, "held responsible for the debasement of taste and the sentimentalisation of culture" (38). Documenting the failure to "examine the forces that conspire to condemn women to be pre-emininet consumers in consumer society" and the widespread assumption that "women's habit of consumption [are] nearly as unavoidable as death," her work is in alignment with McRobbie's (40).

In the case of *Twilight*, we can see how the whole phenomenon has been gendered feminine and dismissed by the bastions of "high culture," as well as how the predominantly female fandom has produced virulent, often sexist, reactions. Much like Nathaniel Hawthorne's "damned mob of scribbling women" comment, critics have framed Meyer as a hack (Stephen King perhaps the most infamous for doing so) and have exuded critiques colored by what Huyssen names "male fears of engulfing femininity" (6). *Twilight*ers are described using words such as hysteria, fever, and obsession, words that Melissa Click aptly calls "Victorian era gendered words" (6). The *Twilight* fandom is presented as "hyperfeminine: uncontrollable, silly, and irrational" (Sheffield 211). Rendering the dismissal of the saga in gendered terms that reflect the historical repudiation of women and femininity, much of the invective comes across as misogynistic, with the "shrieking throngs of manic fans" noted for their "fervor" that "always seems to be cranked to 'squeal.'"[6] Much in the way Anne Rice's fans were caricatured and maligned (for example, Skal notes the "striking preponderance of obese women" drawn to Rice who have a "displaced oral aggression" that reveals "the relationship between vampirism and eating disorders"), *Twilight* fans are depicted as desperate, sex-starved girls who shriek and gasp over "anything possessing a penis."[7] They are further portrayed as vulnerable vessels likely to be harmed by some of *Twilight*'s more insidious messages, a construction that, as Williamson argues, has a long historical precedent when it comes to female fans (55). While the relatively young age of many *Twilight*ers makes this depiction understandable (and even somewhat tenable), it nevertheless furthers the association between femininity and irrationality. For a recent contrast, one need only think back as far as *Harry Potter*, whose fandom was far more gender-balanced and thus garnered far less public dismissal. The response to *Twilight* is markedly different, resulting in "reports of girls and women seemingly out of their minds and out of control" that work to "disparage female pleasures and curtail serious explorations of the strong appeal of the series" (Click, Aubrey, and Behm-Morawitz 3).

Perhaps the response was no more derisive than that levied at *Twilight*ers for "ruining" Comic-Con, one of the largest fandom events in the United States. As Sheffield and Merlo note, this dismissal is typical of "a troubling gendered tendency to represent the (mostly) female *Twilight* fandom as unworthy of entry to traditional fandom spaces— including fandom's largest event" (207). This "gendered rhetoric of superiority" that imbues *Twilight* backlash has been rather kindly referred to as "coded sexism" (Sheffield 208, 219). However, much of the response has been far from coded, dripping instead with misogyny. This response, as noted by Click, positions "girls and women as unexpected and unwelcome media consumers" and thus call upon feminist scholars to not let "the gendered mockery of *Twilight* fans continue unchallenged" ("Rabid" n.p.).

This call has been heeded, and challenges are emerging both online and in print, not only in this book you are now reading, but also in the previously published *Bitten by Twilight* as well as in many panels devoted to *Twilight* at *The Popular Culture Association Conference* and the *National Women's Studies Association Conference*. Of course, the critique of consumer culture and the ways in which females have been framed as consumers is an enduring strand of feminism. Less common, though, is analysis of females and femininity in relation to fan culture. Martens, noting the paucity of feminist work that examines "themes of pleasure, fantasy and consumerism," is in line with Click's call for more of a sustained focus on the "fangirl." "Fanboys," she writes, "have greater visibility in popular culture because their interests and activities have become an unspoken standard. Fangirls' interests and strategies, which do not register when positioned against fanboys,' are ignored — or worse, ridiculed" ("Rabid" n.p.).

Though girl studies emerged in the 1970s along with a growth in focus on female genres and authors (Radway's *Reading the Romance* being a prime example), scholars, as Click notes, "continue to fight the persistent cultural assumptions that male-targeted texts are authentic and interesting, whereas female-targeted texts are schlocky and mindless" (*Bitten by Twilight* 8). McRobbie focuses on this bias in her work, detailing the "almost exclusive interest in boys" in studies of youth culture and subcultures (x). And, as McRobbie documents, when girls do appear in studies it is either fleetingly or else "in ways which uncritically reinforce the stereotypical image of women" (1). As noted above, the mainstream media is certainly guilty of reinforcing stereotypical ideas about female fans in regards to *Twilight*. Yet, challenges to this narrow depiction run the gamut from revealing that the fandom is not as uniform (nor as exclusively female) as it is often presented to be, to exploring how the fandom has furthered female voice and interests as well as allowed for expressions of alternative femininity. As with earlier studies that suggested fan culture can be empowering and gender subversive, emerging studies of *Twilight* examine how fans are not merely passive consumers or dupes, but active, engaged producers of culture.

Fans' Productive Engagement with Twilight

The series has inspired a number of lively, popular blogs, various musical artists, several short film clips and spoofs, a plethora of fan fiction, and a community of excited and exciting fans. As the editors of *Bitten by Twilight* emphasize, "*Twilight* fans are active in their engagement with the series"—they not only attend events and read at length about the series, the films, the author, and the actors, but also have opened businesses, organized conventions, created thriving online and face-to-face communities, and contributed to a vast collection of fan fiction (11). Much like Buffy before it, *Twilight* invites interpretation, albeit for different reasons. Sharing with Buffy melodramatic aspects and a concern with personal issues and relationships, the series provokes very personal responses in fans—indeed, according to Maggie Parke, this is one of the reasons why fans so closely scrutinized the adaptation of the books to films. Moreover, given the cultural moment at which *Twilight* takes place, with internet culture and the explosive growth in social networking mediums such as *Facebook* and *Twitter*, the phenomenon is taking place in a participatory environment that imbues contemporary culture generally, calling on people to update their status and "Tweet." Meyer certainly embraced this environment, utilizing the internet and in-person events to reach out to fans in unprecedented ways. The phenomenon has also allowed for communication across age brackets, with mothers and daughters bonding over the texts, with "*Twilight* Moms" communicating with young fans, with grandmothers attending events with their grandchildren. This communal feel was particularly apparent at *Summer School in Forks* and is further evidenced in the ubiquity of "becoming-a-fan stories" shared in person, online, and in print. The popularity of painstakingly handwritten signs and homemade shirts or self-designed *Twilight* gear further speaks to fans' productive engagement with the series, as does the devotion and creativity of the thriving *Twi*-net world. These are not a "damned mob of scribbling women," but a group of dedicated, creative, and engaged fans proving McRobbie's claim that fan subcultures "possess the capacity to change the direction of young people's lives, or at least sharpen their focus by confirming some felt, but as yet unexpressessed intent or desire" (xv). Naming such subcultures "popular aesthetic movements," McRobbie's work denies the usual model of fans (and especially female fans) as passive consumers.

Though consumerism is certainly a key part of the phenomenon, fans do much more than "buy that *Twilight* feeling." In keeping with Williamson's conception of "fandom for fandom's sake," which she argues rejects "the notion of culture for profit," fans' engagement with *Twilight* often resists or at least extends attempts by Summit and others to commercialize the phenomenon (184). Perhaps the most pervasive activity in this regard can be found online, where fans spend huge amounts of time writing, reading, and dialoguing about *Twilight*, something that runs counter to capitalist norms and motives, as these activities are in the main done for their own sake rather than for profit. Given the way that girls have been targeted as a key market, a trend that began in earnest in the early 1990s, fan resistance or indifference to the consumerist aspects of *Twilight* fandom is heartening. Fans' willingness to camp for days in a *Twilight* tent city (as fans did for the *Eclipse* premiere), or to spend hours writing about the saga, reveals that fans are not a part of this cultural zeitgeist as mere consumers, but they are also a part of it in order to engage with others. Yes, those camping in Los Angeles while I write this had to buy pricey tickets for the premiere, but they also had to sleep on cement for days—this is not merely about consumption of a vampire craze or the chance to see a celebrity, but this is more of a pilgrimage, a fan activity that admittedly benefits consumer culture, but is about much more than that.

Though *Twilight* incorporates many of the consumerist messages girls and females are subject to, it also stresses the importance of friendship, community, family, dedication, trust, commitment, and love. These are things consumer culture tells us we can buy, but most of us know better. Fans may buy that *Twilight* T-shirt or bumper sticker in order to convey their love of a certain character or the saga in general, but what they really want is to continue the imaginative experience that the books represent for them, to fortify the sense of community that the fandom has wrought, to not so much "buy that *Twilight* feeling" but to live it via their immersion in the *Twilight* word.

Conclusion:
You Have a Choice,
and It Need Not Be
Edward or Jacob

The word *seduction* dates at least back to the 15th century, deriving from the Latin *seducer,* and literally means "to lead away." It is associated with alluring others into disobedience or disloyalty through the use of persuasion or trickery — and especially so in relation to seducing others into sexual activity. Seduction is further associated with excitement, allure, mystery, and romance. It has positive connotations in relation to escapism, to bringing about freedom from social mores, and to becoming emancipated from sex/gender or religious constrictions. The *morality* of seduction in academic debates is often read against who is doing the seduction and why, who is being seduced, and what the socio-historical contexts of the seduction is. The history of seduction (especially in its literary representations) has usually served as a warning to females of the social consequences of not being "a good girl."

Yet, women have played their fair share as seducers as well. From the Sirens of Greek mythology who lured sailors to their death to the many female ghosts, vampires, werewolves, and monsters of literature and film, female seductresses have literally or figuratively lured many to their demise. While both men and woman have been represented as seducers, the male seducer is often framed as charming, irresistible, brooding, and mysterious (think of the Bryonic hero — who has his descendents in Edward and Jacob), while the female seductress more often is dangerous, monstrous, evil, and immoral (think Medusa — who has her descendent in Victoria).

We can look to Eve as a quintessential victim of seduction — at least in the traditional readings of her actions, or to the numerous "fallen women" in Victorian literature who lost their families, livelihoods, and/or lives due to falling under the seductive spell of a male suitor. Fairy tales are also rife with warnings, *Little Red Riding Hood* being the most obvious example. In the *Twilight* saga,

Bella is an admixture of all of these seduced females— she, like Eve, chooses to defy authority, metaphorically biting the apple. She "falls" into vampirism and frolics with wolves. She is seduced, throughout the four books, by romance, adventure, and, in particular, by a sparkling vampire-knight, Edward Cullen. Her seduction (and by extension, the seduction of millions of readers around the world) begs examination.

What does it mean that a text grounded in Victorian ideas about gender and sexuality is so alluring to modern readers? What does it mean that so many *love* this tale of seduction that, as so many tales are, is riddled with domineering males, violence against women, and admonitions that female sexuality *must* be policed? Why are we, as readers, seduced to turn page after page, to flock to the films, to buy *Twilight* T-shirts and bumper stickers? Are we, as Radway suggests, accomplices to our own subordination? Does our love of this romantic, supernatural tale suggest that feminism indeed has it wrong — that all females *really* want is to be loved, to marry, to mother?

The massive popularity of the texts indicates the saga has touched a cultural nerve. And though this popularity is worrying in regards to the above suggestions, I think the dismissal (and even hatred) of the *Twilight* phenomenon deserves critical examination. Readers certainly love the romantic tale at the saga's core, but that is not the only thing that explains its mass appeal — they also are undoubtedly seduced by the fact that the saga speaks, on multiple levels, to the reality of their times, to their lives as females, to the ability to still thrive in a patriarchal world that frames them as silly girls (much as Edward frames Bella). The series is also relevant to our so-called post-feminist milieu, a time claimed to be, as McRobbie documents, "beyond feminism," in which we are supposedly living in "a more comfortable zone where women can choose for themselves" ("Post-Feminism and Popular Culture" 259). This emphasis on "choice" reverberates in post-feminist arguments that claim women are now free to choose whatever path they desire — a claim that flattens out the differences between varying choices, as if "choosing" to bare one's breasts for *Girls Gone Wild* is "empowering" and just as salient as "choosing" what career to pursue. Such false paths to liberation, as documented in Levy's *Female Chauvinist Pigs*, frame choice itself as feminist, rather than assessing what types of choices are being offered and in what contexts. Or as Katha Pollit puts it, "These days anything is feminist as long as you 'choose' it ... no matter how dangerous or silly or servile or self-destructive it is."[1] Indeed a rhetoric of "choice" has been consistently used to bolster pro-patriarchal, anti-choice ideology in recent decades.[2] Meyer seems to have taken this concept of choice to heart, as if *any* choice is a feminist choice. For example, when asked, "Is Bella an anti-feminist heroine?" Meyer replies:

> When I hear or read theories about Bella being an anti-feminist character, those theories are usually predicated on her choices. In the beginning, she chooses romantic love over everything else. Eventually, she chooses to marry at an early age and then

chooses to keep an unexpected and dangerous baby. I never meant for her fictional choices to be a model for anyone else's real life choices. She is a character in a story, nothing more or less....

Do her choices make her a negative example of empowerment? For myself personally, I don't think so....

In my own *opinion* (key word), the foundation of feminism is this: being able to choose. The core of anti-feminism is, conversely, telling a woman she can't do something solely because she's a woman....

One of the weird things about modern feminism is that some feminists seem to be putting their own limits on women's choices. That feels backward to me. It's as if you can't choose a family on your own terms and still be considered a strong woman. How is that empowering? Are there rules about if, when, and how we love or marry and if, when, and how we have kids? Are there jobs we can and can't have in order to be a "real" feminist? To me, those limitations seem anti-feminist in basic principle.

Above, Meyer firstly problematically denies the power of "fictional choices," arguing that Bella is *just* a character. While Meyer may not have *meant* Bella to be a model, she undoubtedly is, and to countless females the world over. Second, Meyer's use of the word *empowerment* signals her immersion in our post-feminist moment, a milieu that has de-politicized the concept. No longer is female empowerment so much about equal pay and access to contraception; now it's about the "right" to get "va-jazzled" or the "choice" to have a nose job. (In the *Twilight* saga, it is about the choice between Edward and Jacob.) Third, the claim that the foundation of feminism is choice is a gross oversimplification that suggests Meyer has learned what she knows of feminism from the mainstream media (or perhaps Google, her research tool of choice). Fourth, her rehashing of the tired suggestion that feminists are anti-love, anti-marriage, and anti-family substantiates one of the most enduring and damaging misconceptions about the feminist movement.

With this comment, and her saga, Meyer unfortunately *chooses* to promote many facile, misleading notions about feminism as if Bella's choice to be a young vampire wife were *real feminism*, while those of us who critique existing power structures *choose* to hate on young mothers. As such, Meyer's work is part and parcel of the post-feminist move to make feminism "seem redundant" by "means of the tropes of freedom and choice which are now inextricably connected with the category of 'young women'" (McRobbie 255). This paradigm encourages young women to make *certain* choices—to remain abstinent until marriage, to prioritize family and children, to beautify their bodies. As McRobbie asserts, "Popular texts normalize post-feminist gender anxieties so as to re-regulate young women by means of the language of personal choice" (262). This new female subject hailed by post-feminism (and by Meyer's saga), as McRobbie writes, "is, despite her freedom, called upon to be silent, to withhold critique, to count as a modern sophisticated girl, or indeed this withholding of critique is a condition of her freedom" (260). While it may seem that Bella (and her devoted readers) is free to choose, she is really only free to choose from a limited array of options *if* she wants to remain a viable subject, a good citizen, and a good girl. Choice in this context has a profoundly regulatory dimension —choose wrong, and you will court all sorts of danger —(as in *Twilight*, when *wrong* choices lead to rape, abuse, infertility, and death).

Yet, as critical readers we can choose to enjoy the saga while simultaneously examining (and resisting) its more delimiting messages. We need not deny the pleasure of these texts; rather, as the work of cultural studies theorists suggests, we can be active, engaged textual consumers, forging new, post–*Twilight* identities that may or may not accord with the choices made by any of the characters that populate Meyer's saga — that may, instead, be more Sookie Stackhouse than Bella Swan, more grrrl-power Red Riding Hood than dwarf-serving Snow White.

Chapter Notes

Introduction

1. See Michel de Certeau, *The Practice of Everyday Life* (Berkeley: University of California Press, 1984).

2. For details on the growing popularity of these movements and the ways in which religion in general and the Mormon religion in particular are promoting "traditional marriage," see Kathryn Joyce, *Quiverfull: Inside the Christian Patriarchy Movement* (Beacon: Boston, 2009), 195.

3. For a book-length analysis of this bent, see Kathryn Joyce, *Quiverfull: Inside the Christian Patriarchy Movement* (Beacon: Boston, 2009).

4. Susan Bordo refers to this episode, framing it as indicative of our present cultural moment. See her *Twilight Zones: The Hidden Life of Cultural Images from Plato to O.J.* (Berkeley: University of California Press, 1997), 9.

5. Ananya Mukherjea, "Team Bella: Desire, Collectivity, Identity, and the Sociology of What Makes the Story So Compelling for Its Fans," Summer School in Forks: A *Twilight* Symposium. Forks, Washington. June 26, 2009.

Chapter 1

1. See Paul Barber, *Vampires, Burial, and Death* (New Haven: Yale University Press, 1988), for more on the differences between folkloric and fictional vampires.

2. Various scholars have noted the anti–Semitic connotations of these representations. For example, see Judith Halberstam, *Gothic Horror and the Technology of Monsters* (Durham: Duke University Press, 2000), 92.

3. For example, Milly Williamson argues that the 20th century saw the emersion of increasingly sympathetic vampires and that the roots of this sympathetic vampire lie in Byron and the legacy of melodrama. Milly Williamson, *The Lure of the Vampire: Gender, Fiction, and Fandom from Bram Stoker to Buffy* (London: Wallflower Press, 2005), 28–30.

4. For example, Jewelle Gomez's *The Gilda Stories* features a queer, feminist female vampire, and Andrew Fox's *Fat White Vampire Blues* features various fat vampires, working-class vampires, and vampires of color. See Williamson, *The Lure of the Vampire*, 33.

5. For example, see Sue-Ellen Case, "Tracking the Vampire," pp. 380–400 in *Writing on the Body: Female Embodiment and Feminist Theory*, ed. Katie Conboy, Nadia Medina, and Sarah Stanbury (New York: Columbia University Press, 1997); Christopher Craft, "'Kiss Me with Those Red Lips': Gender and Inversion in Bram Stoker's *Dracula*," pp. 169–194 in *Dracula: The Vampire and the Critics*, ed. Margaret L. Carter (Ann Arbor: University of Michigan Research Press, 1988); and Kathryn Kane, "A Very Queer Refusal: The Chilling Effect of the Cullens' Heteronormative Embrace," pp. 103–18 in *Bitten by Twilight: Youth Culture, Media, and the Vampire Franchise*, ed. Melissa A. Click, Jennifer Stevens Aubrey, and Elizabeth Behm-Morawitz (New York: Peter Lang, 2010).

6. For an analysis of the saga in relation to the American Dream, see Sara Buttsworth's "CinderBella: Twilight, Fairy Tales, and the Twenty-First Century American Dream," in *Twilight and History*, ed. Nancy R. Reagin (Hoboken, NJ: Wiley and Sons, 2010), 47–69.

7. For example, see Williamson's chapter "Vampire Fandom," 97–118.

8. See McClelland, 185. Buffy seems to be an exception to the rule. See, for example, Jes Battis, who argues that Buffy offers a model of a queer, chosen family that "both depends upon and rejects conventional notions of the nuclear family"; both Buffy and Angel shows that Buffy episodes "revolve around radical conceptions of family, and depend for their coherence on the establishment of non-traditional families" that admit those with differences "without censuring them for their peculiarities." Jes Battis, *Blood Relations: Chosen Families in Buffy the Vampire Slayer and Angel* (Jefferson, NC: McFarland, 2005), 7–13.

9. The anthology *Twilight and History*, edited by Nancy R. Reagin, includes numerous essays that read the saga in relation to such contexts.

10. James Twitchell discusses *Little Red Riding Hood*, suggesting that vampire stories function in part as fairy tales. James Twitchell, *Dreadful Pleasures: An Anatomy of Modern Horror* (Oxford: Oxford University Press, 1985), 141, 157–58. See also Catherine Orenstein's *Little Red Riding Hood Uncloaked* (New York: Basic Books, 2002). Orenstein's study reveals that in many early versions of the story, Red Riding Hood was not depicted as passive victim. Indeed, in these versions, she has more agency than the "damsel in distress" Bella.

11. For example, see George Levine and U.C. Knoepflmacher, eds., *The Endurance of Frankenstein: Essays on Mary Shelley's Novel* (Berkeley: University of California Press, 1974), and U. C. Knoepflmacher, "Thoughts on the Aggression of Daughters," in *The Endurance of Frankenstein.*

12. Shannon Winnubst argues that the vampire poses a threat to such privileges.

See her "Vampires, Anxieties, and Dreams: Race and Sex in the Contemporary United States," *Hypatia* 18, no. 3 (2003): 1–20.

13. For a more detailed discussion of vampire lore in relation to souls, reflections, and shadows, see Paul Barber, *Vampires, Burial, and Death: Folklore and Reality* (New Haven: Yale University Press, 1988), 178–88.

14. K. J. Swanson, "'Why Are You Apologizing for Bleeding?': Confronting the Evangelical Embrace of *Twilight*," Southwest/Texas Popular Culture and American Culture Association, Hyatt Regency Albuquerque, New Mexico, February 11, 2010.

15. Here, as Nina Aurbach's quote reveals, the saga is in keeping with *Dracula*'s bolstering of hierarchies: "*Dracula* is in love less with death or secuality than with hierarchies, erecting barriers hitherto foreign to vampire literature; the gulf between male and female, antiquity and newness, class and class, England and non–England, vampire and mortal, homoerotic and heterosexual love, infuses its genre with a new fear: fear of the hated unknown." From *Our Vampire, Ourselves* (Chicago: University of Chicago Press, 1995), 67.

16. Many have read Stoker's *Dracula* similarly — as an unconscious interpretation of his dreams. See Alan Johnson, "Bent and Broken Necks: Signs of Design in Stoker's *Dracula*," in *Dracula: The Vampire and the Critics*, ed. Margaret L. Carter (Ann Arbor: University of Michigan Research Press, 1988).

17. It is interesting to note that she does not deflect her text's engagement with Austen or Bronte texts. To the contrary, she emphasizes these works as inspirational. It seems she wants to distance herself from vampire narratives in general and to deflect suggestions that her works are derivative of this genre, even though they clearly are.

18. Johnson notes there are a number of critical essays that "deny that Stoker really knew what he was doing as he wrote it" (231).

19. For example, Montague Summers writes of *Dracula*, "It is hardly possible to

feel any great interest in the characters, they are labels rather than individuals." *The Vampire: His Kith and Kin* (New Hyde Park, NY: University Books, 1960), 334.

20. Jessica Valenti notes the tendency of men to be called upon to act as "virginity warriors" in the abstinence movement. See Jessica Valenti, *The Purity Myth: How America's Obsession with Virginity Is Hurting Young Women* (Berkeley: Seal, 2009), 25.

21. It seems the Cullen family of five could also echo the crew of light.

22. For more on this line of argument, see Phyllis A. Roth's "Suddenly Sexual Women in Bram Stoker's *Dracula*," pp. 57–67 in *Dracula: The Vampire and the Critics*, ed. Margaret L. Carter (Ann Arbor: University of Michigan Research Press, 1988).

23. "What's With the Vampire Obsession? 'True Blood' Writer Explains," *Star Pulse*, September 2009, available online at www.starpulse.com/news/index.php/2009/09/04/what_s_with_the_vampire_obsession_true_b (accessed on August 18, 2010).

24. For further discussion of vampires and werewolves in this vein, see Mark Collins Jenkins, *Vampire Forensics: Uncovering the Origins of an Enduring Legend* (Washington, D.C.: National Geographic Society, 2010). Admittedly, vampires are sometimes presented as uncontrollable, too, especially in teen films of the 1980s, such as *The Lost Boys, Fright Night*, and *Near Dark*.

25. Some lore also claims lycanthropes will become vampires when they die, as noted by Montague Summers. See *The Vampire: His Kith and Kin* (New Hyde Park, NY: University Books, 1960), 167.

26. As in *The Werewolf* (1913(and *The White Wolf* (1914). See Twitchell, 219.

Chapter 2

1. Christine Seifert calls the saga "abstinence porn" in "Bite Me! Or Don't," *Bitch Magazine*, 2008, available online at http://bitchmagazine.org/article/bite-me-or-dont (accessed on August 12, 2010).

2. *The Official Website of Stephenie Meyer*, available online at www.stephe-niemeyer.com/Twilight_faq.html#pretty (accessed on August 13, 2010).

3. Ibid.

4. For more on the argument that the series circulates around key romantic myths, see Tricia Clasen, "Taking a Bite Out of Love: The Myth of Romantic Love in the *Twilight* Series," in *Bitten by Twilight: Youth Culture, Media, and the Vampire Franchise*, ed. Melissa A. Click, Jennifer Stevens Aubrey, and Elizabeth Behm-Morawitz (New York: Peter Lang, 2010), 120.

5. *The Official Website of Stephenie Meyer*, available online at www.stephe-niemeyer.com/ecl_faq.html (accessed on August 13, 2010).

Chapter 3

1. As the *Geena Davis Institute on Gender in Media* has documented, the ratio of female to male characters in children's media is, at best, three to one. Literature, I would argue, has a similar, if not worse, imbalance. *Geena Davis Institute on Gender in Media*, available at www.thegeena-davisinstitute.org/about_us.php (accessed on July 27, 2010).

2. Joanna Russ, "What Can a Heroine Do," *Images of Women in Fiction: Feminist Perspectives*, ed. Susan Koppleman (Bowling Green, OH: Bowling Green State University Popular Press, 1972).

3. *The Official Website of Stephenie Meyer*, available online at www.stephe-niemeyer.com/bd_faq.html (accessed on July 27, 2010).

4. We learn of Jessica's jealousy and Tanya's lust most specifically in *Midnight Sun*. Further, Jessica shows herself to not be a true friend in *New Moon* when she abandons Bella during her depression.

5. Burton Hatlen argues this point in relation to *Dracula*: "If asked to justify their power and privilege, male members of this ruling elite would point immediately to women like Lucy Westenra and Mina Harker. They are pure sweetness and light. They are immune from such human feelings as lust, envy, anger, and (until Count

Dracula appears, at least) fear. The *function* of English society is, we are asked to believe, to produce such delicate blooms as these young ladies, which can grow only in the most sheltered of locations; and any society which *can* produce such angels must be, we are also asked to believe, *ipso facto* good." See his "The Return of the Repressed/Oppressed in Bram Stoker's *Dracula*," in *Dracula: The Vampire and the Critics*, ed. Margaret L. Carter (Ann Arbor: University of Michigan Research Press, 1988), 121.

6. See Natalie Wilson, "Womb Fiction: Late Twentieth Century Challenges to the Woman as Womb Paradigm," *Womanhood in Anglophone Literary Culture: Nineteenth and Twentieth Century Perspectives*, ed. Robin Hammerman (Cambridge: Cambridge Scholars Press, 2007), 343–72.

7. See Susan Douglas and Meredith Williams, *The Mommy Myth: The Idealization of Motherhood and How it Has Undermined Women* (New York: Free Press, 2004).

8. As Kristin Rowe-Finkbeiner argues, "Motherhood brings to the fore social inequalities that must be addressed politically." See her *The F Word: Feminism in Jeopardy* (Emeryville: Seal Press, 2004), 150. Meyer notes that she didn't write anything for six years at her website, *The Official Website of Stephenie Meyer*, available online at www.stepheniemeyer.com/Twilight.html (accessed August 13, 2010).

9. *The Official Website of Stephenie Meyer*, available online at www.stepheniemeyer.com/Twilight.html (accessed August 13, 2010).

10. *The Official Website of Stephenie Meyer* available online at www.stepheniemeyer.com/nm_thestory.html (accessed August 13, 2010).

Chapter 4

1. Indeed, in *Eclipse*, Renee tells Bella, "The way you move — you orient yourself around him without even thinking about it. When he moves, even a little bit, you adjust your position at the same time. Like

magnets ... or gravity. You're like a ... satellite, or something. I've never seen anything like it" (68).

2. Radway makes a similar argument, asserting, "The genre fails to show that if the emotional repression and independence that characterize men are actually to be reversed, the entire notion of what it is to be male will have to be changes." She frames romance as inadvertently giving the messages that what women need to do is find a man that is already tender, and thus "a potential argument for change is transformed into a representation and recommendation of the status quo." Janice A. Radway, *Reading the Romance: Women, Patriarchy, and Popular Literature* (Chapel Hill: University of North Carolina Press, 1984), 148.

3. Thomas B. Byers makes this argument in "Good Men and Monsters: The Defense of *Dracula*," in *Dracula: The Vampire and the Critics*, ed. Margaret L. Carter (Ann Arbor: University of Michigan Research Press, 1988), 154, arguing that Stoker's novel upholds the idea that male power comes from "the highest patriarch of all — God the Father" (154).

4. Meyer offers extended back stories for many of her character at *The Twilight Lexicon*. Emmet is said to be a former railroad worker, from Tennessee, attacked by bear when hunting. www.Twilightlexicon.com/?p=23 (accessed on August 15, 2010).

5. See, for example, *Center for Relationship Abuse Awareness*, www.stoprelationshipabuse.org/signs.html (accessed on August 15, 2010).

6. Radway further argues that mothering prompts women to find solace in the romance genre, writing, "It is the constant impulse and duty to mother others that is responsible for the sense of depletion that apparently sends some women to romance fiction"; she also suggests that they become mothered through the act of reading via identifying with a heroine who is able to establish herself as an object for concern and recipient of care (84).

7. For exploration of representations of the family in Buffy, see, for example, Jes Battis, *Blood Relations: Chosen Families in*

Buffy the Vampire Slayer and Angel. As Battis argues, the Buffy family "both depends upon and rejects conventional notions of the nuclear family"; both *Buffy* and *Angel* "revolve around radical conceptions of family, and depend for their coherence on the establishment of non-traditional families" that admit those with differences "without censuring them for their peculiarities" (7).

8. "What if Edward Is Ruining It for Mere Male Mortals?" *Professor What If*, http://professorwhatif.wordpress.com/2009/05/29/what-if-edward-is-ruining-it-for-mere-male-mortals/ (accessed on August 16, 2010).

9. This stance was in particular evident at the 2009 Comic-Con in San Diego, where protestors held signs reading, "*Twilight* ruined Comic-Con."

10. Bill Amend, *Foxtrot*, 2009, www.gocomics.com/foxtrot/2009/10/25/ (accessed on August 16, 2010).

Chapter 5

1. I use the word *sexophrenic* to merge sexualized and schizophrenic, in order to indicate American culture's dysfunctional and delusional attitudes about sexuality. For discussion of the hypersexualization of contemporary culture, see, for example, Ariel Levy, *Female Chauvinist Pigs: Women and the Rise of Raunch Culture* (New York: Free Press, 2005); M. Gigi Durham, *The Lolita Effect: The Media Sexualization of Young Girls and What We Can Do About It* (New York: The Overlook Press, 2008); and Jessica Valenti, *The Purity Myth: How America's Obsession with Virginity is Hurting Young Women* (Berkeley: Seal, 2009).

2. It is important to clarify terms here — being sexualized is far different than being sexual —*sexualization* is something that is done to someone from the outside and has the tendency to objectify the person into a sex object.

3. For example, see Carrol L. Fry, "Fictional Conventions and Sexuality in *Dracula*," in *Dracula: The Vampire and the Critics*, ed. Margaret L. Carter (Ann Arbor:

University of Michigan Research Press, 1988), 35.

4. Gail B. Griffin, "'Your Girls That You All Love Are Mine': Dracula and the Victorian Male Sexual Imagination," in *Dracula: The Vampire and the Critics*, ed. Margaret L. Carter (Ann Arbor: University of Michigan Research Press, 1988).

5. We might read all women as "fallen" prior to their turn to vampires — Rosalie due to her vanity, desires, and ultimate rape; Esme due to her pregnancy and suicide attempt; Alice due to her insanity; Bella due to her overt sexual desire.

6. Winnubst discusses fluidity as haunting male body (6).

7. Neesha Meminger, "Disney, Twilight and Bollywood: Reinforcing the Purity Myth or Fantasy of Safe Sexual Exploration for Young Girls (and Their Mothers)?" Racialicious, 2009, available online at www.racialicious.com/2009/11/26/disney-Twilight-and-bollywood-reinforcing-the-purity-myth-or-fantasy-of-safe-sexual-exploration-for-young-girls-and-their-mothers/ (accessed on August 16, 2010).

8. See, for example, "Characteristics of Abused Women," *Abused No More*, 2006, available online at http://lifemadesimple.typepad.com/abusednomore/2006/11/characteristics.html (accessed on August 16, 2010).

9. *Twilight Lexicon*, www.twilightlexicon.com/?p=22 (accessed on August 16, 2010). All subsequent references to Esme's story are taken from Stephenie Meyer's personal correspondence with *Twilight Lexicon*.

10. Paper forthcoming.

11. However, as the "Team Edward" and "Team Jacob" phenomenon reveals, readers' affiliations vary. Some find Edward's more sustained controlling behavior problematic while others excuse this based on his vampire nature.

12. You "win" this quiz if you are *not* critical of other people, if you are very patient, if you keep your mouth shut, if you care about what you and others look like.

Chapter 6

1. See Dan Glaister and Sarah Falconer, "Mormon Who Put New Life into Vampires," *Guardian UK*, July 2008, www. guardian.co.uk/books/2008/jul/20/news. booksforchildrenandteenagers (accessed August 16, 2010).

2. Section 89 of *The Doctrine and Covenants*, commonly known as "Word of Wisdom," further stipulates that in addition to be obedient, the LDS faithful should not masturbate, partake in premarital sec, or imbibe strong drinks.

3. This anachronism (London sewers were not yet in existence in the 1640s), points to Meyer's lack of research in ways that echo her lack of research on the Quileute people. For further details on the historical inconsistencies of the novel, see Eveline Brugger's "Where Do the Cullens Fit In?" *Twilight and History*, ed. Nancy Reagin, (Hoboken, NJ: Wiley and Sons, 2010), 238–39.

4. The notion of the Panopticon comes from Foucault. See Michel Foucault, *Discipline and Punish: The Birth of the Prison*, trans. Alan Sheridan (New York: Vintage Books, 1977).

5. In fact, as Krakauer notes, roles of authority are almost exclusively held by elderly, white males (4).

6. For an extended argument of why society is decidedly not post-feminist, see Susan Douglas, *Enlightened Sexism: The Seductive Message that Feminism's Work Is Done* (New York: Henry Holt, 2010).

7. Laake is particularly illuminating on the topic of how Mormonism frames females and feminism. As she documents, even as late as 1992 Mormon leaders were decrying feminism. Citing Dallin Oaks' condemnation of Mormon feminists' fight for priesthood power, she emphasizes that the Relief Society, sometimes argued to be a site of female power within the church, is "controlled and directed by male priesthood leaders" (235).

8. Also interesting to note is the fact that Smith claimed, "I have ripped open beds and pillows" in his search for the first stolen copy of the *Book of Mormon*. While Edward's pillow ripping is done on his honeymoon, it can be read as a distant echo of Smith's earlier search for his manuscript — both events include seeking salvation, one through finding one's holy work and the other through proving that one is not a damned monster. Bella's black and blue, feather-covered body might also be read as an echo of when Smith was tarred and feathered. In 1832 he was tarred and feathered by "Mormon baiters" and beaten senseless, and in 1833 he was tarred and feathered again (Brodie 119; Krakauer 98).

9. Brodie further argues that Smith's religion "solved the knotty problem of the origin of the red man, which has been a puzzle ever since 1500" (44). His claim that indigenous peoples were descended from Hebrews as a remnant of the Lost Ten Tribves of Israel went along with current popular theory of the time (45).

10. Brodie also documents that Smith pulled a skeleton from one of the "Indian mounds" and told his followers that he was a white Lamanite named Zelf who had the "curse of the red skin" taken from him (149).

11. See "Remarks by President Brigham Young," *Journal of Discourses* 26, no. 7 (October 9, 1859). Young's speech was delivered in the Tabernacle in Salt Lake City and included the following:

> You see some classes of the human family that are black, uncouth, uncomely, disagreeable and low in their habits, wild, and seemingly deprived of nearly all the blessings of the intelligence that is generally bestowed upon mankind. The first man that committed the odious crime of killing one of his brethren will be cursed the longest of any one of the children of Adam. Cain slew his brother. Cain might have been killed, and that would have put a termination to that line of human beings. This was not to be, and the Lord put a mark upon him, which is the flat nose and black skin. Trace mankind down to after the flood, and then another curse is pronounced upon the same race — that they should be the "servant of servants;" and they will be, until that curse is re-

moved; and the Abolitionists cannot help it, nor in the least alter that decree. How long Is that race to endure the dreadful curse that is upon them? That curse will remain upon them, and they never can hold the Priesthood or share in it.... The children of Cain cannot receive the first ordinances of the Priesthood. They were the first that were cursed, and they will be the last from whom the curse will be removed.

12. Peggy Fletcher Stack, "Faithful Witness: New Film and Revived Group Help Many Feel at Home in Their Church," *The Salt Lake Tribune*, July 6, 2007.

13. Eric Jepson, "Saturday's Werewolves," *Sunstone Magazine*, November 11, 2009, available online at www.sunstonemagazine.com/saturdays-werewolves/ (accessed on August 1, 2010).

14. Tyler Chadwick, "Where *Twilight* Meets Mormon Studies," *A Motley Vision: Mormon Arts and Culture*, December 2, 2009, available online at www.motleyvision.org/2009/twilight-meets-mormon-studies/ (accessed on August 16, 2010).

15. See John Granger, "Stephenie Meyer New Moon Q&A: Imprinting," *Forks High School Professor*, November 18, 2009, available online at http://fhsprofessor.com/?p=315 (accessed on August 16, 2010). Granger writes that the saga "serves as an apology or defense of man-child marriages embedded within the story, consciously or unconsciously. John Krakauer's book *Under the Banner of Heaven* was published the week Mrs. Meyer had her dream and it is filled to the brim with nightmare stories about polygamist crimes against young women as well as the nightmare of the Mountain Meadows massacre. *Twilight* is, I suggest, on several levels a Mormon woman's response to Krakauer's attack on her faith."

16. Brodie, 124. Brodie claims that Emmar harangued Smith so much on this topic that it seems Section 132 of *The Doctrine and Covenants* is a direct attempt to persuade her "while at the same time compelling her to refrain from indulging in any extracurricular sex herself" (124). Krakauer notes that polygamy was canonized as Section 132 of *The Doctrine and Covenants*, detailing that Smith called it "the most holy and imp doctrine ever revealed to man on earth" and taught that men needed at least three wives to attain "fullness of exaltation" in heaven (6).

17. As Krakauer details, between 1840 and 1844, "God instructed the prophet to marry some forty women," several of which "were still pubescent girls" (120). Polygamy became so common the in ensuing years amongst the LDS that it was observed in 1856 that "all are trying to get wives, until there is hardly a girl fourteen years old in Utah, but what is married" (204).

18. Meyer refers to free will as a gift from God in Lev Grossman's article "Stephenie Meyer: A New J.K. Rowling," *Time Magazine*, April 2008, available online at www.time.com/time/magazine/article/0,9171,1734838,00.html (accessed on August 17, 2010).

19. Anita Wheeler, "*Twilight* Legends Panel," *Twi-Con*, Dallas, August 2, 2009.

20. Paula Gunn Allen discusses how Christianity was framed as civilizing by the colonizers. See *The Sacred Hoop: Recovering the Feminine in American Indian Traditions* (Boston: Beacon Press, 1986), 50.

21. Maxine Hanks, "Mormon Vampires? Religion and *Twilight*," Summer School in Forks: A *Twilight* Symposium, Forks, Washington, June 27, 2009.

22. Ibid.

Chapter 7

1. As Zinn notes, the United States has signed more than 400 treaties with Native Americans and violated every one. Howard Zinn, *A People's History of the United States: 1492–Present* (New York: Harper Perennial, 1980), 526. Ward Churchill notes the government penchant for imprisoning Native men and sterilizing Native women in *Fantasies of the Master Race: Literature, Cinema and the Colonization of American Indians* (Monroe, ME: Common Courage Press, 1992), 8.

2. See, for example, Patti Jo King, "Charlatans, Hucksters, and Spiritual Orphans: The Historical Tenets of Narcissism, Greed, and Pathos Behind Native Cultural Exploitation," Southwest Texas Popular Culture and American Culture Association, Albuquerque, New Mexico, February 13, 2010; and Ruth Frankenberg, "Whiteness as an 'Unmarked' Cultural Category," in *The Meaning of Difference: American Constructions of Race, Sex and Gender, Social Class, Sexual Orientation, and Disability*, 5th ed., ed. Karen E. Rosenblum and Toni-Michelle C. Travis (Boston: McGraw Hill, 2008), 83.

3. For a history of whites being cast to play Native Americans, see Bob Herzberg, *Savages and Saints: The Changing Image of American Indians in Westerns* (Jefferson, NC: McFarland, 2008), 2, 46.

4. Rob Schmidt, "The Truth about Tinsel Korey," *Newspaper Rock: Where Native America Meets Pop Culture*, 28 July 2009, available online at www.bluecorncomics. com/2009/07/truth-about-tinsel-korey. html (accessed on August 17, 2010).

5. Jowett makes this argument as well (23).

6. Charlaine Harris, "A Reflection on Ugliness," in *Seven Seasons of Buffy: Science Fiction and Fantasy Writers Discuss Their Favorite Television Show*, ed. Glenn Yeffeth (Dallas: Benbella, 2003), 117.

7. "Stephenie Meyer Answers Questions from *Twilight* Moms Members: Part 2," *Twilight Moms*, www.twilightmoms.com/ media/interviews/stephenie-meyer/steph enie-meyer-answers-questions-from-tei-lightmom-members-2/ (accessed on August 17, 2010).

8. John Granger, "Stephenie Meyer *New Moon* Q and A: The Volturi," *Forks High School Professor*, November 18, 2009, available online at http://fhsprofessor.com/?p= 311 (accessed on August 17, 2010).

9. Sherman Alexie, interview, *Atlantic Unbound*, June 2001, www.theatlantic. com/past/docs/unbound/interviews/ba 2000–06–01.htm (accessed on August 17, 2010).

10. "The Story Behind the Writing of *New Moon*," *The Official Website of Stephe-*

nie Meyer, www.stepheniemeyer.com/nm_ thestory.html (accessed on August 17, 2010).

11. "The Story Behind *Twilight*," *The Official Website of Stephenie Meyer*, www. stepheniemeyer.com/twilight.html (accessed on August 17, 2010).

12. Anita Wheeler, "*Twilight* Legends Panel," *Twi-Con*, Dallas, August 2, 2009.

13. See in particular the Book of Nephi in *The Book of Mormon*.

14. Brianna Burke, "The Great American Love Affair: Indians in the *Twilight* Saga," in *Reading Twilight: Analytical Essays*, ed. Giselle Liza Anatol (New York: Palgrave Macmillan, 2010).

15. The fact that imprinting only happens to male wolves and females are the passive objects in the pairing further serves to misrepresent indigenous people as patriarchal in the extreme.

16. As I have written elsewhere:

The fact that the Cullens carry what McIntosh (1988) refers to as "an invisible weightless knapsack of special provisions, maps, passports, codebooks, visas, clothes, tools, and blank checks' is key to their power and success" (79). In the final book of the series, Bella is able to draw on this "knapsack" to prepare a bevy of provisions for her daughter Renesmee. Fearing her new vampire family may lose their battle with the Volturi (a powerful vampire coven), Bella is able to secure falsified birth certificates, passports, and a driver's license so that Renesmee can escape to safety if necessary. Packing these in a small black leather backpack along with "twice the yearly income for the average American household" (*BD* 672) in cash, Bella literally packs a knapsack of special provisions that would not be possible without her white vampire privilege. The metaphor used by Wise relating whiteness to money in the bank is particularly apt in relation to the representation of privilege in Meyer's series. Wise writes, "The virtual invisibility that whiteness affords those of us who have it is like psychological money in the bank, the proceeds of which we cash in every day while others are in a state of perpetual overdraft" (120). As mentioned above, Bella cashes in on these privileges in *Breaking Dawn* in various ways, using her "proceeds" to draw on important networks, secure documents, and withdraw cash.

From Natalie Wilson, "Civilized Vampires versus Savage Werewolves: Race and Ethnicity in the *Twilight* Series," in *Bitten by Twilight: Youth Culture, Media, and the Vampire Franchise*, ed. Melissa A. Click, Jennifer Stevens Aubrey, and Elizabeth Behm-Morawitz (New York: Peter Land, 2010), 58.

17. This championing of traditional marriage is in keeping with George W. Bush's 2004 claim that civilization depends on such marriage. See Angela McRobbie, "Post-Feminism and Popular Culture," *Feminist Media Studies* 4, no. 3 (2004): 256.

18. John Granger, "Why We Love *Twilight*: The Artistry and Meaning of the Bella Swan Novels," Summer School in Forks, Forks, Washington, June 27, 2009.

Chapter 8

1. For this line of argument, see Rob Latham, "Consuming Youth: The Lost Boys Cruise Mallworld," pp. 129–147 in *Blood Read: The Vampire as Metaphor in Contemporary Culture*, ed. Joan Gordon and Veroniza Hollinger (Philadelphia: University of Pennsylvania Press, 1997).

2. For coverage of this framing, see Melissa A. Click, "'Rabid,' 'Obsessed,' and 'Frenzied': Understanding Twilight Fangirls and the Gendered Politics of Fandom," FlowTV, December 2009, Department of Radio, Television, and Film at the University of Texas at Austin, available online at http://flowtv.org/2009/12/rabid-ob-sessed-and-frenzied-understanding-Twilight-fangirls-and-the-gendered-politics-of-fandom-melissa-click-university-of-missouri/ (accessed on August 11, 2010).

3. Paige Dickerson, "'New Moon' Premiere Like Being in a Movie for Quileute Tribal Members," *Peninsula Daily News*, November 18, 2009, available online at www.peninsuladailynews.com/article/20091118/news/311189994 (accessed on August 17, 2010).

4. See Fred Botting, "Gothic Culture," pp. 199–213 in *The Routledge Companion to Gothic*, ed. Catherine Spooner and Emma McEvoy (London: Routledge, 2007).

5. Milly Williamson compares fandom to academia, for example (11, 93–95).

6. See *Twi-Con Forums*, 2009, available online at http://Twicon.freeforums.org/disappointed-in-Twicon-t687.html (accessed on August 18, 2010).

7. See David J. Skal, *V is for Vampire: The A–Z Guide to Everything Undead* (New York: Plume, 1996), 175; Genevieve Koski, "I Attended This on Purpose: Twi-Con 2009," *A.V. Club*, August 2009, available online at www.avclub.com/articles/i-attended-this-on-purpose-Twicon-2009,31768/ (accessed on August 18, 2010).

Conclusion

1. Qtd. in Linda Hirshman "Crazy Choices: Why on Earth Do Women Stay in Abusive Relationships?" *Slate,* April 8, 2009, available online at www.slate.com/id/2215693 (accessed on August 19, 2010).

2. See Elizabeth A Pritchard, "Speaking Out: Faith-Based Patriarchy and the Rhetoric of 'Choice,'" *Journal of Feminist Studies in Religion* 19, no. 1 (2003): 65–70.

Bibliography

Abbott, Stacey. *Celluloid Vampires: Life after Death in the Modern World.* Austin: University of Texas Press, 2007.

Aldiss, Brian. "Foreword: Vampire — The Ancient Fear." In *Blood Read: The Vampire as Metaphor in Contemporary Culture*, edited by Joan Gordon and Veronica Hollinger, ix–xi. Philadelphia: University of Pennsylvania Press, 1997.

Alexie, Sherman. Interview. *Atlantic Unbound*. June 2001. Available online at www.theatlantic.com/past/docs/unbound/interviews/ba2000–06–01.htm. Accessed on August 17, 2010.

Allen, Paula Gunn. *The Sacred Hoop: Recovering the Feminine in American Indian Traditions.* Boston: Beacon Press, 1986.

Anderson, Eric Gary. "Driving the Red Road: Powwow Highway." In *Hollywood's Indian: The Portrayal of the Native American in Film*, edited by Peter C. Rollins and John E. O'Connor, 136–52. Lexington: University Press of Kentucky, 1998.

Andrade, Manuel J. "Quileute Texts." *Columbia University Contributions to Anthropology* 12 (1931): 1–211.

Auerbach, Nina. "My Vampire, My Friend: The Intimacy Dracula Destroyed." In *Blood Read: The Vampire as Metaphor in Contemporary Culture*, edited by Joan Gordon and Veronica Hollinger, 11–16. Philadelphia: University of Pennsylvania Press, 1997.

_____. *Our Vampires, Ourselves.* Chicago: University of Chicago Press, 1995.

_____. *Woman and the Demon: The Life of a Victorian Myth.* Cambridge: Harvard University Press, 1982.

Baird, Robert. "Going Indian: Discovery, Adoption, and Renaming Toward a 'True American,' from *Deerslayer* to *Dances with Wolves*." In *Dressing in Feathers: The Construction of the Indian in American Popular Culture*, edited by S. Elizabeth Bird, 195–209. Oxford: Westview Press, 1996.

Barber, Paul. *Vampires, Burial, and Death: Folklore and Reality.* New Haven: Yale University Press, 1988.

Barthes, Roland. "Death of the Author." In *Image, Music, Text*, translated by Stephen Heath, 142–48. New York: Hill and Wang, 1978.

Bartlett, Wayne, and Flavia Idriceanu. *Legends of Blood: The Vampire in History and Myth.* Westport: Praeger, 2006.

Battis, Jes. *Blood Relations: Chosen Families in* Buffy the Vampire Slayer *and* Angel. Jefferson, NC: McFarland, 2005.

Baudelaire, Rimbaud Verlaine. "Metamorphoses of the Vampire." In *Selected Verse and Prose Poems*, 79–80. New York: Citadel Press, 1993.

Beauvoir, Simone de. *The Second Sex.* New York: Vintage, 1952.

Behm-Morawitz, Elizabeth, Melissa A. Click, and Jennifer Stevens Aubrey. "Relating to *Twilight*: Fans' Responses to Love and Romance in the Vampire Franchise." In *Bitten by Twilight: Youth Culture, Media, and the Vampire Franchise*, edited by Melissa A. Click, Jennifer Stevens Aubrey, and Elizabeth Behm-Morawitz, 137–54. New York: Peter Lang, 2010.

Berkhofer, Robert F., Jr. *The White Man's Indian: Images of the American Indian from Columbus to the Present*. New York: Vintage Books, 1978.

Bettelheim, Bruno. *The Uses of Enchantment: The Meaning and Importance of Fairy Tales*. New York: Knopf, 1976.

Bird, Elizabeth S. "Constructing the Indian, 1830s–1990s." In *Dressing in Feathers: The Construction of the Indian in American Popular Culture*, edited by Elizabeth S. Bird, 1–12. Oxford: Westview Press, 1996.

_____. "Not My Fantasy: The Persistence of Indian Imagery in *Dr. Quinn, Medicine Woman*." In *Dressing in Feathers: The Construction of the Indian in American Popular Culture*, 245–61. Oxford: Westview Press, 1996.

_____, ed. *Dressing in Feathers: The Construction of the Indian in American Popular Culture*. Oxford: Westview Press, 1996.

Bordo, Susan. *Twilight Zones: The Hidden Life of Cultural Images from Plato to O.J.* Berkeley: University of California Press, 1997.

Bore, Inger-Lise Kaviknes, and Rebecca Williams. "Transnational Twilighters: A Twilight Fan Community in Norway." In *Bitten by Twilight: Youth Culture, Media, and the Vampire Franchise*, edited by Melissa A. Click, Jennifer Stevens Aubrey, and Elizabeth Behm-Morawitz, 189–205. New York: Peter Lang, 2010.

Botting, Fred, "Gothic Culture." In *The Routledge Companion to Gothic*, edited by Catherine Spooner and Emma McEvoy, 199–213. London: Routledge, 2007.

Braidottie, Rosi. *Nomadic Subjects: Embodiment and Sexual Difference in Contemporary Feminist Theory*. New York: Columbia University Press, 1994.

Brodie, Fawn M. *No Man Knows My History: The Life of Joseph Smith*, 2nd ed. New York: Vintage Books, 1995.

Brugger, Eveline. "Where Do the Cullens Fit In?" In *Twilight and History*, edited by Nancy Reagin, 227–44. Hoboken, NJ: Wiley and Sons, 2010.

Burke, Brianna. "The Great American Love Affair: Indians in the *Twilight* Saga." In *Reading Twilight: Analytical Essays*, edited by Giselle Liza Anatol. New York: Palgrave Macmillan, 2010.

Butler, Judith. *Bodies That Matter*. New York: Routledge, 1993.

Buttsworth, Sara. "CinderBella: Twilight, Fairy Tales, and the Twenty-First Century American Dream." In *Twilight and History*, edited by Nancy R. Reagin, 47–69. Hoboken, NJ: Wiley and Sons, 2010.

Byers, Thomas B. "Good Men and Monsters: The Defense of Dracula, Dracula." In *Dracula: The Vampire and the Critics*, edited by Margaret L. Carter, 149–57. Ann Arbor: University of Michigan Research Press, 1988.

Case, Sue-Ellen. "Tracking the Vampire." In *Writing on the Body: Female Embodiment and Feminist Theory*, edited by Katie Conboy, Nadia Medina, and Sarah Stanbury, 380–400. New York: Columbia University Press, 1997.

Charnas, Suzy McKee. "Meditations in Red: On Writing *The Vampire Tapestry*." In *Blood Read: The Vampire as Metaphor in Contemporary Culture*, edited by Joan Gordon and Veronica Hollinger, 59–67. Philadelphia: University of Pennsylvania Press, 1997.

Chodorow, Nancy. *The Reproduction of Mothering: Psychoanalysis and the Sociology of Gender*. Berkeley: University of California Press, 1978.

Churchill, Ward. *Fantasies of the Master Race: Literature, Cinema and the Colonization of American Indians*. Monroe, ME: Common Courage Press, 1992.

Clasen, Tricia, "Taking a Bite Out of Love: The Myth of Romantic Love in the Twilight Series." In *Bitten by Twilight: Youth Culture, Media, and the Vampire Franchise*, edited by Melissa A. Click, Jennifer Stevens Aubrey, and Elizabeth Behm-Morawitz, 119–34. New York: Peter Lang, 2010.

Click, Melissa A. "'Rabid,' 'Obsessed,' and 'Frenzied': Understanding *Twilight* Fangirls and the Gendered Politics of Fandom." *FlowTV*, December 18, 2009. Department of Radio, Television, and Film at the University of Texas at Austin.

http://flowtv.org/2009/12/rabid-obsessed-and-frenzied-understanding-twilight-fangirls-and-the-gendered-politics-of-fandom-melissa-click-university-of-missouri/. Accessed on August 11, 2010.

Cobb, Amanda J. "This Is What It Means to Say Smoke Signals: Native American Cultural Sovereignty." In *Hollywood's Indian: The Portrayal of the Native American in Film*, edited by Peter C. Rollins and John E. O'Connor, 206–28. Lexington: University Press of Kentucky, 1998.

Coward, Rosalind. "Female Desire: Women's Sexuality Today." In *Feminist Literary Theory: A Reader*, edited by Mary Eagleton, 145–48. Oxford: Basil Blackwell, 1986.

Craft, Christopher. "'Kiss Me with Those Red Lips': Gender and Inversion in Bram Stoker's *Dracula*." In *Dracula: The Vampire and the Critics*, edited by Margaret L. Carter, 169–94. Ann Arbor: University of Michigan Research Press, 1988.

Creed, Barbara. *The Monstrous Feminine: Film, Feminism, Psychoanalysis*. London: Routledge, 1993.

Day, William Patrick. *Vampire Legends in Contemporary American Culture: What Becomes a Legend Most*. Lexington: University Press of Kentucky, 2002.

de Certeau, Michel. *The Practice of Everyday Life*. Berkeley: University of California Press, 1984.

Deloria, Vine, Jr. "Comfortable Fictions and the Struggle for Turf." In *Natives and Academics: Researching and Writing about American Indians*, edited by Devon A. Mihesuah, 864–83. Lincoln: University of Nebraska Press, 1998.

Dijkstra, Bram. *Idols of Perversity: Fantasies of Feminine Evil in Fin-de-Siècle Culture*. New York: Oxford University Press, 1986.

Douglas, Susan. *Enlightened Sexism: The Seductive Message That Feminism's Work Is Done*. New York: Henry Holt, 2010.

_____. *Where the Girls Are*. New York: Three Rivers Press, 1994.

Douglas, Susan, and Meredith W. Michaels. *The Mommy Myth: The Idealization of Motherhood and How It Has Undermined Women*. New York: Free Press, 2004.

Durham, M. Gigi. *The Lolita Effect: The Media Sexualization of Young Girls and What We Can Do About It*. New York: The Overlook Press, 2008.

Dyer, Richard. *Heavenly Bodies: Film Stars and Society*. Houndmills: Macmillan, 1986.

_____. "The Matter of Whiteness." In *Entertainment, Media and Minorities: The Politics of Race in News and Entertainment*, edited by Stephanie Greco Larson, 45–56. Lanham, MD: Rowman and Littlefield, 2006.

_____. *White*. London: Routledge, 1997.

Fiske, John. "Popular Discrimination." In *Modernity and Mass Culture*, edited by James Naremore and Patrick Brantlinger, 103–116. Bloomington and Indianapolis: Indiana University Press, 1991.

Foucault, Michel. *Discipline and Punish: The Birth of the Prison*, translated by Alan Sheridan. New York: Vintage Books, 1977.

Fox, Andrew. *Fat White Vampire Blues*. New York: Ballantine Books, 2003.

Frankenberg, Ruth. "Whiteness as an 'Unmarked' Cultural Category." In *The Meaning of Difference: American Constructions of Race, Sex and Gender, Social Class, Sexual Orientation, and Disability*, 5th ed., edited by Karen E. Rosenblum and Toni-Michelle C. Travis, 81–87. Boston: McGraw Hill, 2008.

Frost, Brian J. *The Essential Guide to Werewolf Literature*. Madison: The University of Wisconsin Press, 2003.

_____. *The Monster with a Thousand Faces: Guises of the Vampire in Myth and Literature*. Bowling Green, OH: Bowling Green State University Popular Press, 1989.

Fry, Carrol L. "Fictional Conventions and Sexuality in *Dracula*." In *Dracula: The Vampire and the Critics*, edited by Margaret L. Carter, 35–38. Ann Arbor: University of Michigan Research Press, 1988.

Frye, Northrop. *Anatomy of Criticism*. Princeton: Princeton University Press, 1957.

Gelder, Ken. *Reading the Vampire*. Routledge: London, 1994.

Glaister, Dan, and Sarah Falconer. "Mormon Who Put New Life into Vampires." *Guardian UK*, July 2008. www.guardian.co.uk/books/2008/jul/20/news.books forchildrenandteenagers. Accessed on August 11, 2010.

Gomez, Jewelle. *The Gilda Stories*. Ann Arbor: Firebrand Books, 2004.

_____. "Recasting the Mythology: Writing Vampire Fiction." In *Blood Read: The Vampire as Metaphor in Contemporary Culture*, edited by Joan Gordon and Veronica Hollinger, 85–92. Philadelphia: University of Pennsylvania Press, 1997.

Gordon, Joan, and Veronica Hollinger. "Introduction: The Shape of Vampires." In *Blood Read: The Vampire as Metaphor in Contemporary Culture*, edited by Joan Gordon and Veronica Hollinger, 1–7. Philadelphia: University of Pennsylvania Press, 1997.

Granger, John. *Spotlight: A Close-Up Look at the Artistry and Meaning of Stephenie Meyer's Twilight Saga*. Allentown: Zossima, 2010.

Gresh, Lois H. *Twilight Companion: The Unauthorized Guide to the Series*. New York: St. Martin's Griffin, 2008.

Griffin, Gail B. "'Your Girls That You All Love Are Mine': *Dracula* and the Victorian Male Sexual Imagination." In *Dracula: The Vampire and the Critics*, edited by Margaret L. Carter, 137–48. Ann Arbor: University of Michigan Research Press, 1988.

Halberstam, Judith. *Gothic Horror and the Technology of Monsters*. Durham: Duke University Press, 2000.

Hall, Stuart. "The Whites of Their Eyes: Racist Ideologies and the Media." In *Gender, Race, and Class in Media*, edited by Gail Dines and Jean M. Humez, 18–22. Thousand Oaks: Sage, 1995.

Hanks, Maxine. "Introduction." In *Women and Authority: Re-Emerging Mormon Feminism*, edited by Maxine Hanks, xi–xxix. Salt Lake City: Signature Books, 1992.

_____. "Mormon Vampires? Religion and Twilight." Summer School in Forks: A *Twilight* Symposium. Forks, Washington. June 27, 2009.

Harris, Charlaine. "A Reflection on Ugliness." In *Seven Seasons of Buffy: Science Fiction and Fantasy Writers Discuss Their Favorite Television Show*, edited by Glenn Yeffeth, 116–20. Dallas: Benbella, 2003.

Hatlen, Burton. "The Return of the Repressed/Oppressed in Bram Stoker's *Dracula*." In *Dracula: The Vampire and the Critics*, edited by Margaret L. Carter, 117–35. Ann Arbor: University of Michigan Research Press, 1988.

Herzberg, Bob. *Savages and Saints: The Changing Image of American Indians in Westerns*. Jefferson, NC: McFarland, 2008.

Hodges, Devon, and Janice L. Doane. "Undoing Feminism in Ann Rice's Vampire Chronicles." In *Modernity and Mass Culture*, edited by James Naremore and Patrick Brantlinger, 158–75. Bloomington and Indianapolis: Indiana University Press, 1991.

Hollinger, Veronica. "Fantasies of Absence: The Postmodern Vampire." In *Blood Read: The Vampire as Metaphor in Contemporary Culture*, edited by Joan Gordon and Veronica Hollinger, 199–212. Philadelphia: University of Pennsylvania Press, 1997.

Housel, Rebecca. "The Tao of Jacob." In *Twilight and Philosophy: Vampires, Vegetarians, and the Pursuit of Immorality*, edited by Rebecca Housel and J. Jeremy Wisnewski, 237–46. Hoboken, NJ: John Wiley and Sons, 2009.

Huyssen, Andreas. "Mass Culture as Woman: Modernism's Other." January 15, 1986. www.mariabuszek.com/kcai/PoMoSeminar/Readings/HuyssenMassCult.pdf. Accessed August 11, 2010.

Ingraham, Chrys. *White Weddings: Romancing Heterosexuality in Popular Culture*. New York: Routledge, 1999.

Inness, Sherrie A. *Tough Women: Women Warriors and Wonder Women in Popular Culture*. Philadelphia: University of Pennsylvania Press, 1999.

Jaimes, M. Annette. "Introduction: Weapons of Genocide." In *Fantasies of the Master*

Race: Literature, Cinema and the Colonization of American Indians, edited by M. Annette Jaimes and Ward Churchill, 1–4. Monroe, ME: Common Courage Press, 1992.

Jameson, Frederic. "Magical Narratives: Romance as Genre." *New Literary History* 7 (1975): 135–63.

Jenkins, Mark Collins. *Vampire Forensics: Uncovering the Origins of an Enduring Legend.* Washington, D.C.: National Geographic Society, 2010.

Johnson, Alan. "Bent and Broken Necks: Signs of Design in Stoker's *Dracula*." In *Dracula: The Vampire and the Critics*, edited by Margaret L. Carter, 231–43. Ann Arbor: University of Michigan Research Press, 1988.

Jones, Beth Felker. *Touched by a Vampire: Discovering the Hidden Messages in the Twilight Saga.* Colorado Springs: Multnomah Books, 2009.

Jowett, Lorna. *Sex and the Slayer: A Gender Studies Primer for the Buffy Fan.* Middleton, CT: Wesleyan University Press, 2005.

Joyce, Kathryn. *Quiverfull: Inside the Christian Patriarchy Movement.* Beacon: Boston, 2009.

Kane, Kathryn. "A Very Queer Refusal: The Chilling Effect of the Cullens' Heteronormative Embrace." In *Bitten by Twilight: Youth Culture, Media, and the Vampire Franchise*, edited by Melissa A. Click, Jennifer Stevens Aubrey, and Elizabeth Behm-Morawitz, 103–18. New York: Peter Lang, 2010.

Katz, Jackson. "Advertising and the Construction of Violent White Masculinity." In *Gender, Race, and Class in Media*, edited by Gail Dines and Jean M. Humez, 133–41. Thousand Oaks: Sage, 1995.

_____. *The Macho Paradox.* Naperville, IL: Sourcebooks, 2006.

Kendall, Diana. "Framing Class: Media Representations of Wealth and Poverty in America." In *The Meaning of Difference: American Constructions of Race, Sex and Gender, Social Class, Sexual Orientation, and Disability*, 5th ed., edited by Karen E. Rosenblum and Toni-Michelle C. Travis, 138–42. Boston: McGraw Hill, 2008.

King, Patti Jo. "Charlatans, Hucksters, and Spiritual Orphans: The Historical Tenets of Narcissism, Greed, and Pathos behind Native Cultural Exploitation." Southwest Texas Popular Culture and American Culture Association. Albuquerque, New Mexico. February 13, 2010.

King, Stephen. *Danse Macabre.* New York: Everest House, 1981.

Knoepflmacher, U. C. "Thoughts on the Aggression of Daughters." In *The Endurance of Frankenstein: Essays on Mary Shelley's Novel*, edited by George Levine and U. C. Knoepflmacher, 88–119. Berkeley: University of California Press, 1974.

Koski, Genevieve. "I Attended This on Purpose: *Twi-Con* 2009." *A.V. Club*, August 2009. Available online at www.avclub.com/articles/i-attended-this-on-purpose-twicon-2009,31768/. Accessed August 17, 2010.

Kristeva, Julia. *Powers of Horror.* Translated by Leon S. Roudiez. New York: Columbia University Press, 1982.

Lamb, Sharon, and Lyn Mikel Brown. *Packaging Girlhood: Rescuing Our Daughters from Marketers' Schemes.* New York: St. Martin's Press, 2006.

Larson, Stephanie Greco. "Native Americans in Film and Television Entertainment." In *Media and Minorities: The Politics of Race in News and Entertainment*, 45–56. Lanham, MD: Rowman and Littlefield, 2006.

Latham, Rob. "Consuming Youth: The Lost Boys Cruise Mallworld." In *Blood Read: The Vampire as Metaphor in Contemporary Culture*, edited by Joan Gordon and Veronica Hollinger, 129–47. Philadelphia: University of Pennsylvania Press, 1997.

Leogrande, Cathy. "My Mother, Myself: Mother-Daughter Bonding via the Twilight Saga." In *Bitten by Twilight: Youth Culture, Media, and the Vampire Franchise*, edited by Melissa A. Click, Jennifer Stevens Aubrey, and Elizabeth Behm-Morawitz, 156–71. New York: Peter Lang, 2010.

Levin, Diane E., and Jean Kilbourne. *So Sexy So Soon: The New Sexualized Child-*

hood and What Parents Can Do to Protect Their Kids. New York: Ballantine Books, 2008.

Levine, Elana. "Afterword." In *Bitten by Twilight: Youth Culture, Media, and the Vampire Franchise*, edited by Melissa A. Click, Jennifer Stevens Aubrey, and Elizabeth Behm-Morawitz, 281–86. New York: Peter Lang, 2010.

Levine, George, and U. C. Knoepflmacher, eds. *The Endurance of Frankenstein: Essays on Mary Shelley's Novel.* Berkeley: University of California Press, 1974.

Levy, Ariel. *Female Chauvinist Pigs: Women and the Rise of Raunch Culture.* New York: Free Press, 2005.

Light, Alison. "'Returning to Manderley'— Romance Fiction, Female Sexuality and Class." In *Feminist Literary Theory: A Reader*, edited by Mary Eagleton, 140–45. Oxford: Basil Blackwell, 1986.

Linn, Susan. *Consuming Kids: The Hostile Takeover of Childhood.* New York: The New Press, 2004.

Martens, Lydia. "Feminism and the Critique of Consumer Culture, 1950–1970." In *Feminism, Domesticity and Popular Culture*, edited by Stacy Gillis and Joanne Hollows, 33–47. New York: Routledge, 2009.

Martens, Marianne. "Consumed by Twilight: The Commodification of Young Adult Literature." In *Bitten by Twilight: Youth Culture, Media, and the Vampire Franchise*, edited by Melissa A. Click, Jennifer Stevens Aubrey, and Elizabeth Behm-Morawitz, 243–60. New York: Peter Lang, 2010.

Marx, Karl. *Capital: A Critique of Political Economy.* Translated by David Fernbach. London: Penguin, 1978.

McClelland, Bruce A. *Slayers and Their Vampires: A Cultural History of Killing the Dead.* Ann Arbor: University of Michigan Press, 2009.

McElvaine, Robert S. *Eve's Seed: Biology, the Sexes, and the Course of History.* New York: McGraw Hill, 2001.

McRobbie, Angela. *Feminism and Youth Culture: From "Jackie" to "Just Seventeen."* Boston: Unwin Hyman, 1991.

_____. "Post-Feminism and Popular Culture." *Feminist Media Studies* 4, no. 3 (2004): 255–64.

Meyer, Stephenie. *Breaking Dawn.* New York: Little, Brown, 2008.

_____. *Eclipse.* New York: Little, Brown, 2007.

_____. *Midnight Sun.* 2008. www.stepheniemeyer.com/pdf/midnightsun_partial_draft4.pdf. Accessed on August 18, 2010.

_____. *New Moon.* New York: Little, Brown, 2006.

_____. *The Short Second Life of Bree Tanner.* New York: Little, Brown, 2010.

_____. *Twilight.* New York: Little, Brown, 2005.

Modleski, Tania. "Feminity as (Mas)querade: A Feminist Approach to Mass Culture." In *High Theory, Low Culture: Analysing Popular Television and Film*, 37–52. Manchester: Manchester University Press, 1986.

_____. *Loving with a Vengeance: Mass Produced Fantasies for Women.* Hamden, CT: Archon Books, 1982.

Moretti, Franco. *Signs Taken for Wonders: Essays in the Sociology of Literary Forms.* London: Verso, 1983.

Mukherjea, Ananya. "Team Bella: Desire, Collectivity, Identity, and the Sociology of What Makes the Story So Compelling for Its Fans." Summer School in Forks: A *Twilight* Symposium. Forks, Washington. June 26, 2009.

Neale, Stephen. *Genre.* London: BFI Books, 1989.

O'Donnell, Ruth. "*Twilight*: Historical Contexts and Psychoanalytic Interpretations." Southwest/Texas Popular Culture and American Culture Association. Hyatt Regency, Albuquerque, New Mexico. February 11, 2010.

Orenstein, Catherine. *Little Red Riding Hood Uncloaked.* New York: Basic Books, 2002.

Parke, Maggie. *The Event Film: Twilight, Filmmakers, Fans, and the Phenomenon.* Unpublished PhD dissertation. National Institute for Excellence in the Creative Industries, Bangor University, Wales, UK.

Pateman, Matthew. *The Aesthetics of Culture in* Buffy the Vampire Slayer. Jefferson, NC: McFarland, 2006

Pettitt, George A. "The Quileute of La Push, 1775–1945." *Anthropological Records*, vol. 14, no. 1. Berkeley: University of California Press, 1950.

Postman, Neil. *Amusing Ourselves to Death: Public Discourse in the Age of Show Business*. New York: Penguin, 1986.

Powell, Jay, and Vickie Jensen. *Quileute: An Introduction to the Indians of La Push*. Seattle: University of Washington Press, 1976.

Pritchard, Elizabeth A. "Speaking Out: Faith-Based Patriarchy and the Rhetoric of 'Choice.'" *Journal of Feminist Studies in Religion* 19, no. 1 (2003): 65–70.

Radway, Janice A. *Reading the Romance: Women, Patriarchy, and Popular Literature*. Chapel Hill: University of North Carolina Press, 1984.

Reagin, Nancy. *Twilight and History*. Hoboken, NJ: Wiley and Sons, 2010.

Roth, Phyllis A. "Suddenly Sexual Women in Bram Stoker's *Dracula*." In *Dracula: The Vampire and the Critics*, edited by Margaret L. Carter, 57–67. Ann Arbor: University of Michigan Research Press, 1988.

Rowe-Finkbeiner, Kristin. *The F Word: Feminism in Jeopardy*. Emeryville: Seal Press. 2004.

Russ, Joanna. "What Can a Heroine Do?" *Images of Women in Fiction: Feminist Perspectives*, edited by Susan Koppleman. Bowling Green, OH: Bowling Green State University Popular Press, 1972.

Russell, Bertrand. *Why I Am Not Christian: And Other Essays on Religion and Related Subjects*. New York: George Allen, 1957.

Schmidt, Rob. "The Truth about Tinsel Korey." *Newspaper Rock: Where Native America Meets Pop Culture*, July 28, 2009. www.bluecorncomics.com/2009/07/truth-about-tinsel-korey.html. Accessed on August 17, 2010.

Seifert, Christine. "Bite Me! Or Don't." *Bitch Magazine*. 2008. http://bitch-magazine.org/article/bite-me-or-dont. Accessed on August 12, 2010.

Shapiro, Marc. *Stephenie Meyer: The Unauthorized Biography of the Creator of the Twilight Saga*. New York: St. Martin's Griffin, 2009.

Sheffield, Jessica, and Elyse Merlo. "Biting Back: *Twilight* Anti-Fandom and the Rhetoric of Superiority." In *Bitten by Twilight: Youth Culture, Media, and the Vampire Franchise*, edited by Melissa A. Click, Jennifer Stevens Aubrey, and Elizabeth Behm-Morawitz, 207–22. New York: Peter Lang, 2010.

Siering, Carmen D. "Taking a Bite out of *Twilight*." *Ms. Magazine* (Spring 2009): 50–52.

Silverstein, Olga, and Beth Rashbaum. *The Courage to Raise Good Men*. New York: Viking, 1994.

Simmons, Rachel. *Odd Girl Out: The Hidden Culture of Aggression in Girls*. New York: Harcourt, 2002.

Skal, David J. *The Monster Show: A Cultural History of Horror*. New York: W. W. Norton and Company, 1993.

_____. *V is for Vampire: The A–Z Guide to Everything Undead*. New York: Plume, 1996.

Smith, Andrea. "Rape and the War against Native Women." In *The Matrix Reader: Examining the Dynamics of Oppression and Privilege*, edited by Abby Ferber, Christina M. Jimenez, Andrea O'Reilly Herrerra, and Dena R. Samuels, 280–91. Colorado Springs: University of Colorado, 2009.

Snitow, Ann Barr. "Mass Market Romance: Pornography for Women Is Different." In *Feminist Literary Theory: A Reader*, edited by Mary Eagleton, 134–40. Oxford: Basil Blackwell, 1986.

Spooner, Catherine, and Emma McEvoy, eds. *Fashioning Gothic Bodies*. Manchester: Manchester University Press, 2004.

_____. *The Routledge Companion to Gothic*. London: Routledge, 2007.

Stevens, Jennifer Aubrey, Scott Walus, and Melissa A. Click. "Twilight and the Production of the 21st Century Teen Idol." In *Bitten by Twilight: Youth Culture, Media, and the Vampire Franchise*, edited by Melissa A. Click, Jennifer Stevens Aubrey, and Elizabeth Behm-Morawitz, 225–41. New York: Peter Lang, 2010.

Stoker, Bram. *Dracula*. London: Penguin, 1994.

_____. "Dracula's Guest." In *Best Ghost and Horror Stories*, edited by Richard Dalby, Stefan Dziemianowicz, and S. T. Joshi, 208–20. Mineola, NY: Dover, 1997.

Summers, Montague. *Vampire: His Kith and Kin*. New Hyde Park, NY: University Books, 1960.

Swanson, K. J. "'Why Are You Apologizing for Bleeding?': Confronting the Evangelical Embrace of *Twilight*." Southwest/Texas Popular Culture and American Culture Association. Hyatt Regency, Albuquerque, New Mexico. February 11, 2010.

Topel, Fred. "Alex Meraz on the *Twilight* Saga: *New Moon*." *Can Magazine*, November 17, 2009. www.canmag.com/nw/15021-twilight-saga-new-moon-alex-meraz-interview. Accessed on December 10, 2009.

Tough Guise. Directed by Sut Jhally. Written by Jackson Katz and Jeremy Earp. Media Education Foundation, 1999.

Tsing, Anna Lowenhaupt. "Monster Stories: Women Charged with Perinatal Endangerment." In *Uncertain Terms: Negotiating Gender in American Culture*, edited by Faye Ginsburg and Anna Lowenhaupt Tsing, 282–99. Boston: Beacon, 1990.

Twitchell, James B. *Dreadful Pleasures: An Anatomy of Modern Horror*. Oxford: Oxford University Press, 1985.

Valenti, Jessica. *The Purity Myth: How America's Obsession with Virginity Is Hurting Young Women*. Berkeley: Seal, 2009.

Veeder, William. "Foreword." In *Dracula: The Vampire and the Critics*, edited by Margaret L. Carter, ix–xviii. Ann Arbor: University of Michigan Research Press, 1988.

Weissman, Judith. "Women and Vampires: *Dracula* as a Victorian Novel." In *Dracula: The Vampire and the Critics*, edited by Margaret L. Carter, 69–77. Ann Arbor: University of Michigan Research Press, 1988.

Whitt, Laurie Ann. "Cultural Imperialism and the Marketing of Native America." In *Natives and Academics: Researching and Writing about American Indians*, edited by Devon A. Mihesuah, 139–71. Lincoln: University of Nebraska Press: 1998.

Wilcox, Linda P. "The Mormon Concept of a Mother in Heaven." In *Women and Authority: Re-Emerging Mormon Feminism*, edited by Maxine Hanks, 3–21. Salt Lake City: Signature Books, 1992.

Wildman, Stephanie M., and Adrienne Davis. "Making Systems of Privilege Visible, White Privilege: Essential Readings on the Other Side of Racism." In *White Privilege*, 2nd ed., edited by Paula S. Rothenberg, 95–101. New York: Worth Publishers, 2005.

Williamson, Milly. *The Lure of the Vampire: Gender, Fiction, and Fandom from Bram Stoker to Buffy*. London: Wallflower Press, 2005.

Willis-Chun, Cynthia. "Touring the Twilight Zone: Cultural Tourism and Commodification on the Olympic Peninsula." In *Bitten by Twilight: Youth Culture, Media, and the Vampire Franchise*, edited by Melissa A. Click, Jennifer Stevens Aubrey, and Elizabeth Behm-Morawitz, 261–79. New York: Peter Lang, 2010.

Wilson, Natalie. "Civilized Vampires versus Savage Werewolves: Race and Ethnicity in the *Twilight* Series." In *Bitten by Twilight: Youth Culture, Media, and the Vampire Franchise*, edited by Melissa A. Click, Jennifer Stevens Aubrey, and Elizabeth Behm-Morawitz, 55–70. New York: Peter Lang, 2010.

_____. "Womb Fiction: Late Twentieth Century Challenges to the Woman as Womb Paradigm." In *Womanhood in Anglophone Literary Culture: Nineteenth and Twentieth Century Perspectives*, edited by Robin Hammerman, 343–72. Cambridge: Cambridge Scholars Press, 2007.

Winnubst, Shannon. "Vampires, Anxieties, and Dreams: Race and Sex in the Contemporary United States." *Hypatia* 18, no. 3 (2003): 1–20.

Wise, Tim. "Membership Has Its Privileges: Thoughts on Acknowledging and Challenging Whiteness." In *White Privilege*, 2nd ed., edited by Paula S. Rothenberg, 119–22. New York: Worth, 2005.

Wiseman, Rosalind. *Queen Bees and Wannabes: Helping Your Daughter Survive Cliques, Gossip, Boyfriends, and the New Realities of Girl World*. New York: Three Rivers Press, 2002.

Worley, Sara. "Love and Authority among Wolves." In *Twilight and Philosophy: Vampires, Vegetarians, and the Pursuit of Immorality*, edited by Rebecca Housel and J. Jeremy Wisnewski, 107–18. Hoboken, NJ: John Wiley and Sons, 2009.

Zinn, Howard. *A People's History of the United States: 1492–Present*. New York: Harper Perennial, 1980.

Index

229